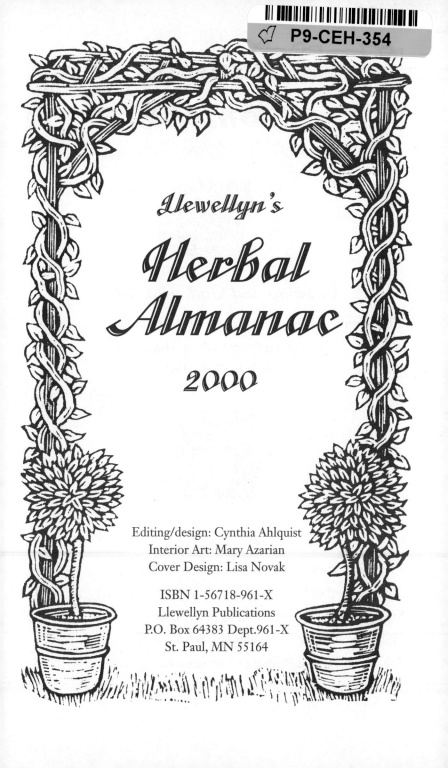

Llewellyn's
Herbal Almanac
2000

Editing/design: Cynthia Ahlquist
Interior Art: Mary Azarian
Cover Design: Lisa Novak

ISBN 1-56718-961-X
Llewellyn Publications
P.O. Box 64383 Dept.961-X
St. Paul, MN 55164

Table of Contents

Growing and Gathering Herbs

Culinary Herbs

Herbs for Health

Herbs for Beauty

Herb Crafts

Herb History, Myth, and Magic

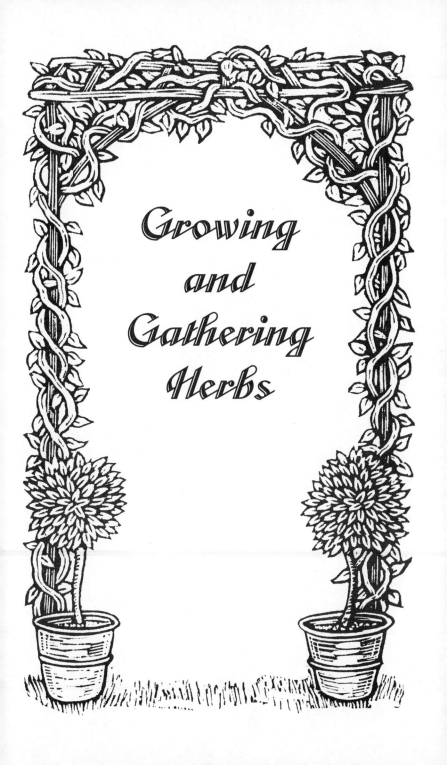

Growing
and
Gathering
Herbs

The Windowsill Herb Garden

By Carly Wall, C.A.

*H*erb lovers come in many varieties. One of the reasons, I
think, is that herbs them-
selves are so versatile. There's an herb
and a particular use for that herb for
every interest. There are herbs for medicinal use, and if that weren't enough,
there is medicinal herb usage in aromatherapy, Chinese traditional healing,
Native American healing, and every
other culture. There are also herbs for
crafts and pleasure, for beauty, and for
food. You name it, you can find some
type of interest and tie herbs to it.

Once you get your interest piqued,
of course you are going to start thinking
about growing a few plants of your own.
The problem is that not everyone has
garden space or wants an outdoor garden. Perhaps you live in an apartment,
or your yard space is limited, and perhaps you just don't enjoy outdoor gardening, or are unable to keep up with

the hard work that outdoor gardening entails. You may work long hours and have limited time, or you may have health reasons that prevent you from doing such strenuous work. Or maybe you just like having growing things surround you year-round. The solution? A windowsill herb garden.

Having your garden indoors is much easier than you think if you know a few key tricks. First and foremost, you have to remember that the plants are solely dependent upon you for their life. You need to give them plenty of space, the correct lighting, and the perfect balance of food and water. When gardening outdoors, you get a little help from Mother Nature. Indoor plants are in an environment most of them aren't really suited to. You have to make the environment suitable. It isn't complicated, but you do have to make a commitment to care for your garden on a daily basis. There are other considerations, too. Here are a few things to keep in mind:

- Windowsills provide sunlight ideal for seedlings, but you'll need much more light to keep healthy plants growing. If you want more than one or two pots, artificial lighting is what you'll definitely need. Even if you use a windowsill, plan on having back-up grow lights since the herbs will need a steady source of light for up to five hours a day (and this doubles for artificial lighting).

- You can fit more on a windowsill if you purchase a special windowsill extender. You can also get more light and heat by using tin foil to line the tray. It'll reflect light up onto plant stems and leaves. A mirror behind plants has the same effect.

- If you forego the use of a tabletop or shelf with artificial light and use natural sunlight, the plants will turn toward the light source. Make sure you turn them every day so growth will be even.

- Radiators and baseboard heaters will turn your pretty green plants into parched, dry, and withered stems—but you can compensate by letting the pots stand in trays of water-soaked pebbles so that the evaporating water will humidify the surrounding air. You can also mist regularly so that leaves get that needed moisture.

- ⇗ Make sure that you leave space between plants so that air circulates freely. Fungal diseases can catch hold quickly in a moist, crowded area.

- ⇗ Don't let cold drafts do in your plants. They need cool rooms, but cold drafts can cause tender herbs to shrivel. Also, in northern climes and in cold weather, don't let herb leaves touch cold windows, especially at night. Also, never close a curtain over the plants and trap them in this cold window area—at night the temperature will drop dramatically. On warm days, open the window and give your plants a good breeze—they'll appreciate it.

- ⇗ Pinch back the stems to keep plants bushy. You can use the pinched stems of culinary herbs to add flavor to your dishes. Remove dead or yellowing leaves or broken branches to discourage disease and to keep your plant looking its best.

Getting the Right Light

You can go out and spend the money to buy special grow lights, but many indoor gardeners say that you can do just as well using fluorescent tubes. They're great because they give off little or no heat, consume much less electricity, and have a long thin shape (available in various lengths to fit the area you want to have).

You have to use the right combination, though. Most indoor gardeners swear by the combo of the cool-white and the warm-white tubes. This combination gives the plants the needed blue-violet and the orange-red waves. The tubes should be changed after a year, since the efficiency falls off after that time period.

Too much light is just as bad as too little. How do you know the right amount? Most plants do best when there is a time period of darkness. The easiest method is to buy an inexpensive light timer. A good amount of light would be about twelve to fourteen hours per day. The timer would come on in the morning and shut off automatically after twelve to fourteen hours, letting the plant get adjusted to a regular routine.

Place the lights four to six inches from the plants. Because the lights on a fluorescent decrease near the ends, plants needing less light can go there. You can also use overturned pots to boost smaller plants closer to the light source while keeping larger plants at a good distance.

How to Water

Watering regularly will help your plants stay green and healthy. Touch the soil to find out when to water. When it is dry to the touch, soak the soil thoroughly. Use only unsoftened water at room temperature. Remember to mist every day, too (unless you have the moistened gravel tray underneath) to keep humidity up for the plant and to clean off dust from leaves. Incidentally, if you go away for a few days, you can fill the gravel tray with water and the pots will water themselves by soaking up the water as needed. With the lights being on automatic timers, your plants won't miss you for up to a week.

Feeding Your Herbs

Herbs don't require much in the way of feeding—perhaps a liquid fertilizer every other month. The stronger flavors will come through if you only fertilize when the leaves begin losing color or growth slows down.

When potting, make sure you use a good potting mix, which consists of a mixture of organic material (compost, or peat moss), and minerals (sand, vermiculite). You can purchase premixed soil packages or buy your ingredients and mix them yourself in a five-gallon plastic pail.

Once you have all these things down pat, you are sure to have an abundance of fresh, flavorful herbs to use or just enjoy growing. It's fun to watch them as they develop, and to become familiar with their growth habits and special needs. Here are twenty herbs you can pick from or try them all. Good luck with your indoor gardening!

LEMON BALM: Lemon balm is a tender perennial that likes a warm room and moist conditions. Use the leaves in tea to calm your nerves, or chop the leaves to add flavor to salads and soups.

BASIL: Basil is a tender annual. You can grow either the green or the purple bush type indoors from seed. Plants are big enough to harvest in eight weeks. Use in tea, for flavoring tomato dishes, and to make herbal vinegars.

CHERVIL: This hardy annual can be started from seed indoors. It likes a cool room, and since it needs less light, it likes to be placed at the end of the florescent tube or in indirect sun. Harvest the leaves in six to eight weeks, and keep it pinched back to prevent it from going to seed. Use the leaves in potpourris, or use it in cooking as a substitute for parsley. It's great in soups or stews when added at last minute (long cooking turns it bitter). It's also good for making herbal butter.

CHIVES: You can pot up starts or grow these from seed easily. They are perennial plants that withstand cool rooms, but they also need lots of feeding. Make sure you feed them once a month. It will take two and a half to three months to get the plants ready for harvesting, but once they get going one pot will supply a family with all the flavor of fresh onions that it needs. Use the snipped leaves to flavor omelets, baked potatoes, soups, or add to salads.

CILANTRO: An annual, you can pot up starts or start by seed. This also grows best in cooler rooms, and seeds germinate between 55–68 degrees. Use the seeds for spicy flavor in soups and stews. It is also used in chili sauces, curries, and other exotic dishes.

DILL: Another annual, the best dill to grow indoors is the fernleaf type. It is a dwarf with bushy habits. Start it by seed and it can handle warmer rooms well. Use chopped leaves in sour cream, on cucumbers, in salads, and when making dill pickles.

GARLIC: You can grow either the regular or the elephant type. Plant the cloves an inch deep, two inches apart. Dig up the roots when the tops fall. To use garlic, roast it to make garlic butter for toasted garlic bread. You can also use the green shoots as you do chives. The elephant garlic is less pungent and can be sliced and tossed into salads.

GREENS: As long as you're growing herbs, you might as well throw in some greens, too. You can grow lettuces, mustard greens, or spinach. That way, you can have a salad and sprinkle on the herbs to liven it up. Sow your seeds and keep them evenly moist. Pick tender greens when they reach four to six inches high. Use greens in salads. Steam spinach and mustard greens, then top them with butter. Growing greens is a great way to add vitamins to your diet and have fresh salad year around.

LEMONGRASS: This tender perennial loves lots of light and water and grows easily. Divide plants and pot up starts. Use the lemon-flavored leaves to flavor fish, soups, and sauces. You can also make an excellent hot or cold tea with lemongrass, or add it to potpourris or perfumes.

MARJORAM, SWEET: Marjoram seeds germinate quickly, but expect the plant to grow slowly. It's an annual and doesn't like dampness. It's a little picky, but it has many medicinal and other uses. It's a member of the mint family. Use the leaves in Italian dishes and to spice up salads, casseroles, or veal dishes.

MINT: A perennial, mint grows best in pots because you can keep control of the plants that way! They spread rapidly in the ground. The seeds are slow to germinate, but the plants rapidly grow, and there are a wide variety of flavors to choose from. Peppermint and spearmint are two favorites. Use mint sprigs whenever you need to garnish drinks or fruit dishes, make hot tea to settle stomachs and nausea, or to make jelly.

OREGANO: A perennial, these tiny seeds grow very slowly—up to four months before the plants are ready to use. You have to be very careful to get true oregano, as sometimes wild marjoram is substituted for the true oregano. Use this "pizza" herb to make your own pizza. It's a favored Italian flavoring and its hot, spicy taste is great in tomato dishes, soups, salads, or casseroles.

PARSLEY: A biennial, parsley is best grown from seed. Soak the seeds in warm water before sowing. Use the leaves chopped in almost any dish, and also whenever you need some color. Use them as a garnish when you have company over for dinner.

ROSEMARY: This tender perennial makes a wonderful potted herb. Avoid peat in the potting soil, as this is too acid for the rosemary. It also has to have good drainage. The plants like cool locations with plenty of light. Mist the leaves daily, but water only when the soil is dry to the touch. Rosemary also doesn't like to be crowded with other plants. Use the pungent leaves in stuffings, preserves, or with lamb or pork dishes. It makes a good tea. It is also good in homemade shampoos.

SAGE: This perennial can be potted up from starts or cuttings. It should have good drainage. Use the leaves in stuffings, and to flavor sausage, cheese, and bean dishes. Use sage tea for a sore throat gargle.

SAGE, PINEAPPLE: A tender perennial, take from cuttings or pot up small plants. Keep it pinched back to promote bushy growth. Use the leaves and flowers for drinks, chicken, and in jams and jellies. It has a great pineapple scent and taste.

SPROUTS: The great thing about sprouts is that you can harvest your crop in a couple of days. You also don't need any soil. There are two kinds of sprouts. First are the tiny green-leafed sprouts, formed from alfalfa, cress, mustard, or radish. Second, there are the ones eaten before the leaves form, like lentils, mung beans, wheat, or rye. To make sprouts, purchase seeds from the health food store or specialty shop. Soak the seeds in water for a few hours, or overnight for the larger seeds. Next, place them in a Mason jar with cheesecloth covering it, or cut a screen to fit the opening. Keep the jar on its side at room temperature, or 70–75 degrees. Rinse with water and drain well every day. When they sprout, keep them in plenty of light (except mung beans, which must be kept in the dark). Sprouts are ready in a few days. Use them on sandwiches, salads, or other vegetable dishes.

STRAWBERRIES: You can grow a good strawberry crop from a small strawberry jar or a couple rows of plants planted in trays. The strawberry jar is a ceramic vase with pockets for the plants. Keep the crowns just above the soil. The alpine and sweetheart varieties are good for indoor growers since they are runnerless and everbearing. When the fruits ripen and turn red, you can add the berries to cereal, eat them with cream, or collect enough berries for a small batch of strawberry jam. The leaves can be used medicinally for a wide range of things—diarrhea and urinary tract problems to name a few.

TARRAGON: Tarragon is a perennial. You must pot up the plants and they can be divided in the fall. Divide your plant every three years. You have to really search to get a true tarragon plant. If it isn't strongly scented, it isn't a true tarragon. Use the licorice-tasting leaves in sauces, omelets, marinated meats, or make tarragon butter for vegetables.

THYME: This perennial is very slow to germinate (up to four weeks), so you may want to start out with a small plant. Use thyme in most cooking. It's essential to the bouquet garni and is a great seasoning for stews, soups, or fish. It is also antiseptic and is good in gargles and for headaches. In tea form it is a good digestive.

A Child's Garden of Herbs

～ By Carolyn Moss ～

irst things first: why do we want a child's garden of herbs? Well, if you have children in the family, they will naturally use the garden to play and explore, or they may simply enjoy the flowers in your window box if that is all that space permits. However, even the youngest of children, certainly from the age of three or four, can get so much more out of it if they are involved. Anyone who has seen the kick kids get out of growing a bit of cress on some damp tissue will realize there is a lot of untapped enthusiasm here. Sure, not all of them will garden from childhood through to their dotage without a break, but an early introduction pays huge dividends when your grown "kids" want to return to the soil later on in life. They will also have a stock of happy memories of a shared experience. As parents, providing that positive memory bank is one of the

best things we can do prior to sending our young out into the world. Any child who experiences bees humming round thyme, marjoram, and lavender early enough in life will have an evocation of childhood forever.

So we want a garden for our children, and one in which they can be involved. In planning such a garden there are a number of key issues to consider: the plants must be fun; there must be something to actually harvest, be it flowers or things to eat; plants must be easy to grow and must be fast-growing; and ideally, the plants will have a touch of magic.

I could go on, but you get the idea of the sort of things we must consider and, surprise, surprise: herbs can be found that fulfil all these qualities. Here are some planting ideas that will hopefully help you give your kids an herb garden childhood.

When choosing plants for a child's garden, always glance at the above list and decide whether or not the criteria are fulfilled. It is always good to include some flowers here in addition to the herbs. Sunflowers are, of course, a staple "kid" plant, and they can enjoy both the growth and watching the birds get a seed feast in the fall. Also, try anthirrynums to see the little snap dragon mouths of the flower heads open and close. A great way of getting the fun factor into the garden is to plant a theme garden. These are very popular with children and lend themselves to a small, self-contained patch. How about one of the following?

A Fairy Garden

This will contain lots of tiny plants, including the fairy favorite, thyme. Try Corsican mint (*Mentha requienii*) and the creeping thymes. If you want a larger plot, also search in the alpine collections of nurseries for some wonderful tiny flowers. Place a mirror among the plants to reflect the moonlight, and maybe a large shell of water for the fairies to bathe in. How about some soapwort (*Saponaria officinalis*) for them to wash with? Leave out some cakes on Midsummer's Eve and see if the fairies visit to decorate them.

A Peter Rabbit Garden

Plan this with your child after presenting the Beatrix Potter book as a gift. Include chamomile, from which Peter Rabbit's mother made tea, lavender, parsley (which Peter had when he had over-eaten), the rabbit's favorite of lettuce, radishes, and some of the miniature vegetables now available, such as carrots.

A Pizza Garden

This would appeal to a slightly older child and can include oregano, basil, and thyme. Also try some of the lovely cherry tomatoes that can grow in hanging baskets or tubs. Grow some small onions and garlic or chives. The whole thing can be laid out in a cartwheel pizza shape with a few spears of wheat in the middle to teach the children about how bread is made.

A Bee Garden

Many flowers and herbs do, of course, attract bees, but it is fun to plant a patch of those that attract an exceptional number. Always ensure, of course, that no one is allergic to bee stings. However, if the bees are not disturbed, they are unlikely to worry you. I have never been stung in my garden in many years of poking round among the flowers. Bees particularly like the foxglove (*Digitalis purpurea*) and it is fun for children to see the bee crawl right up into the long flower head. Just remember that foxglove is poisonous, and caution children not to eat it or handle the flowers. Bees also adore mint, thyme, marjoram, oregano, bee balm (*Monarda didyma*), elecampane (*Inula helenium*), and viper's bugloss (*Echium vulgare*). A bee skep or miniature hive would make a lovely gift for a child with a bee garden. I have also found wooden and terracotta bees on sticks to put in the ground for decoration.

The Five Senses

A wonderful project, either for home or school, is a garden that appeals to all five senses. I include a starting list to give you the idea, and you will often find that your children are far more creative than adults in finding more plants to fulfil this theme. Although I have not planted this garden as such, my children got quite carried away with the idea and we had a period of trying to fit every plant we came across into one of the categories.

Sight

For sight one could have any of the spectacular plants, such as the sunflower, mullein (sometimes known as Aaron's rod, *Verbascum thapsus*), or angelica. Alternatively, or in addition, the very beautiful plants could be included, such as a perfect rose. Roses are particularly versatile as climbing, and miniature versions may be fitted in where space is at a premium.

Smell

For smell there is again an almost infinite variety to choose from, but some of the strongest scented herbs would be the curry plant (*Helichrysum stoechas*), lemon balm (*Melissa officinalis*), southernwood (*Artemisia abrotanum*), lavender, and, to contrast with something rather overpowering, if not exactly unpleasant, clary sage (*Salvia sclarea*).

Touch

For touch the fun really starts. You could go for the almost unbelievably soft lambs ears (*Stachys lanata*). Also slightly furry are the leaves of the mullein. You could also try the rough leaves and stems of borage (*Borago officinalis*) or comfrey (*Symphytum officinale*). Neither of these are for small gardens, although a slightly more manageable dwarf comfrey is available (*S. officinale sp.*). Of course, there is always the fiercely spiky English holly (*Ilex aquifolium*).

Taste

Taste is another easy sense to appeal to with a herb garden. For children the mint and lemon flavors are favored, with a large variety of mints to choose from and various lemon herbs from balm (*Melissa officinale*) and lemon verbena (*Lippia triphylla*) to a number of thymes. Also try chives and basil, which most children like to use in the kitchen. As we are talking herb gardens I have not listed the many fruits and vegetables that you could include in your child's garden. Especially quick growing, though, are salad stuff such as radishes and lettuce.

Hearing

I must admit that when first planning a herb garden of the five senses the one which made me struggle the most was that of hearing. However, I have now come up with two categories. The first are those plants whose seed pods make a satisfying rattle when dried. This includes poppies and, to a lesser extent, love-in-a-mist (*Nigella damascena*). The other category is the result of some lateral thinking and comprises those herbs that attract the bees and so, on a warm day, are never quiet!

The Children's Garden Year

In addition to theme gardens, a tried and tested way of keeping children interested is to have garden related activities on hand throughout the year. They will, of course, only have flowers to pick and leaves to eat for often very short seasons. Here, then, are ideas to keep them interested for twelve months.

JANUARY: Get children involved in planning their own herb garden and show them lots of books and catalogues with ideas.

FEBRUARY: Make pressed herb cards for Valentine's Day.

MARCH: Grow bright green herbs on the windowsill for St. Patrick's Day. These could include chives, parsley, and, of course, shamrock. Start making labels for the plants. Plastic labels with waterproof markers or the more expensive metal labels can be obtained from nurseries. Painted wood, coated with waterproof varnish, would be lovely for a theme garden label.

APRIL: Dye eggs with herbs for Easter breakfast. Tansy (*Tanace-tum vulgare*) will give green, goldenrod (*Solidago virgaurea*) gives yellow, and onion skins give a lovely reddish brown.

MAY: Make up baskets filled with herbs for May Day and leave them as special gifts for someone.

JUNE: Make cakes and leave them out, by the thyme plants, for the fairies to decorate on Midsummer's Eve. Take cuttings and pot them up as gifts, being sure to include labels with name of plant and growing advice.

JULY: Just enjoy the garden at its best. A lovely anonymous quote I came across just about sums it up: "If you can't find time to sit down beside a wild flower and keep it company for a couple of hours, you might as well go someplace and sell life insurance."

AUGUST: Start gathering the harvest. Show your children how to cut the stems from thyme and marjoram, or whatever, and tie it into small bunches to dry for the winter store.

SEPTEMBER: Get a head start on holiday gifts and start making some herb oils and vinegars. These useful infusions cost a fortune in gourmet shops.

OCTOBER: Hang bunches of herbs to protect against evil—especially marigold (*Calendula officinalis*) and tansy. Rue (*Ruta graveolens*) is also one of the main traditional protectants against bad spirits, but is not recommended for a child's garden as it can cause a serious skin complaint in some.

NOVEMBER: Let them boast to the family at how the turkey dressing is made with herbs from their very own patch.

DECEMBER: Decorate a crib with manger herbs—pennyroyal (*Mentha pulegium*), thyme, and lady's bedstraw (*Galium verum*). Give small posies of herbs as gifts.

I do hope you can enjoy making a herb garden with your children or grandchildren just as much as I have done. The only rule is to turn a blind eye to the weeds occasionally, leaving you time to smell the lavender.

Foraging for Green Salads

≈ By Carly Wall, C.A. ≈

*E*ating wild foraged greens has some kind of excitement for me. For one, it's something you can truly get for nothing. These "weeds" contain all kinds of vitamins and minerals our bodies are starved for. They also make up an exotic, gourmet meal or dish. All it takes is a few minutes to find and harvest them. Think of it; you never have to buy the seed, plant or care for it, weed on boiling hot days, or till or fertilize the soil. It's just out there, growing, waiting for you to take it—out there just for the asking!

For me, the best and most potent herbs come from the wild, so, when it comes to eating, for these reasons (low-cost, great taste, health benefits), I'll choose wild every time.

There's another reason, too, I have to confess. Wild foraging also brings another gourmet treat to my table. After the first warm rain, when

the temperatures hover in the 60s for a few days, I see signs of the wild mushroom forager. Their cars will be parked willy-nilly alongside the road near where I live (close to a wildlife preserve so there are plenty of woodlands). If you wait long enough, you are sure to see these foragers emerge from the trees and meadows, staggering back to their vehicles with their booty of mushrooms stuffed in their sacks, jaunty hats on their heads and walking sticks in hand.

Of course, morel mushrooms are quite delicious. The trouble is, everyone knows that, so there is plenty of competition when you go out to hunt for them. If you long for the taste of these delicious tidbits, you have to be lucky enough to know where a good patch grows, and you have to get there at just the right time, before anyone else. You also have to be good at spotting them as well as having the stamina to tromp around up slopes and down in search of them.

For me, it's much too hard to do, so I've invented another way around it. I'd rather forage wild greens from my back yard (where they grow in abundance) and trade some greens with a willing mushroom hunter. Of course, they always want to trade, because morels taste so good with a wild salad. Morels dredged in egg and rolled in flour, fried to crisp brown perfection in bacon grease, with a fresh foraged green salad as an accompaniment—now that's a gourmet meal!

Before you even think about foraging wild, make sure you can identify the plants. If you can't be certain, get a good book with pictures and ask an experienced forager or contact your local agricultural office. Some plants can be dangerously poisonous, so you have to know your stuff. Also important is that you pick only from a pesticide-free area, away from roadsides.

Spring and Summer

Of course, the morels come up in early spring, so the greens we harvest then will be the tender dandelion greens, purslane, wild strawberries, wild onion, and plantain.

DANDELION (*Taraxacum officinale*): The dandelion is so useful and delicious, I can't understand why some people are dismayed to see them in their yards. This perennial has lance-shaped leaves and a well-known yellow bloom. Harvest tender leaves in early spring, and after a frost in the fall, when the bitterness of summer has passed. Dandelion greens always improve the taste of salads; they have a slightly bitter, endive flavor. The leaves are higher in beta carotene than carrots, have high iron and calcium levels, and contain vitamins B1, B2, B12, and C as well as high amounts of potassium, phosphorus, magnesium, and zinc. Toss the greens into mixed salads and add the blossoms if you wish for color and flavor.

PURSLANE (*Portulaca oleracea*): In Europe, this used to be a well-known cultivated garden vegetable, but the smooth, succulent, creeping stems now grow wild everywhere with abandon, and are largely a forgotten herb. What a shame, for purslane makes a great addition to raw salads with its sweet-sour taste. Just chop the fleshy rounded, paddle-like leaves and the stems into your salad for a taste treat. It is also a nutrition powerhouse, boasting iron, vitamin C, calcium, and riboflavin. It is a great source of omega-3 fatty acids, which boost the immune system. Purslane appears late spring and dies in the fall, reseeding itself for next year, so you never want to strip your wild patch completely, but leave a few plants to reseed so you won't do without in the following year.

WILD STRAWBERRIES (*Fragaria virginiana*): A member of the rose family, the strawberry also has the nickname earthberry. No one could mistake this plant's succulent red and juicy berries. They grow wild in open and sunny meadows and edges of woodlands and fences. The wild strawberry has a short season—about two weeks. The red berries add interest and bright flavor to perk up salad greens, especially when served with a sweet dressing. The fruit is a mild laxative, as well as being high in potassium and magnesium. While you're at it, pick some strawberry leaves for a tea to have with your salad. The tea is high in vitamins C and K, and tastes divine when sweetened with honey.

WILD ONION (*Allium spp.*): Before I became herb-literate, I used to curse the wild onion for popping up all over my gardens in spring. Then I got smart and started to add them to my green salads. Now I can't find enough of them! There are poisonous look-alikes for these but they are odorless, so be sure you can smell the onion on these wild things. Wild onions are easy to recognize. They have little shoots that resemble young onions or chives. Use these as you would chives or scalllions. Chop the leaves and/or bulbs finely and toss over salads freely. You can also add wild onions to olive oil and let them infuse for a week or so to get a flavored oil, or add to vinegar the same way to flavor vinegar and use this in making your own dressing. In the spring the plant has a mild onion flavor, but the later you pick it, the more garlicky the flavor becomes. The wild onion contains beta carotene, calcium, copper, zinc, and selenium.

PLANTAIN (*Plantago spp.*): The large, shiny round leaves of the plantain are very appealing in early spring, but they become tough as the season wears on. Plantain provides plenty of nutrients though—calcium and beta carotene—as well as helping to reduce cholesterol and helping prevent heart disease. It has also been deemed useful for kidney and urinary tract problems. Another plus is that because of its high chlorophyl content, it helps prevent bad breath. The dark green leaves can be chopped and added to mixed green salads for color.

Autumn

LAMB'S QUARTERS (*Chenopodium album*): Originally from Europe, the seeds of this plant were carried over to the U.S.A., and it quickly became a prolific weed. It's a branching herbaceous annual that grows on average to five feet high. The leaves have a white wax underneath and the young leaves are slender. Use the tender leaves from the tips (or from young shoots under a foot tall) from late spring until late fall frosts kill the plant. It has a delicious flavor—like spinach only not bitter at all. It's also a powerhouse of nutrition, containing more iron than spinach, as well as trace minerals, B vitamins, vitamin C, and it provides plenty of fiber. Use it as you would spinach in fresh salads.

Sweet Clover Flowers (*Trifolium, Melilotus spp.*): You can find common clovers on lawns and fields everywhere. They bloom spring to fall, and the flowers are sweet and tasty as long as you pick the brightly-colored heads. Chop them finely and toss them into your salad for bright color appeal and an added surprise flavor. High in protein, clover contains minerals like magnesium, manganese, zinc, copper, and selenium.

Miner's Lettuce (*Montia perfoliata*): The oval, cupped leaves of this plant are quite pretty. It grows in shady places that stay moist, like near springs and at the bottom of mountainous slopes. A major food source to Californians during the Wild Western days of yore, miner's lettuce has a mild flavor and is quite tender and delicious. It is really good when mixed with the stronger greens like the dandelion. The flowers are spicy, peppery, and are great for perking up salads too. It's a great source of vitamin C.

There are plenty of other greens out there, but these will get you started, so get going. Pick some greens (enough to keep and enough to trade) and find yourself a mushroom hunter quick, before the season passes you by!

Dandelion Green Salad with Carrots

Salad

3   cups rinsed/spun dry salad greens, torn

1   cup rinsed/spun dry tender dandelion greens, torn

½   cup coarse grated carrot

4   pieces of bacon, crisp fried and crumbled

Dressing

½   cup mayonnaise

1   tablespoon bacon grease, melted

2   teaspoons sugar (or to taste)

1   tablespoon raspberry or tarragon vinegar

Toss salad ingredients, except for bacon, in bowl. Sprinkle crumbled bacon on top. In another bowl, whisk together dressing ingredients well. Add dressing to greens, and toss well. Serves four.

Culinary
Herbs

Extraordinary Culinary Herbs

⇒ By Penny Kelly ⇐

When I first left home and started cooking for myself, I cooked only to stay alive, not because I enjoyed it. Seven years later my interest in cooking was still at a low point, but I didn't know how low that was until the first dinner party I ever gave. I served up spaghetti with Campbell's tomato soup over it. Fortunately, the three couples seated around the table were friends. When one of the men said to me, "Hey, where are the salt and pepper shakers?" and I replied that I didn't have any, the conversation at the table came to a halt. They just couldn't believe I didn't use salt and pepper at the table. Someone else asked me if I had ever thought of using herbs.

"What for?" I said.

"For taste!" she replied, then continued in an ever-so-curious tone, "You know, this almost tastes like spaghetti with tomato soup on it."

"It is!" I said with some cross between naiveté and enthusiasm that she recognized my cooking.

The whole group broke into laughter and someone said in a good-natured way, "If you like spaghetti like this, then you would love how it tastes with a few herbs added."

Thinking back, I squirm in belated embarrassment at the memory of my early version of Italian spaghetti, and what a terrific sense of humor those friends brought to my dinner table. Their gentle teasing wakened me to the possibility that there was more to food than pure survival, and not too long afterward I got out the recipe book I had gotten as a wedding gift and looked through it. I took the suggested list of herbs that the cookbook said should be in every kitchen, went to the Spice Island display at the grocery store, got everything on the list, and almost had a heart attack when I discovered how much it was going to cost at the checkout. I couldn't believe a few leaves could be so expensive. Once I had them in my kitchen, I found a few recipes that called for an herb here and there, and ever so slowly started using a few of the basic ones. I couldn't tell the difference in the flavor of the dish, but I definitely felt like a more accomplished cook.

One day a couple of years later I decided to put in a small garden. While buying tomato and pepper plants at the nearest garden center, I came across a small section of herb seedlings and decided to try growing a few things. Into the cart went parsley, three kinds of basil, sage, thyme, oregano, marjoram, and lavender.

When I harvested the first cuttings from these and dried them, I was astounded at depth of flavor and aroma they gave to my soups, salads, roasts, and casseroles. There was no comparison between the rich green parsley from my garden and the pale stuff I had been buying at the store.

Growing my own herbs expanded from those early few to almost four dozen culinary herbs and led eventually to a bit of research into the nature of culinary herbs, and what they do. Many culinary herbs started out either as preservatives in the days when refrigeration was not yet available, or as some type of digestive aid. They are also full of vitamins and minerals, and contain a wide variety of chemical substances that have beneficial effects on the body/mind system.

When you put parsley into your soup, the broth becomes a rich, healing, and flavorful tea that is mixed with the other flavors such as carrot or potato, beef or chicken. Not only have you added calcium, iron, and potassium, you have put in Vitamin B and prodigious amounts of Vitamin A.[1] If you add fresh parsley to your salad, you get the added benefit of all of the above plus Vitamin C, which is normally destroyed by heat.

In addition to the nutritional aspects offered by herbs, there are dozens of other effects offered by culinary herbs. For instance, parsley soothes the entire gastrointestinal tract, aiding digestion, which then results in less gas and sweeter breath. It works as a powerful diuretic, cleaning the kidneys, dissolving kidney stones, helping eliminate bladder problems, and shrinking hemorrhoids.[2] You get the gentle, persistent benefit of all this simply by adding it to your food regularly.

Thyme is another culinary herb that is worth growing and keeping in your diet. A major component of thyme is thymol, an antiseptic, antifungal ingredient in many of Edgar Cayce's healing programs. It has a sweetening effect on butters, sauces, salads, meats, and all sorts of baked dishes. Besides the sweetening effect, it soothes the urinary tract, raises your spirits, temporarily heats up the body, which helps keep you warm on cold days, and the thymol is expelled through the lungs, which helps keep asthma and bronchitis to a minimum. Adding fresh or dried thyme to your salad will help keep your gums healthy, your breath fresh, and helps to cut down on post-nasal drip.

Sage is another common culinary herb with potent taste and wide-ranging effects. It is a major ingredient in poultry seasoning, along with marjoram, black pepper, coriander, and celery seed. It is a bit strong when added fresh to salads, but it is excellent for soups, stews, casseroles, and meat dishes. Sage protects against colds and sore throats. Like parsley, it enriches the natural flavor of foods and aids in the digestion of foods, especially the animal fats that are so maligned these days but so important to good, complete nutrition. For women of menopause age, sage helps prevent hot flashes. For those with diabetes it lowers blood sugar. Sage eases arthritis aches and pains, and imparts to all who partake of it a bit of natural resistance to staphylococcus infections. Dried sage added in spartan amounts to summer salads helps to prevent sweating, and the old stories promise that sage, like ginseng, is a great overall tonic that brings wisdom, clear thinking, health, and long life.

Basil, one of my favorite herbs, is added to every salad, most soups, and a number of other dishes I make because it has just plain wonderful taste. Besides aiding in a more complete digestion, it lends a sense of relaxation and ease to life because of its mild sedative properties. Basil soothes irritated tummies, cuts down on a tendency toward gas and constipation, relieves the general heaviness of breathing that nags people with respiratory disorders after a meal, and helps your body to continuously heal itself. Best of all, it adds flavor that carries you into the realms of the sublime. I grow six different kinds of basil, treasure them all, and never get tired of its uplifting scent.

The use of marjoram goes back a long way, first as a medicine and later as a flavoring agent for foods. Like thyme and sage, marjoram contains thymol, and is used as a both medicinal and culinary herb all over the world. Several herbal references contradict one another in identifying marjoram, oregano, and sweet marjoram. One book says that the common name for the species called *Origanum vulgare L.* is "marjoram." Two other books refer to this same species as "oregano." Regardless, all three are very similar in effect, yet quite unique in flavor and taste. *Origanum vulgare L.* is very strong and is used freely in Italian cooking, while sweet marjoram, *Origanum majorana*, is more delicate and is used in many French dishes.

All have a reputation for strengthening the brain while having a mild detoxification effect on the entire body/mind system.

Dried or fresh marjoram added to salads not only imparts a distinct and delicious flavor, it helps keep the gall bladder healthy and functioning and fights fatigue and tension, while eliminating gas and stomach upsets. Used in soups, sauces, and meat dishes, it helps the systems of the body stay in balance by keeping the bladder in good working order, keeping menstrual periods regular, stimulating liver function, and acting as a diuretic. It also serves to keep teeth and gums healthy by fighting abscesses, and reducing inflammations and the pains of arthritis.

Onions are now considered a vegetable, but were once grown as a medicinal for their powerful juice. Onions are chockfull of vitamins, minerals, essential oils, and a number of antiseptic compounds. Cooking them greatly reduces their potency, yet they are still excellent for the lungs, the circulatory system, and the gastrointestinal tract. They help keep cholesterol down, clear the bronchial passageways, and keep blood sugar in balance. Adding onions to your culinary creations helps clean out your arteries, and keeps the blood in a fluid condition so it circulates more easily. Chopping onions to add to soups and salads, whether raw or cooked, helps fights colds and flu, tones the kidneys, lowers blood pressure, and adds a bit of sexual energy.

Garlic is similar to onion but better, stronger, and its list of benefits is longer. In addition to everything onions do, garlic also kills candida organisms, works as an antibiotic to destroy staphylococcus and streptococcus bacteria, gets rid of worms and parasites, and breaks up the purulent matter that is generated by infections, ulcers, and abscesses. What is even more magical is that garlic literally prevents arteriosclerosis, reduces hypertension and sinus congestion, and prevents, arrests, then helps break up tumors! From my point of view there is just no reason to leave garlic and onions out of your diet, especially when we have parsley, thyme, and sage to erase the smell on our breath.

The last items that go in the category of "culinaire extraordinaire" are rosemary and celery. Rosemary leaves have an amazing assortment of helpful effects when added to your meals.

Foremost is its ability to improve memory! Following that, it will help ward off headaches, prevent muscle spasms, and lift depression. It also works wonders for the liver, gall bladder, stomach, and intestines, improving digestion and thus making for better assimilation of whatever you've eaten. For years it has been recognized as good for your hair and skin, probably because it strengthens the walls of blood vessels and capillaries and thus results in better circulation to the far reaches of the body.

Celery, especially raw, but also in the form of seeds or juice, is a powerful antiarthritic agent, as well as diuretic assistant for those with congestive heart failure and other circulation problems. Adding celery seeds to your soups, gravies, salads, and dressings is a good way to get some of the benefits of celery. The body needs sodium for its basic nerve functions, but table salt is the wrong kind of sodium. Celery contains organic sodium and thus does not have the serious side effects in the body that table salt has. What's more, this organic sodium has the ability to eliminate inorganic calcium deposits in the body, relieving many problems with arthritis.[3] Celery also helps maintain muscle, keep lungs clear, and helps the body absorb needed nutrients from all the food it is fed.

It has been a long journey since the time of that first dinner party. The interesting thing is that where I once ate only to survive, I now prepare meals that I believe will help me thrive.

Endnotes

1   Mabey, Richard. *The New Age Herbalist*. New York: Simon and Schuster, 1988. A great book on using herbs for nutrition, healing, relaxation, and body care.

2   Kaye, Connie and Neil Billington. *Medicinal Plants of the Heartland*. An excellent discussion of what is actually in many of herbs, both culinary and medicinal.

3   See *Medicinal Plants of the Heartland*.

Making Herbal Butters

~ By Carly Wall, C.A. ~

*U*sually, on the first fine spring day, my mind is full of exciting herbal possibilities. There is the herb garden to check, new plants to grow, and the most exciting—new ways to put the herbs to use. If you don't make the effort, you'll never use the herbs. You have to set reasonable goals for yourself, choosing one or two new ways per year to incorporate herbs into your life. Otherwise, you could become overwhelmed; after all, there are thousands of herbs and thousands of uses.

As I look out my home office window, the herb garden looks a little barren at first. I decide it's time for a break and so I put on my jacket and boots and take a walk.

The grass is greening up a little. In the herb garden I push aside the winter debris and wet leaves to find my first hint that spring is indeed around the corner! Tiny green shoots of chives are

growing and pushing their way out of the ground. The chives are always up first. Now my eyes are adjusting, and I notice other things around me. The winter has been kind to my rosemary plants this year—they've survived. My thyme is green in places. I look around and suddenly see that the clematis vines I planted last year have made it, too.

Sometimes it takes time to adjust our eyes from the dreary winter days to the spring landscape. It is almost as if we have been put to sleep ourselves by winter's cold winds. Gardeners, just like their garden beds, seem to hunker in for the winter. All it takes to wake up again is one turn around outside on the first mild spring morning, and again the mind races with gardening ideas.

I plan to haunt certain plant nurseries again and to dream up new garden designs. In the meantime there's plenty of work to be done clearing out the old and preparing for the new.

As I clear away the debris, I realize that my eating habits change in spring. I begin to long for fresh green things. It does not take long to snip a few of the pungent, oniony-flavored tips of chives. I can mince them, add them to omelets, sprinkle them over baked potatoes, or toss them into soup bowls with a few croutons. If you don't happen to have chives, many groceries now carry fresh and dried herbs if you want to try them before growing your own plants.

I'm still looking for that one special project to try this year and I finally hit on the idea. I'll experiment with herbal butters! They are delicious, unusual (yet easy), and they brighten up a spring table, too. They are also quite elegant for formal occasions and parties. Did I mention versatile? You can use a wide variety of herbs for these butters. Fresh or dried herbs both work well.

If you too decide to experiment with herbal butters, you'll discover they are an easy way to add zest to your cooking—and it's the easiest way to try out herbal flavors. You can make them with one herb or a combination of your choosing, and use them in various ways. That's the challenge and adventure. Perhaps you'll create an herbal butter that will become a tradition.

Choose Your Butter

The best choice for herbal butters is the unsalted sweet butter (the real stuff). It lets delicate flavors of the herbs come through. You can also use margarine or salted butter too, depending upon on how you plan to use your finished product.

Various Uses for Herbal Butters

Basically, herbal butters are flavored butters you can use just like butter, only with that extra kick. They are wonderful drizzled on all vegetables: tomatoes, zucchini, eggplant, potatoes, carrots, peas, or corn. They also make a good baste for all types of meat: lamb, beef, pork, chicken, fish, and other seafood. Last, they flavor rice and egg dishes wonderfully, and are great slathered on thick slices of homemade breads, crackers, toast, and biscuits. There's nothing better than flavored butters for the grill, or to use to make toast or to make toasted french bread slices.

Making the Flavored Butters

Here's the basic recipe:

- ¼ pound sweet cream butter, softened
- 2 teaspoons fresh lemon juice
- 3 tablespoons finely minced herbs

If using dried herbs, mix in with the lemon juice to moisten. Cream everything together with a wooden spoon until well blended. You can either use a melon ball scoop to make butter balls (in which case, drop the balls into a bowl of ice water—then drain) or roll the whole thing into a log from which to cut rounds. If you roll it into a log, you can roll it in additional minced herbs for a decorative touch. A neat idea is to use minced chives for the recipe, then roll the log in minced chive blossoms to coat the outside. The pretty purple blossoms are eye-catching.

Wrap the log tightly in plastic wrap (or place the balls in plastic baggies) and refrigerate or freeze. If fresh herbs are used, keep in the refrigerator up to three days. If using dried herbs, keep refrigerated a week or so. You can freeze the butters for up to three months. Be sure to let the flavors blend before using (at least four hours, but overnight is best). Let the butter stand at room temperature twenty minutes before serving.

What Herbs Work Well Together?

I like to make a parsley-garlic butter to toast french bread slices. This goes nicely with pasta dishes. Another great combination is to use rosemary/chive butter to rub all over a whole chicken before roasting (be sure to keep basting). Dill butter is great with grilled salmon. Mint butter is great in cooked carrots or peas and for spreading on bread in making cucumber sandwiches. Try making a sweet violet butter. Here is a recipe to brighten up the table and to give you an idea of the varied uses of herbal butters:

Lemon Balm Muffins with Rose Petal Butter

2	cups flour
1¼	teaspoon baking soda
½	teaspoon salt
½	cup sugar
1	teaspoon lemon zest
2	eggs
½	cup applesauce
½	cup lemon juice
3	tablespoons minced lemon balm

Spray muffin tins with nonstick cooking spray. Blend together dry ingredients. In another bowl whisk the eggs until blended. Add applesauce, lemon juice, and minced lemon balm. Add wet mixture to dry ingredients. Mix well and drop into muffn tins. Bake at 375°F for 20-25 minutes. Serve with rose butter.

Stevia for Your Sweet Tooth

❧ By Penny Kelly ❧

There isn't much to be found in traditional herb manuals on the plant known as stevia. Out of almost two dozen herbal reference books in my library, only one contained any mention of stevia, and that amounted to two sentences: "*Stevia rebaudiana* is a tropical annual with very sweet leaves that yield the substance stevioside. This white, crystalline substance is 250–300 times sweeter than sucrose."[1] And it is!

I found stevia late last June at a local nursery and brought home half a flat, about twenty-five plants in all. It was already somewhat overgrown and stringy when I put it in the garden at a spacing of about fifteen inches between plants, but it grew well without special attention or extra nutrients. It grew to about knee height and formed straight stems and small oval leaves about an inch long that seemed to grow fairly far

apart along the stems. The plants were not very dense or bushy overall, but this might have been due to the fact that they needed to go in the ground long before I found them and planted them.

Even from a very young stage, however, the leaves were incredibly sweet. Once or twice I picked several leaves, put them in a two-quart pitcher of water in the refrigerator, and noticed a subtle richness in the taste of the water when they were left in overnight. Sliced lemons added to this water the next day created a simple drink that was really delicious without being "sweet."

When the summer ended, I wasn't sure what to do with all the stevia, so I set about experimenting.

Since it was a tropical annual, there was no point in trying to mulch the plant for overwintering. Getting a basket and my shears, I cut the majority of the stems from about eighteen of the plants and brought them in to dry. When the eighteen I had brought in were fully dry, I stripped the leaves from the stems and at this point had a large, cafeteria-type tray of dried leaves about two inches deep. The stems were as sweet as the leaves, so I started experimenting with the stems.

My first idea was to make a cup of tea, divide it into two half-cups, and then stir one of them with a few stevia stems to see if it would make it any sweeter—but it didn't. The stems were sweet in my mouth, but not sweet enough to sweeten the tea. I couldn't tell a bit of difference between the cup of plain tea and the cup that had been stirred with the stems. I decided not to try to do anything further with the stems and they went into the compost bucket.

Next I crushed a single leaf as completely as I could using my fingers and put the herb in a half cup of ordinary black tea. After a moment of stirring I tasted it and found that there was a subtle change compared to the half that was still plain tea.

Crushing a second leaf and adding that to the cup with one leaf already in it created a noticeable change. The tea in the control cup of plain tea tasted flat with a sharp edge, while the tea with the two crushed stevia leaves tasted round and full.

I took a third leaf, crushed it, and added it to the first two, and by that time the taste of the stevia was overpowering. I noticed that it tended to leave a bitter aftertaste along the sides and back of my tongue when there was too much sweetener present.

Now, using a cup of coffee as my test cup, I ground a handful of the stevia in a small food grinder. The idea was to put the finely ground herb in a sugar bowl and be able to dip some out with a spoon. This worked well except that you had to be careful not to put too much in the coffee. Only an eighth teaspoon produced a strong sweetening effect. After a few sips I gave it to someone else to try and he said it was good, but another test with someone different produced an immediate wrinkled nose and the question, "What did you put in this? It leaves an aftertaste!"

My next idea was that maybe using the herb directly was a bad idea. Perhaps I could get the same sweetening effect by steeping the leaves in hot water to make a syrupy tea. I put a quarter cup of the dried leaves into a measuring cup, then poured two cups of boiling water over them and covered all with a small plate. After steeping for twenty minutes I had a light brown liquid sweetener without the aftertaste!

A tiny taste of the leaves that had been strained out of the steeped liquid still provided a blockbuster dose of sweetness, so I took that same quarter cup of soggy leaves, poured another two cups of boiling water over top, and let them steep overnight. In the morning I had a second batch of liquid sweetener that was just as good as the first batch.

The remaining leaves went into the food grinder and netted me nearly two cups of finely ground stevia, which I decided to experiment with in some muffins, using the following quantities:

2   cups flour (whole wheat or white or other)

½   teaspoon salt

1   tablespoon baking powder

½   cup oil (or ⅓ cup butter)

½   cup milk (to start)

I made a batch of muffin batter and divided it evenly into three small bowls. To the first bowl I added a teaspoon of stevia, to the second bowl I added a half teaspoon of stevia, and the third bowl got only two tablespoons of the liquid I had steeped using stevia leaves. Once the sweetener was in I had to add a little more milk to each of the three bowls to get the "drop biscuit" consistency I wanted. I had added a minimum of liquid at the start because I wasn't sure what effect the stevia—especially the liquid—would have. After baking I gathered all the family members to sample the results, including four adults and three children.

Without exception, the vote for favorite went to the muffins made with the liquid stevia. This group of muffins was rich tasting and yet not too sweet. The next favorite were the muffins made with a half teaspoon of stevia. They were tasty with an undefinable sweetness that would have served well as a dinner or shortcake muffin. Almost without exception, everyone who bit into the muffins made with one teaspoon of the herb had some kind of reaction from "wow" to "whoa" to "ugh!" The consensus was that it was just too sweet.

When my experimenting was completed I sat down to ruminate on the plusses and minuses of my experience with stevia again. To my surprise, the only minus was that I like to collect my own seeds and the plants did not produce seeds in the allotted Michigan growing season. The plusses were several. The biggest one was that I liked the idea of being able to grow a plant that I could keep on hand in dried form and make a liquid sweetener from it whenever I needed to. Another plus was that lots of people come here to the farm, many of them have special or restricted diets, and I liked the idea of having access to a variety of sweeteners that would not aggravate an already aggravating condition.

1   Bremness, Leslie. *Herbs*. Eyewitness Handbook Series. New York: Dorling Kindersley, 1994.

Herbal Syrups for Beverages

➤ By Carly Wall, C.A. ➤

What did people do before the invention of bottled soft drinks? They made their own instant drinks from fruits and herbs. It's so easy and economical, you have to wonder why these homemade "time-savers" have fallen to the wayside.

I wondered this myself, and decided to drag out some of grandma's favorite old syrup recipes, which I share with you here. She liked using lemon syrup for her famous icy lemonade, to be sipped on the porch on hot summer days. She liked mint, so that was a regular around her household, too.

How did these syrups originate? There was a need for fast drinks on hot days. On top of that, kitchens were pretty busy in summers during canning season, so these drinks were easy to make; all the kids had to do was mix a couple tablespoons of the flavored syrup with water and they were ready.

Syrups are bases of flavored sugars in liquid form that are easy to mix with either hot or iced water, or sparkling water or ginger ale for that little fizz on special occasions.

Some syrups were reserved for cold and flu season if the right herbs were used, and honey was used as the base for the syrup. In this case, the syrup was taken from the spoon, or added to hot water to help with coughs and sore throats. Lemon-flavored herbs, as well as horehound, hyssop, or wild cherry bark, were a few that were particularly favored for these concoctions. Since I've made cough syrups plenty of times over the years, I was interested in the drinks for pleasure that old-timers created to have on hand.

I discovered there were two types; the regular-flavored syrup and something called shrub, which was a flavored syrup made with vinegar. The vinegar gives a little tang to the taste (this mix was also good for cold and flu season). Both these syrup drink bases were versatile, meaning that not only could you use them for instant drinks, but you could pour the syrups over ice cream, add them to yogurt or hot cereals, or drizzle them over pancakes or biscuits. Try a few different flavors and combinations and see if you and your family don't find them enjoyable. They're an easy way to use herbs, and it's much more healthy than guzzling tons of soda. At least you know that in these drinks the herbal additions will give you a boost of vitamins as well as other added benefits. For an even healthier drink, you can make the syrup from honey to avoid refined sugar altogether. Have fun!

Basic Base Syrup Recipe

2   cups water (or fruit juice)
½   cup dried herb of choice
2   cups sugar

Bring water or juice to boil. Add herb. Remove from heat and cover. Steep 20 minutes. Strain and squeeze out the herbs. discard the plant material. Place the liquid back on the heat and bring to a boil again, adding the sugar. Boil 15 minutes. Pour into sterilized jars and seal. After opening, keep refigerated up to one year. To use, add two tablespoons to eight ounces iced or hot water, sparkling water, or ginger ale.

Basic Honey Syrup Recipe

1   cup water (or fruit juice)
½   cup dried herb of choice
3   cups honey

Place the herb into the water or juice and bring to a boil. Let steep covered for about 20 minutes. Strain. Return to heat and bring to a boil again, then turn down to simmer. Add the honey and mix well. Pour into sterilized jars and seal. After opening, keep refrigerated up to a year. For drinks, add two tablespoons to iced or hot water, sparkling water, or ginger ale.

Basic Shrub Recipe

1½   cups fruit juice
 ½   cup dried herb of choice
 1   pound sugar
 ½   cup apple cider vinegar

Bring fruit juice to boil. Remove from heat, and add the herbs. Cover and steep 20 minutes. Strain herbs out and return liquid to heat, bringing to a boil again. Add sugar and vinegar, and boil for 15 minutes. Pour into sterilized jars and seal tightly with fresh, sterilized canning lids. Invert for 5 minutes. Lids should seal. If not, place in a boiling water bath for ten minutes. Refrigerate after opening. It keeps up to a year. To use, add two tablespoons to iced or hot water or sparkling water or ginger ale.

Here are a few old-time recipes to get you started. Note that you can turn any of these drinks into creamy coolers by adding two tablespoons plain yogurt or real cream to the ice water, along with the two tablespoons of syrup your choice. Orange flavors are especially delicious this way.

Mint Syrup

3   cups boiling water

4   cups chopped mint leaves

4   cups sugar

1   tablespoon mint extract

     Green food coloring, optional

Cover the chopped mint with boiling water. Cover and let steep 30 minutes. Strain. Bring liquid to boil with the sugar; boil 10-15 minutes. Add mint extract and food coloring. Pour into sterilized bottles.

Floral Syrup

2½   cups water

1   pound clean, pesticide-free edible flowers (lavender, rose, jasmine, chamomile, etc.)

1¾   cup sugar

Bring the water to boil and add the flowers. Remove from heat and cover to steep 15–20 minutes. Strain. Return liquid to heat and bring to boil again, adding sugar. Stir.

Lemonade Syrup

2   cups sugar

1   cup water

1   lemon peel

½   cup lemon verbena (or spearmint leaves)

     Juice of 6 lemons

Combine all together except for the lemon juice. Boil for 5 minutes. Strain out the lemon peel and herbs. Add the lemon juice and mix well. Pour into sterile jars. If you want the mix more yellow, simply add yellow food coloring, or, for pink lemonade, add a few drops of red food coloring. You can also purchase different flavoring oils to add to the syrup. Add them just before pouring into sterile jars, mixing well.

Strawberry–Mint Syrup

Fresh cleaned strawberries

2   cups sugar per every 2 cups juice

3   mint tea bags

5   whole cloves

Place strawberries in a pan and add a bit of water. With a potato masher, mash the strawberries and warm on low heat. Strain the juice. For every 2 cups of juice add 2 cups sugar. Place the juice and sugar in the pan and return to heat. Add mint tea bags and cloves, and bring all this to a boil for 15 minutes. Take out the cloves and tea bags and pour the syrup into sterilized jars.

Lavender–Cherry Syrup

1   pound cherries, pitted

½   cup lavender buds

2½   cups water

2   pounds sugar

1   teaspoon almond extract

Bring cherries, lavender, and water to boil 20 minutes. Strain. Add sugar to the cherry/lavender juice, and return to boil for 15 minutes. Add almond extract. Pour into sterilized jars.

Homemade Root Beer Syrup

2   cups water

3   tablespoons sarsaparilla

1   tablespoon sassafras

½   teaspoon coriander

2   cups sugar (or 1 cup blackstrap molasses)

Bring flavorings and water to boil, boil for 20 minutes. Strain. Add the sugar and bring to boil again for 15 minutes. Pour into sterilized jars. Add several tablespoons to ginger ale for a refreshing summer drink.

Jasmine–Almond Syrup

4½   cups water
1½   cups fresh almonds, ground
  1   cup jasmine flowers
  3   tablespoons almond extract
       Juice of 2 oranges
6½   cups sugar

Bring water to boil and add almonds and jasmine flowers. Cover and cool, then use muslin to strain and squeeze out the ground almonds and spent flowers. Return liquid to pan and add almond extract, orange juice, and sugar. Cook until the consistency is a thick syrup. Let cool. If not thick enough, boil again for 5 minutes. Pour into sterilized bottles.

Cinnamon–Bee Balm Syrup

  2   cups water
  2   cinnamon sticks
  ½   cup bee balm
       Juice of 1 lemon
  2   cups sugar

Bring water to boil. Add cinnamon sticks and bee balm and boil 5 minutes. Strain. Return to heat, add lemon juice and sugar. Boil 15 minutes or until syrup is thick. Bottle.

A Kitchen Herbal Primer

⚘ By Caroline Moss ⚘

When planning herb gardens for others, as it is my pleasure to do, I always ask what uses are expected for the herbs. Occasionally I get the answer "for medicines" or "for potpourri." Even more rarely comes the reply "for dyeing" or "to make natural cosmetics." However, by far the most frequent response is "for cooking." Even those who claim not to like "fancy" food or not to want an herb garden will enjoy a little parsley or thyme, but we can do better than that! Now I will help you give yourself a real treat.

In the depths of a cold winter, make a cup of your favourite tea, put a few cookies on your prettiest plate and take a blank piece of paper, some colored pencils, an herb reference book, and some specialist herb nursery catalogues. Sit at a good table and start planning your dream herb garden.

This little exercise is a many-layered pleasure. You have the delight of a very special few hours in the planning. You will have the great sense of fun and achievement later in the year of getting the garden up and running. You will also have the continued joy, for many years to come, of tending, altering, adding to, and, of course, harvesting from your very own herb patch.

In designing your garden, much will, of course, depend on the space available. You can have a lovely selection of herbs to use throughout the year with nothing more than a few pots or a window box. You could set aside a very small, semi-formal herb patch by using a "template" in which to plant. This could be an old ladder, with a plant in each gap, a cart wheel, or paving slabs laid out leaving chess-board spaces of earth. One could plant in a more casual way, while always being aware that the blowsy, cottage garden look still involves careful planning of height and regular tending to ensure that some element of control is maintained. Then again, if you are sure you have a considerable amount of time to spend on maintenance, then you could even try a knot garden, where intricate patterns are achieved by working with carefully trimmed herb hedges, often of box (*Buxus sempervirens*). Make full use of varying leaf colorings and even colored gravel carefully placed to bring out the pattern. Begin with:

- An idea of the space available, but beware! Once you get the bug your herbs will take over your entire garden.

- Information on what plants are possible in your locality. It's no good trying to plant a tree-sized lemon verbena to over-winter outdoors in Vermont.

- A list of the plants you definitely want to include. It would be a shame to plant up a wonderful herb patch only to have to purchase rosemary at the market.

- Details of basic growing patterns, such as the expected heights of plants and any particular requirements. For example, you might want to plant mint in a container or in a separate area.

We now want to get on to the herbs you could include in your garden. As I work in England, I deal with growing in a middling sort of climate. If you have very long, harsh winters or are in the desert states you will need to check local growing guides to ascertain what plants you can deal with, or any extra care they may need.

We will look at how to grow and use several lovely plants that will help you in the kitchen. There are, of course, many dozens more herbs, but these are a good basic selection with which to start, with one or two that are perhaps slightly more unfamiliar. I have only included culinary uses, but may of these herbs do, of course, have valuable medicinal or scented qualities.

Basil (Ocimum basilicum)

TRAITS: Half-hardy annual, six to twelve inches tall.

NATURAL HABITAT: India.

HISTORY AND FOLKLORE: Basil is connected with scorpions in astrology and the ancient herbals. The scorpions were said to enjoying lying under, and even breeding under, the basil.

VARIETIES: There are numerous varieties, including lemon, spice/cinnamon, holy, Greek/bush, opal, purple ruffles, green ruffles, and lettuce leaf basil.

GROWING: It is easily grown from seed. Do not over-water, but do thin to avoid transplanting. Grow indoors as a pot plant in all but the warmest of conditions.

HARVESTING: Pick leaves from the top to avoid flowering and thus prolong life.

PRESERVING: Please don't dry basil—dried basil is horrible. Some basils freeze after painting leaves on both sides with olive oil, although I prefer to treat it as a summer herb and just use it fresh. Infuse the leaves in olive oil or white wine vinegar to add to cooking and salad dressings.

USES: Tear leaves coarsely over tomato salads. Use basil pesto for a pasta sauce or on pizza.

Basil Pesto

2	ounces fresh basil
4	ounces extra virgin olive oil
2	ounces pine nuts
2	cloves garlic
	Salt
2	ounces butter, softened
4	ounces freshly grated parmesan

Blend the basil, oil, pine nuts, garlic, and salt in a food processor. Blend in the butter and parmesan. This makes enough for 1½ pounds of pasta. Add a little hot water if mixing with pasta. It can also be used on chicken or on vegetables such as peppers, tomatoes, or aubergine.

Bay (Laurus nobilis)

TRAITS: Evergreen perennial, over twenty feet tall.

NATURAL HABITAT: Mediterranean.

HISTORY AND FOLKLORE: Bay was sacred to Apollo, the Greek god of prophecy, poetry, and healing. Indeed, Apollo's temple at Delphi had a roof constructed of bay as a guard against disease, witchcraft, and lightning. A wreath of bay became a mark of honor for scholars and athletes, and the word *laureate* means to crown with laurel.

GROWING: Bay really needs to be in containers when small and must be brought under cover if frosty. It is hardy when mature, but the leaves will die in a hard winter. Grow from cuttings (in April) or layering (April or August). Plant in full sun, protected from winds in a moist soil. Be patient. It is slow-growing.

VARIETIES: Look for golden bay (*Laurus nobilis "Aurea"*).

PRESERVING: The leaves dry most successfully.

USES: The leaves are used extensively in cooking. The savory uses of bay are well known, but try adding a leaf to custards or rice pudding. A leaf placed between each piece of meat or vegetable in kebabs is good. Bay is an essential in a bouquet garni (along with thyme and parsley). A leaf placed in the flour bin effectively repels weevils and other bugs.

Bouquet Garni

A jar of these muslin bags makes a good present.

12	(4-inch) squares of muslin
12	bay leaves
12	teaspoons celery seeds
24	cloves
12	tablespoons dried parsley
12	peppercorns
6	teaspoons thyme

Divide the ingredients equally between the squares of muslin. Tie with heavy twine, leaving a long string attached with which to fish the bundle out of the stew pot.

Chives (*Allium schoenoprasum*)

TRAITS: Hardy perennial, six inches tall.

NATURAL HABITAT: Northern Europe and northeastern North America

HISTORY AND FOLKLORE: Chives were used in China as long as 5,000 years ago and introduced into Britain by the Romans.

GROWING: Chives will take virtually any conditions, although they need to be watered well in very dry weather. Feed the soil occasionally and divide clumps every couple of years. This plant will keep in a pot all year round.

PRESERVING: Use only fresh chives.

USES: Finely chop the stems into salad dressings, particularly for potato, tomato, or egg salad. Add to anything where a mild onion flavor is required. Also delicious chopped into cream cheese.

Coriander/Cilantro (Coriandrum sativum)

TRAITS: Annual, from eighteen inches to three feet tall.

HABITAT: Native to southern Europe.

HISTORY AND FOLKLORE: The name comes from the Greek *koros*, meaning an insect, due to the smell of bed bugs in the leaf. The leaves are certainly pungent, but I cannot actually vouch for what a bed bug smells like! As with so many herbs, coriander was introduced into Britain by the Romans, who used it as a meat preservative. In the Middle Ages it was added to love potions, and the Chinese believed that the seeds conferred immortality. The Greeks, notably Pliny, said the best coriander came from Egypt.

GROWING: Plant seeds in full sun in well-drained, fertile soil. The leaves can be used when desired. The seed is ready for use in late August. Treat it as a salad crop with several plantings as it soon goes to seed.

USES: The leaves are widely used in Eastern foods, and the seeds are essential in spice and curry mixes and crushed in boiled basmati rice. Use the leaves in moderation in salad dressings. Some find the flavor of the leaves something of an acquired taste, others love it. Coriander flavors certain German sausages and is wonderful in a carrot soup. To keep leaves fresh in the fridge, Madhur Jaffrey recommends pulling up a whole plant, roots and all, and placing it into jar of water and covering the lot with a plastic bag. Discard yellowing leaves daily and the bulk should keep for weeks.

Spicy Grilled Cheese (Not for the Faint-Hearted)

1   pound grated cheddar cheese

1   carton sour cream

3   cloves crushed garlic

1   chile, seeds removed and finely chopped

1   red onion, finely chopped

1   tomato, chopped

1   bunch fresh coriander

Avocado slices

Mix the cheese, sour cream, garlic, chile, and half the onion. Bake in a greased dish in a hot oven until melted, stirring occasionally. When melted, add the tomato and grill until bubbling. Sprinkle with the remaining onion and coriander. Garnish with avocado slices. Use as dip for tortilla (corn) chips or crackers.

Dill (Anethum graveolens)

TRAITS: Hardy annual, up to five feet tall.

NATURAL HABITAT: Southern Russia and surrounding countries.

HISTORY AND FOLKLORE: Dill was used in the Middle Ages on St John's Eve as a protection against witchcraft. It was known as "meetin' seed" by early American settlers as it was given to young children to chew in long religious meetings. The name dill is derived from a Norse word *dilla*, meaning "to lull."

GROWING: Plant in full sun, protected from the wind, in a rich and well-drained soil. Grows well from seed planted in spring up to June. Do not plant near the closely related fennel, as it will cross pollinate. Thin seedlings to one foot apart.

PRESERVING: The leaves should really only be used fresh, but the seed may be dried or preserved in vinegar.

USES: Add seeds to soup, fish dishes, pickles (such as the famous German-American dill pickles), cabbage, sauerkraut, seed cake, or apple pie. The seeds can be chewed to aid digestion after a meal. The chopped leaf can be added to potato salad, cream cheese, salmon, eggs, or grilled meat.

Dill Pickles

Fill sterilized jars with baby cucumbers or gherkins. Quarter the cucumbers lengthwise if they are too thick. Place a clove of garlic and a flowering head of dill in each jar. Boil up the following solution, fill jars, leaving a half-inch of head space, and seal in a boiling-water bath for twenty minutes.

3   ounces salt

8   ounces white wine vinegar

24 ounces water

Label and date. Keep in cool place for six weeks before using.

Fennel (Foeniculum vulgare)

TRAITS: Hardy perennial, up to four feet tall.

NATURAL HABITAT: Mediterranean.

HISTORY AND FOLKLORE: Hippocrates suggested that fennel be used by wet nurses to increase their milk supply. In medieval times bunches were hung on Midsummer's Eve to ward off evil spirits, and keyholes were filled with the seeds to keep out ghosts.

GROWING: It will take some shade but likes a rich, well-fed soil. It self-seeds throughout the garden and may be grown from seed or propagated from root division.

VARIETIES: Bronze fennel (*F. vulgare "Purpurascens"*) has a lovely purple brown tint and is most attractive in the garden. Florence fennel (*F. vulgare var. dulce*) has a larger bulb that can be eaten raw in salads or cooked as a vegetable.

PRESERVING: Dry the seeds, but otherwise use fennel fresh.

USES: Fennel seeds aid digestion and can be an ingredient in baby's gripe water. The leaves may be finely chopped into mashed potato, salad dressings, or sauces for fish. Use sprigs of the leaf in salads with other greens for a marked aniseed note.

Goosefoot Family/Good King Henry (Chenopodium)

NATURAL HABITAT: Europe, North America, and Mexico.

VARIETIES: *C. bonus-henricus* (Good King Henry, English mercury, goosefoot, smearwort, allgood), *C. album* (fat hen, lamb's quarters, dirty dick, baconweed, pigweed), *C. rubrum* (red goosefoot, sowbane), *C. ambrosioides* (wormseed, American wormseed, epazote, Mexican tea, herba Sancta Maria), *C. quinoa* (quinoa).

HISTORY AND FOLKLORE: Good King Henry may take its name from Germany, where a poisonous but similar plant is known as "Bad Henry." The Brothers Grimm (as in fairytales) said the "Henry" came from the elves Heinz and Heinrich, who had magical powers of a malicious nature, whereas others say it was named for Henry IV of France who promised a chicken in every peasant's pot. This herb was used to fatten the fowl. Fat hen has been found in the stomach of a preserved Iron Age man. Various varieties were commonly used in feeding-up livestock, hence such names as fat hen, pigweed, and bacon weed.

GROWING: Grow Good King Henry in sun or very light shade in a well drained, well dug, rich soil. Plant seeds in spring or take root divisions in the fall. Plant or thin to one foot apart and fertilize. This is an outdoor plant only.

FLOWER: Tiny, green, seed-like flowers in spikes.

USES: Steam Good King Henry flowers lightly and toss in butter like broccoli for an excellent source of iron and vitamins. The very young leaves may be used in salad and older leaves cooked like spinach. It may be added to quiches, soups, and stuffings, and the stems boiled and peeled like asparagus.

Lemon Verbena (Lippia citriodora)

TRAITS: Tender perennial. Can reach six feet tall in a pot to ten feet outside in subtropical conditions.

NATURAL HABITAT: South and Central America, where it is known as *herba luisa*.

GROWING: Grow lemon verbena in a large pot with rich soil. It must be fed from late winter to summer. It will sit outside during the summer in virtually all zones, but needs protection from frost in winter when it must be kept in a light, cool, moist situation. Take cuttings when well established. Lemon verbena may be grown as a house plant. When all the leaves drop off in winter it is not dead! Keep it moist and it will sprout again in February.

USES: This herb has the strongest lemon scent of all the many lemony herbs. The leaves will drop in winter. Save them for tea or potpourri. Try adding just one or two leaves to a pot of ordinary tea. Use in fruit punches or add to any sweet or savory dish where a hint of lemon is required.

Lemon-Glazed Cake

2   tablespoons warm water

3   drops vanilla essence

A few lemon verbena leaves

8   ounces icing sugar

Zest of one lemon, grated

Water or lemon juice if necessary

Crystallized lemon for garnish, if desired

Combine water, vanilla, and lemon verbena and soak overnight. Strain out leaves and stir in sugar and zest. Add water or lemon juice if required to reach a pouring consistency. Pour over a plain sponge cake (a firm pound cake, butter sponge, or madeira cake is best). Garnish with lemon verbena leaves and crystallized lemon.

Lovage (Levisticum officinale)

TRAITS: Hardy perennial, up to seven feet tall.

NATURAL HABITAT: Mediterranean, Greece, south of France.

GROWING: Lovage will take some shade and likes a rich, well-drained soil. It self-seeds easily and can be grown from seeds planted in late summer. Plant them soon after they have been collected as they go bad if kept to plant the following spring.

PRESERVING: Freeze leaves. Dry seeds and roots.

USES: Lovage seeds can be used in baked foods and on mashed potatoes. However, I really grow the plant for its leaves, which are most useful in salads, on chicken, in soup, on their own, or added to other herbs. The leaves are also good chopped over a tomato salad. Try anywhere where a celery flavor would be appropriate.

NOTE: Lovage is not to be taken during pregnancy or by anyone with kidney problems.

Lovage Dip

½ pound cream cheese

½ cup chopped lovage leaves

1 tablespoon chopped chives

Salt and pepper

Blend together. Serve with raw vegetables, chips, and bread sticks.

Lovage Cordial

Steep lovage seeds in brandy and add sugar to taste. This makes an excellent medicine to warm and comfort the stomach. It is also good for a cold. Lovage cordial can be bought commercially. You can also mix it with brandy for a warming drink.

Marjoram (Origanum majorana)

TRAITS: Hardy perennial, up to two feet tall.

NATURAL HABITAT: Mediterranean and western Asia.

HISTORY AND FOLKLORE: The name "oregano" comes from the Greek *oros* (mountain) and *ganos* (joy). The Greeks planted it on graves to bring joy to the departed, and the Romans felt it symbolized happiness and wove it into head circlets for young couples.

GROWING: Marjoram likes the sun and can take a poor soil, as long as it is well drained. It self-seeds easily and can be grown from seed or cuttings.

VARIETIES: Marjoram varieties are notoriously confusing, but anything labelled "oregano" or "Greek marjoram" should have a good strong flavor. Wild marjoram (*O. vulgare*) does not have such a good flavor. Golden marjoram (*O. onites "Auereum"*) is a very attractive garden plant with the same culinary uses. Dwarf marjoram (*O. onites "Compactum"*) is low-growing with an attractive full and bushy habit and is useful for window boxes or small gardens.

PRESERVING: The leaves dry well.

USES: A wonderful plant for attracting bees, majoram can be used in many savory dishes. It is used extensively by Germans, Italians, and Greeks to flavor sausages, salami, pizza, spaghetti sauces, and stuffings.

Mint (Mentha)

TRAITS: Hardy perennial.

NATURAL HABITAT: Pretty much worldwide.

HISTORY AND FOLKLORE: Mint is named for the nymph Menthe, who was turned into the mint plant by the jealous Proserpina when she learned of Pluto's passion for her.

GROWING: This robust plant will take some shade and prefers a rich, damp soil. It spreads violently and sprigs pulled from established plants will root easily. Try sinking large plastic bags or pots in the soil to contain the roots, and don't plant different varieties too close or they may cross-pollinate and lose their character.

VARIETIES: There are too many to mention, but here is a selection: Spearmint (*Mentha spicata*) and peppermint (*M. x piperita*) are the two standard forms. Corsican mint (*M. requienii*) has minute leaves and forms a fresh-smelling carpet. Pennyroyal (*M. pulegium*) a pretty plant for between paving stones, but do not make into tea as it was formally used, with considerable effect, to induce abortion. Eau de Cologne mint (*M. x piperita citrata*) has a lovely fragrance.

PRESERVING: Freeze leaves. They are not good dried, but available fresh for most of the year.

USES: Mint adds a freshness to grilled chicken and is popular in Middle Eastern dishes. A strong, sweet mint tea is also widely drunk in the Middle East, and one of the sharpest, freshest scented mints is often marketed as "Moroccan mint." It is the traditional English sauce with roast lamb, finely chopped and mixed with vinegar and a little sugar. The oil or flavoring is, of course, widely used in sweet dishes.

Parsley (Petrsolinum cirspum)

TRAITS: Hardy biennial, up to one foot tall.

NATURAL HABITAT: Southern Europe.

HISTORY AND FOLKLORE: Said to take so long to germinate as it must go to the Devil and back seven times and only then, if the woman is master in the home, will it grow. The Greeks thought the plant sprang from the blood of Archemeus, the forerunner of death, and thus used it to decorate tombs rather than to eat.

GROWING: Parsley does not like full midday sun. Plant in a rich, well drained soil. It is notoriously slow to germinate, so soak seeds in hot water for a few minutes prior to planting and ensure seeds do not dry out at all prior to shooting. It grows very vigorously in "grow-bags."

PRESERVING: Parsley freezes well in entire sprigs in plastic bags and can be crumbled, still frozen, into cooking. Despite being available in dried form in the shops it really doesn't taste good.

USES: Use parsley chopped in salad dressings, sauces, soups, and especially in fish dishes. Use it in a mixed herb bunch for bouquet garni, and try deep-frying sprigs quickly in hot oil for an unusual, crisp, and delicious garnish. Drain well on absorbent kitchen paper before use. Not recommended for consumption by people with inflammatory kidney disease.

Rosemary (Rosmarinus officinalis)

TRAITS: Usually a evergreen perennial, three to six feet tall.

NATURAL HABITAT: Southern Europe.

HISTORY AND FOLKLORE: Rosemary is the symbol of love and friendship. It is also the herb for Christmas and weddings, as it symbolises remembrance. The normal plants have blue flowers. It is said that originally they were all white-flowered, but the Virgin Mary dried her blue cloak on a rosemary bush and since then almost all have been blue, and grow for only thirty-three years (the life of Jesus) or to around six feet (the height of Jesus).

GROWING: Plant in a sunny, very well drained site, protected from wind. Bring indoors in bad winters or when small. Rosemary likes a lime soil but can take poor conditions. Grow from cuttings, layering, or from seed.

VARIETIES: Look out for the new tall tree type, a prostrate type (try this in hanging baskets), and white or pink flowered varieties. There are also variegated forms with green and gold leaves.

USES: Indispensable with roast meats (chicken, lamb, or pork), rosemary is also delicious in roasted or sautéed potatoes. Some add it to fruit purée, although I don't, but do try herb butters and oil or vinegar infusions. Save branches from which you have removed the leaves to scatter on a barbecue, and use very sturdy stems as barbecue skewers. Include rosemary with vegetables.

Sage (Salvia officinalis)

TRAITS: Hardy evergreen perennial, one to two and a half feet tall.

HISTORY AND FOLKLORE: Sage has often been associated with longevity, hence the proverb: "How can a man grow old who has sage in his garden?"

GROWING: Grow sage in full sun on a dry, well-drained soil. It grows well from cuttings. Cut it back in late summer and replace woody plants every five years or so (like lavender).

VARIETIES: There are many, including: *S. lavandulifolia* (narrow leaf sage), *S. officinalis* "Tricolor" (variegated—green/white/red), *S. officinalis* "Icterina" (variegated—green/yellow), *S. officinalis* "Purpurea" (purple/red sage), *S. elegans/rutilans* (pineapple sage), *S. officinalis* "broad leaf" (broad leafed sage), and *S. officinalis prostratus* (prostrate sage) There are many varieties of the *Salvia* family.

USES: This is an indispensable culinary herb. Use it in stuffings, with cheese dishes, or with sautéed liver. The leaves may be coated in light batter and deep fried for an unusual Italian nibble with drinks. Try in oil, vinegar, and herb butters, but do beware that sage needs to be used with moderation as it can overpower other flavors. The woody branches add a savory aroma to a barbecue.

Salad Burnet
(Sanguisorba minor, S. officinalis)

TRAITS: Hardy perennial, up to two feet tall.

HABITAT: The mountain areas of Europe as far north as Norway.

HISTORY AND FOLKLORE: Salad burnet was carried to the New World by the Pilgrim Fathers. The herbalist Gerard said it would "make the hart merry and glad, as also being put in wine, to which it yeeldeth a certaine grace in the drinking." The botanical name comes from *sanguis*, blood, and *sorbeo*, to staunch, indicating its early use as a wound herb. Culpeper rated it only one step below betony as a valuable herb.

GROWING: Plant seeds in sun or light shade in a well-drained lime (alkaline) soil. Thin to nine inches apart. It will self-seed prolifically if allowed to flower.

PRESERVING: Never use dried salad burnet. Salad burnet should be available virtually all year round unless the weather is particularly harsh.

USES: Salad burnet is decorative in the garden with pretty, delicate leaves, as long as kept under control. It is high in vitamin C and gives a mild cucumber flavor to salads. Add it to herb butters, cream cheese, cream soups, and cream sauce for fish. Infuse it in vinegar (white) to use for salad dressings.

Summer Savory (Satureja hortensis) and Winter Savory (Satureja montana)

TRAITS: Summer savory is an annual up to eighteen inches tall, and winter savory is a hardy perennial up to nine inches tall.

HISTORY AND FOLKLORE: Savory was regarded as the herb of the satyrs, hence the botanical name *Satureja*.

GROWING: Savory needs full sun and a well-drained soil. Sow seeds outside in late spring or take cuttings, which root easily. Take winter savory cuttings from close to the roots. Savory, like so many herbs, responds well to being picked for use and will give several harvests in a season. Grow summer savory as a pot plant.

USES: Winter savory is a good edging plant and is virtually evergreen. Both varieties are largely culinary herbs. The leaves have a slightly peppery flavor, and can be used in any bean dish (green or haricot type), rice, soup, stuffings, sauces, bouquet garni, salads, and dressings. Winter savory is traditional, not to mention delicious, with trout. Try making a bread and onion dressing with savory instead of sage, and roll it into small balls to bake or fry.

Smallage (Apium graveolens)

TRAITS: Hardy biennial, up to three feet tall.

NATURAL HABITAT: Southern Europe—found wild on marshy land, primarily near the sea.

HISTORY AND FOLKLORE: Smallage was used to crown victors of the Nemean games held in honor of the Greek god Zeus, but when the son of the Nemean king was killed by a snake concealed in smallage it was used as a funeral wreath. Smallage was popular throughout history and particularly with the American Shakers, who were expert herbalists, for their medicines.

GROWING: Grow in sun or partial shade in a rich, moist, well-drained soil. Plant seeds in spring. The germination will be slow and may benefit from heat. Transplant to over one foot apart. Smallage will not do well indoors.

USES: The seed may be ground with salt as celery salt, or added to soups and pickles. The Romans puréed the stems with lovage, oregano, onions, and wine, and used the leaves with dates and pine nuts to stuff suckling pig. The chopped leaves may be put to good use in green salads, cream cheese, or chicken salads, and may be added to milk when poaching white fish. (*Editor's note:* avoid consuming high levels during pregnancy, and use with caution if suffering from renal disorders.)

Tarragon (*Artemisia dracunculus*)

TRAITS: More or less hardy perennial, two to three feet tall.

NATURAL HABITAT: Parts of Russia, Mongolia, and China.

GROWING: Tarragon likes a sunny, rich, and dry site. French tarragon (the preferred variety) grows from cuttings only, so if you are offered tarragon seeds it will be the coarse Russian tarragon, which has no culinary value. Protect your plants in winter with straw mulch and bring them indoors in very harsh weather.

PRESERVING: Tarragon leaves may be frozen, dried, or infused in oil or vinegar.

USES: Tarragon is an essential ingredient of the French seasoning mix *fines herbes*, with parsley and chervil. Chop it into Bernaise, tartar, and hollandaise sauces, or mix it into herb butter for steaks and fish. Chop fresh tarragon into omelettes and salad dressings, and try adding it to your favorite chicken dishes. A good starter or light supper is to put a pat of tarragon butter into mushroom caps and bake them uncovered.

NOTE: Tarragon is a member of the *Artemisia* family, which includes the mugworts, wormwoods, southernwoods, and other decorative forms.

Thyme (*Thymus*)

TRAITS: Hardy perennial, up to eight inches tall.

NATURAL HABITAT: Mediterranean, Greece, south of France.

GROWING: Plant in full sun on a well-drained soil, like many Mediterranean herbs, such as sage and marjoram. Thyme will grow from seed, or propagate easily from cuttings.

VARIETIES: There are dozens of varieties, and indeed a whole garden could be devoted to thymes with great effect. Look for: Common thyme (*Thymus vulgaris*), with green leaves and mauve flowers; broad leaf thyme (*T. pulegioides*), with dark oval leaves and dark pink flowers; miniature thyme (*T. minimum*), with tiny leaves, a ground creeping form; and lemon thyme (*T. x citriodorus*), with a lovely lemon scent. Look also for forms with yellow or variegated leaves and bright flowers, often found in the Alpine section of nurseries rather than with the herbs.

PRESERVING: The leaves dry successfully.

USES: Can be added to many cooked, savory dishes such as soups, stews, and sauces. Use it in dressings for roast chicken or turkey. Include a sprig in bags of mixed herbs or bouquet garni for authentic French casseroles.

Herbs for
Health

Herbal Allies for Pregnant Women

～ By Susun Weed ～

Pregnancy is a special time, one that brings joys and pains. Many minor but distressing health complaints can accompany pregnancy, such as morning sickness, varicose veins, skin discoloration, hemorrhoids, constipation, folic acid anemia, iron deficiency anemia, muscle and leg cramps, backache, heartburn, fatigue, mood changes, bladder infections, and high blood pressure. What can the expectant mother use to alleviate these problems that is safe for her unborn child as well as herself?

Most women would agree that drugs are to be avoided during pregnancy. Many over-the-counter remedies, especially antihistamines, acne medicines, and laxatives, have been shown to cause birth defects in animals or humans. Antibiotics may cause fetal abnormalities, and sulfur drugs can cause neonatal jaundice. Tranquilizers

and painkillers can cause birth defects and addict the fetus. Antacids can cause muscle problems in the baby and edema in the mother. (In addition, they mess up a woman's calcium metabolism; see discussion following.)

It is well-accepted that the drug-like actions of alcohol, tobacco, and coffee are best avoided both before conception, during pregnancy, and while lactating. Few women, however, understand that vitamin/mineral supplements are more drug-like than food-like. Though they are widely recommended, even by orthodox MDs, supplements are problematic for pregnant women and ought to be avoided. A study of 23,000 pregnant women, reported in *The New England Journal of Medicine* (1995) found 4.8 times more birth defects among the children of women who consumed 10,000 I.U. or more of vitamin A in supplemental form. (*Editor's note:* The recommended daily dosage of vitamin A is 5,000 I.U.) If that isn't enough to make you hesitate before reaching for the pills, consider this: The amount of iron in four prenatal-formula tablets can kill a child under the age of three.

In addition to drugs and supplements, many common herbal remedies, including goldenseal and flax seed, are best avoided during the weeks of gestation. See page 74 for herbs that may be problematic during pregnancy.

Nevertheless, there are many simple, safe, home and herbal remedies available to ease the discomforts of pregnancy. The remedies of wise women, or "old wives," have persisted for centuries, passed from woman to woman. They are not strict protocols designed to work with the greatest possible number of women. Rather, they are part of the ever-changing wisdom ways of women, meant to be applied to the unique individual in unique and ever-changing ways. Although they have not been subjected to double-blind studies, they are not superstition and dumb custom, but the results of millions of careful observations over thousands of generations. These remedies are the gifts of our foremothers. They are gifts from women who were deeply intuitive, immersed in day-to-day practice, and in tune with women's needs—emotional and spiritual as well as physical.

Wise women believe that most of the problems of pregnancy can be prevented by attention to nutrition. Morning sickness and mood swings are connected to low blood sugar; backaches and severe labor pains often result from insufficient calcium; and varicose veins, hemorrhoids, constipation, skin discolorations, and anemia are also related to lack of specific nutrients.

Excellent nutrition for pregnant women includes not just vital foodstuffs and nourishing herbal infusions, but also pure water and air, abundant light, loving and respectful relationships, beauty and harmony in daily life, and joyous thoughts.

All nutrients are needed in abundance during pregnancy as the gestating woman forms two extra pounds of uterine muscle; the nerves, bones, organs, muscles, glands, and skin of the baby; several pounds of amniotic fluid; the placenta; and a great increase in blood volume. In addition, extra kidney and liver cells are created to process the waste of two beings instead of one.

Wild and organically grown foods are the best source of vitamins, minerals, and other nutrients needed during pregnancy. It is all the better if the expectant mother can get out and gather her own herbs—stretching, bending, breathing, moving, touching the earth, taking time to talk with the plants and to open herself to their spiritual world.

Raspberry (Rubus ideaus and other species)

For centuries herbalists have relied on the leaves of red raspberry to nourish pregnant women and relieve difficulties during pregnancy and birth. Scientific herbalists are baffled by these claims, as they find no chemical constituents in raspberry leaves that are capable of inducing these purported effects. Nonetheless, "if pregnant women believe that it provides relief from various unpleasant effects associated with their condition, no harm is done," says Varro Tyler in *The Honest Herbal*.

Most of the benefits associated with regular use of raspberry throughout pregnancy can be traced to its astringent, strengthening, and nourishing powers. Raspberry leaves contain tannins and fragrine, which give tone to the muscles of the pelvic region, including the uterus. They also contain nourishing vitamins and minerals. Of special note are the concentrations of vitamins A, C, E, and B, plus generous amounts of easily assimilated calcium, iron, phosphorous, and potassium salts.

A strong infusion of dried raspberry leaves increases fertility, tones the uterus, aids in easy birthing, helps prevent miscarriage, alleviates morning sickness, reduces muscle and leg cramps and backache, and counters fatigue. To make it: Put one ounce of the dried raspberry leaves in a quart jar; fill it to the top with boiling water, and cap tightly. After steeping for at least four hours, strain the leaves out of the infusion. Drink the liquid hot or cold, with honey, or any way you like it. Refrigerate leftovers. Capsules, tinctures, and teas of raspberry are not as effective.

Stinging Nettle (Urtica dioica)

Some people dislike nettle because of its strong sting, but it is an herb with myriad benefits for the expectant mother. A strong infusion (prepared by brewing one ounce of dried nettle leaves in a quart of boiling water for at least four hours) helps prevent varicose veins and hemorrhoids, eases leg cramps and backache, reduces the incidence of hemorrhage after birth, and increases the richness of breast milk.

Every cup of nettle infusion supplies amazing amounts of energy as well as huge amounts of calcium, magnesium, and vitamins A, D, C, B, and K. It prevents folic acid anemia and iron deficiency anemia, and is also a digestive aid, a strengthener to the lungs, an ally of the kidneys, and a restorative to the hair and skin. Capsules, tinctures, and teas of nettle are not as effective. (*Editor's note*: If you are using fresh plants, older plants must be cooked thoroughly before ingesting.)

Red Clover (Trifolium pratense)

As a keeper of dairy animals, I was introduced to this herb as an ally to keep my goats' fertility high and their milk production generous. It took only a little imagination for me to begin to use it for women, too. Red clover blossoms are best taken as a strong infusion (one ounce of dried blossoms brewed overnight in a quart of boiling water). The tincture is a sedative. Pills and capsules have very little effect.

To date, I know of dozens of women who, unable to conceive, have found success after drinking up to a quart of red clover infusion every day for at least six weeks. The generous amounts of minerals, proteins, antioxidants, and phytoestrogens in red clover restore health to the entire reproductive system. It's great for men, too. Most notable are the amounts of vitamin E and the presence of selenium and zinc. Red clover has ten times more plant hormones than soy.

Don't stop drinking red clover infusion once you get pregnant, though. The infusion prevents and eases the constipation so common during pregnancy. It also strengthens the liver and improves appetite, especially when morning sickness is a problem, and it relieves anxiety.

Keep on drinking red clover once your child is born, too. There is no more valuable herb to keep breast milk rich and the breasts healthy than red clover. In fact, it is the world's most respected anti-cancer herb, acting not only to eliminate cancer but to stop its occurrence as well.

Seaweeds

One of the best green allies for women in their fertile years is seaweed, both for its mineral richness, and for the special substances it contains that directly counter birth defects. Algin or alginic acid, found in many seaweeds, absorbs radioactive neucleotides and heavy metals. When eaten by the prospective mother and father, seaweed protects them from cancer and protects the fetus from faulty genes. Seaweeds also protect the fetus and parents from the harmful effects of chemicals and carcinogens.

Seaweed is one of the most nutritious plants known. Earl Mindell, in his book *Vitamin Bible*, notes that kelp contains vitamins A, B, C, and E, as well as choline, carotenes, and twenty-three minerals, including calcium, selenium, iron, magnesium, and zinc. He recommends it especially for nourishing the brain, spinal cord, and nerves of the fetus. Eating seaweeds regularly improves the fertility and the health of the pregnant woman, too, strengthening her digestive system, increasing her overall energy, and helping to prevent constipation, muscle cramps, backaches, anemias, hemorrhoids, and depression.

Capsules, tablets, and powdered seaweeds are not as effective as eating seaweed as a vegetable several times a week. In addition to buying seaweed at your health food store, you can harvest it yourself. There are no poisonous seaweeds. For more information on harvesting and using seaweeds, consult the *Sea Vegetable Gourmet Cookbook. (Editor's note:* People with hyperthyroidism should avoid using seaweeds. Check the source of your seaweed carefully to make sure that it has not been collected from a polluted area. Some seaweeds are especially susceptible to absorbing metal poisons.)

Dandelion (Taraxacum officinalis)

This common weed of suburban lawns is one of the best liver tonics known. All parts of the dandelion are medicinal. The roots, leaves, and flowers are brewed into tinctures, medicinal vinegars, cordials, wines, and bitter infusions.

If you dig your own, use them to make a mineral-rich vinegar: Fill a jar with cut dandelion, then fill the jar to the top with pasteurized apple cider vinegar. Cover with a piece of plastic wrap held on with a rubber band. Label with the date, and it's ready to use in six weeks. Try it as a salad dressing, or a condiment for beans. Some women like to drink it first thing in the morning; one to two tablespoonful in a glass of water.

Nourishing the liver is critical during pregnancy. Lack of strong liver functioning is implicated in morning sickness, hemorrhoids, constipation, heartburn, indigestion, lack of energy, headaches, and mood swings. If using the tincture, try a dose of 10–20 drops in a small glass of water just before meals.

The "Carrot Family"

By the "carrot family" I mean fennel seed (*Foeniculum vulgare*); dill seed (*Anethum graveolens*); caraway seed (*Carum carvi*); and coriander seed (*Coriandrum sativum*). The aromatic seeds of members of the "carrot family" of plants are used around the world to ease indigestion, freshen breath, and increase milk supply. As the medicinal value is found in the volatile oil, the seeds are quickly and easily brewed: add a heaping tablespoonful to a mug and fill it with water just off the boil, letting it steep for two to five minutes.

For a somewhat more complicated brew, midwife Elizabeth Davis in her book *Heart and Hands* relates this old wives' remedy to increase milk supply: Boil a half-cup pearled barley in three cups water for twenty-five minutes. Strain and refrigerate. Heat (but do not boil) one cup of barley water and pour it over one teaspoon fennel seeds. Steep no longer than thirty minutes.

It is delightful that the ease imparted by the brew influences the infant through the breastmilk, relieving colic, turning fretfulness into slumber, and countering teething pain. For best results, drink your brew, hot or cold, while nursing your baby. Herbalist Juliette de Bairacli Levy advises mothers of infants and young children to always carry some aromatic seeds in their pockets for the children to chew should they be carsick.

Ginger (Zingiber officinale)

When it comes to quelling nausea or morning sickness (motion sickness, too) there is no better herb than ginger root. Whether you use it fresh or dried, a little ginger goes a long way toward warming the belly and relieving queasy feelings. Some books mistakenly list ginger as an herb that can cause a miscarriage. This misinformation no doubt got started by a woman who had noticed that drinking ginger tea made her menses flow more easily. Midwives agree, though, that ginger is safe, even in early pregnancy.

In addition to quelling morning sickness, ginger helps prevent constipation, keeps the pelvic muscles warmed and toned, relieves intestinal cramping and gas (in infants, too), increases digestive force by encouraging the secretion of digestive enzymes, lowers blood pressure, and restores vitality.

Calcium

Of course calcium is a mineral, not an herb, but it is so important during pregnancy that it deserves our attention. Lack of adequate calcium during pregnancy can cause muscle cramps, backache, high blood pressure, intense labor pains, severe afterbirth pains, loss of teeth, and pre-eclampsia. Lack of calcium also contributes to feeble fetal heart action, a difficult birth, and "cranky" babies with easily irritated nervous and digestive systems. For optimum health of mother and child, eat plenty of foods rich in calcium and other minerals.

The calcium found in foods and herbs is metabolized by the body far more effectively than the calcium in pills. Calcium in plants is found in the form of minerals salts, which are naturally chelated. In addition, the varied forms of these salts aids in assimilation. Of course, no plant contains only one mineral. The mineral salts found in herbs and foods act synergistically with the calcium salts, improving utilization by all the body's tissues.

In general, to improve calcium assimilation, women are advised to consume it with acidic foods (antacids interfere with calcium absorption), plenty of vitamin D (which can be produced by sitting in the sun for fifteen to twenty minutes), magnesium, and daily exercise. Stress, use of antacids, consumption of coffee, use of steroids, drinking fluoridated water, and too much phosphorus in the diet also interfere with calcium assimilation.

Getting 1,500 to 2,000 milligrams of nourishing calcium salts every day is not hard with the help of Wise Woman ways.

🌿 Many wild greens are exceptionally rich in calcium and other mineral salts. The leaves of lamb's quarters, mallow, galinsoga, shepherd's purse, knotweed, bidens, amaranth, or dandelion, when cooked until tender, supply more calcium per half-cup serving than a half-cup of milk.

🌿 Herbal teas and tinctures contain little or no calcium salts. For mineral richness, make herbal infusions by pouring a quart of boiling water over one ounce of dried herb (such as raspberry, nettle, or red clover) and steeping overnight, or make mineral-rich vinegars by steeping fresh herbs in apple cider vinegar for six weeks. The long steeping of the water infusion releases minerals, and the acid of the vinegar does it too. A cup of herbal infusion can have 150–300 milligrams of calcium salts. A tablespoon of medicinal herbal vinegar can contain 75–150 milligrams.

🌿 Cultivated greens are good sources of calcium. They are better if they are cooked thoroughly, and best if they are organic. Kale, collards, mustard greens, oriental greens, broccoli de rape, turnip greens, and even cabbage supply 100–250 milligrams of calcium salts per half-cup serving.

🌿 Fresh dairy products are the best place to get mineral salts, especially calcium, but there is controversy about the assimilability of calcium from pasteurized milk. Fortunately, raw milk cheeses are now easily available.

🌿 When milk is made into yogurt, it becomes superbly digestible and the calcium content increases by 50 percent (up to 450 milligrams of calcium in just one cup). A daily cup of plain yogurt not only prevents pregnancy problems, it also counteracts vaginal and bladder infections. Women who eat yogurt regularly are far less likely to be diagnosed with cancer as well. When buying yogurt, avoid brands containing dried milk powder, skim milk powder, pectin, and other thickeners.

- Other great-tasting sources of calcium include goat milk and goat cheese, canned fish eaten with the bones such as salmon, sardines, and mackerel, and tahini.

- There are roughly 200 milligrams of calcium in two ounces of nuts (not peanuts), one ounce of dried seaweed, two ounces of carob powder, one ounce of cheese, a half cup of cooked greens, a half cup of milk, three eggs, four ounces of fish, or one tablespoon of molasses.

- Many fruits are rich in calcium (though not as rich as the above foods). Dried dates, figs, raisins, prunes, papaya, and elderberries are the best.

- Avoid foods high in oxalic acid such as spinach, swiss chard, beet greens, rhubarb, and brewer's yeast. They interfere with your ability to absorb calcium.

- Do not use bone meal or oyster shell tablets as sources of supplemental calcium. They have been found to be high in lead, mercury, cadmium, and other toxic metals that can cause birth defects in your child.

For more information about herbs and pregnancy, including herbs to use during birth, to improve lactation, and to help the newborn infant, see: *Wise Woman Herbal for the Childbearing Year*, by Ash Tree Publishing. To receive a free brochure of classes and correspondence courses available from Susun S. Weed, contact her at P.O. Box 64, Woodstock, NY 12498, U.S.A.

Herbs Women May Wish to Avoid During Pregnancy and While Lactating

AGAVE (*Agave spp.*) and **YUCCA** (*Yucca spp.*): Contain large quantities of irritating saponins.

ALOES (*Aloe spp.*): Purging, cathartic.

AUTUMN CROCUS (*Colchicum autumnale*): Also known as saffron; large doses can cause miscarriage.

BEARBERRY (*Berberis vulgaris*): Bark contains similar alkaloids to goldenseal; berries and leaves are okay.

BIRTHROOT (*Trillium species*): Contains oxytocin.

BLACK COHOSH (*Cimicifuga racemosa*): May irritate the uterus.

BLUE COHOSH (*Caulophyllum thalictroides*): Contains oxytocin.

BUCKTHORN (*Rhamnus cathartica, Rhamnus frangula*): Purging cathartic.

CASCARA SAGRADA (*Rhamnus purshiana*): Purging cathartic.

CASTOR OIL (*Ricinus communis*): Purging cathartic.

COMFREY (*Symphytum officinale*): Alkaloids in roots are dangerous to the liver; leaves are safe to use.

COTTON ROOT BARK (*Gossypium harbaceum*): Contains oxytocin.

DONG QUAI (*Angelica sinensis*): Contains coumarins that may irritate uterus and liver.

EPHEDRA OR MA-HUANG (all species): Increases blood pressure; may cause heart palpitations, insomnia, and headaches.

EVENING PRIMROSE OIL (*Oenothera biennis*): Induces labor.

FLAX SEEDS (*Linum usitatissimum*): Large doses may stimulate uterine contractions.

FEVERFEW (*Chrysanthemum parthenium*): Contains essential oils that can damage liver and kidneys.

GOLDENSEAL (*Hydrastis canadensis*): Contains irritating alkaloids that stress liver and kidneys.

JUNIPER BERRIES (*Juniperus communis*): Very harsh on the kidneys.

LICORICE (*Glycyrrhiza glabra*): Increases blood pressure; large doses can cause heart failure, headache, lethargy, water retention, and excessive excretion of potassium.

MINTS, such as basil, catnip, rosemary, thyme, savory, peppermint, oregano, ground ivy, sage, and spearmint—contain essential oils that, used internally (or extracted into a tincture) may harm the kidneys and liver; the infusion, taken in large enough quantity, may stimulate uterine contractions.

Mistletoe (*Viscum album*): Large doses can have detrimental effects on the heart.

Mistletoe, American (*Phoradendron flavescens*): Raises blood pressure, causes uterine contractions.

Mugwort/Cronewort (*Artemisia vulgaris*): Used to help bring on labor.

Nutmeg (*Myristica fragrans*): Large doses of this spice contains essential oils that could adversely effect the brain, liver, and kidneys.

Osha (*Ligusticum porterii*): May irritate the uterus.

Parsley (*Petroselinum crispum*): A well-known, and quite effective, abortifacient

Poke root (*Phytolacca americana*): Large dose (more than four drops) may stress kidneys.

Pennyroyal (*Mentha pulegium or Hedeoma pulegiodes*): Essential oil may harm kidneys and liver; may cause miscarraige. See mints.

Rue (*Ruta graveolens*): Contains essential oils that can damage the kidneys and liver.

Senna (*Cassia senna*): Potent purging cathartic.

Southernwood (*Artemisia abrotanum*): Essential oils, similiar to those in wormwood, are easily extracted into tinctures and can adversely affect the brain.

Tansy (*Tanacetum vulgare*): Essential oils in tinctures may damage kidneys and liver.

Thuja (*Thuja occidentalis*): Contains essential oils that can damage the kidneys and liver.

Turkey rhubarb (*Rheum palmatum*): Purgative; may cause uterine contractions.

Wormwood (*Artemisia absinthium*): essential oils can adversely affect the brain.

(*Editor's note:* This list is not meant to be complete.)

A Medicinal Herbal

≫ By Ellen Evert Hopman ≪

Aloe (Aloe vera)

Aloe, or *Aloe vera* in Latin, is sometimes called "the burn plant" because of its soothing effect on burns, from sunburn to the burns encountered in the kitchen. Since ancient times this plant has been used to soothe and heal skin conditions of all kinds. Aloe has fleshy, long leaves with spines on the edges. A native of Africa, it is easily grown on a sunny windowsill in the home. Use the inner gel as a soothing rub for burns, insect bites, cuts, scratches, itchy irritated skin conditions, wounds, and wrinkles. Several teaspoons of the juicy inner gel can be eaten for a mild laxative effect, preferably before bed and with a large glass of water.

The outer skin of the aloe plant is a more powerful laxative and should only be used in extreme situations. Take two inches from the tip of a leaf,

using both the inner gel and the skin, and put it in the blender with a cup of water and a half teaspoon of powdered ginger. Take the mixture before retiring at night. Avicenna, an Arab physician of the Middle ages, recommended mixing powdered aloe, powdered myrrh, cayenne pepper, and goldenseal as a tooth powder for those affected with gum disease. This mixture is both hot and extremely bitter, so care should be taken to avoid touching the mixture to your tongue. It can be brushed directly onto the gums several times a day and has the effect of killing bacteria, stimulating the circulation, and hastening the growth of new gum tissue. (*Editor's note:* Aloe should not be used internally by anyone with hemorrhoids or other fissures in the body. Overdose can cause fissures in the colon and kidney damage. Avoid during pregnancy.)

Astragalus/Ligusticum

Chinese medicine, with its five thousand year herbal tradition, has bequeathed to us powerful immune enhancers that have withstood the tests of time. One of these is *Astragalus membranaceous*, known as "huang-chi" or "yellow chi" in Chinese. The chi is the vital force of the body, its universal energy, and astragalus has been known throughout the centuries as a chi tonic.

Astragalus root is known to strengthen the immune system by increasing the white blood cell count. It also raises the metabolism, promoting the healing of wounds and injuries. Astragalus is used for chronic asthma, seasonal allergies, and any chronic weakness of the lung involving shortness of breath. It is helpful for night sweats, spleen deficiency, Hodgkin's disease, AIDS, and wasting conditions, such as dysentery and kidney disease. Pregnant women can take the herb to build immune resistance in their unborn babies.

People with a tendency to develop colds throughout the winter will benefit from the use of astragalus. It can help any condition of low resistance and immune weakness. To prepare the root, use two teaspoons per cup of water and simmer for twenty minutes in a non-aluminum pot with a tight-fitting lid. One quarter cup can be taken four times a day, between meals. Astragalus root can also be added to chicken soup and vegetable broths.

Astragalus root is often combined with ligusticum root, another Chinese medicinal herb that is becoming common in the West. Ligusticum root has resins and essential oils that are slightly irritating to the body and thus tend to increase the blood flow in internal organs. The effect is that the internal organs are warmed and the entire metablism is stimulated, wastes are moved through and out of the body, and congestion is relieved.

Burdock Root

Burdock, known as *Arctium lappa* in Latin, is a common "weed" found growing along roadsides and in disturbed areas. Remember that what we call a weed is usually a plant whose attributes have yet to be appreciated. Remember also that it is unwise to pick plants less than 1,000 feet from a roadside as they can be polluted by lead and other contaminants from car exhaust. Look for your burdock at the edges of fields and waste areas.

Burdock is a biennial plant that produces maroon-colored flowers and sticky burrs in its second year. The roots should be gathered from a first-year plant and can be eaten in small quantities as a vegetable. In Japan, the roots are known as *gobo* and are used to make sushi.

Burdock root is a gentle and effective blood cleanser. Use the roots as a daily tonic for acne, eczema, psoriasis, and boils. Burdock is also a gentle remedy for the liver and for long-standing glandular infections like mononucleosis.

Contrary to popular belief, the itch of poison ivy is a systemic condition, and the itch can be carried to other parts of the body via the blood. The spread of the poison ivy rash can be halted by taking burdock as a tea. As with all roots, the method of preparation is to chop and then simmer the roots in water for about twenty minutes in a well-covered, non-aluminum pot. The usual proportions are two teaspoons of root per cup of water. An adult can drink up to a cup a day of the tea. A child would take half of that amount.

Burdock leaves should not be taken internally as a tea but they can be made into a poultice for bruises, sores, inflammations, and poison ivy. Grind the leaves in a blender with a little water and then add enough powdered slippery elm bark or buckwheat flour to make a pie dough consistency. Roll with a rolling pin onto a clean cotton cloth and apply to the skin.

Recent in vitro studies have found that burdock is effective against the HIV virus, making it a "weed" that merits our attention and respect.

Catnip

Catnip, or *Nepeta cataria* in Latin, is well known as a feline aphrodisiac, but how many people know of its virtues when it comes to the human species? A member of the mint family, and native to Eurasia, it is a perennial that is easily grown in gardens, provided the gardener can find a way to keep the cats away. When given the chance, a cat will wallow in a catnip bed and flatten it in order to release the plant's aromatic oils. Apparently catnip grown from seed is less attractive to felines. Transplanted catnip will be attacked and eaten as soon as the cats discover it.

Now to the human uses. Catnip tea, made from the leaves and flowers, is relaxing to the nerves, settling to the digestive tract, and helps to expel gas. It is a true fever remedy as it brings on perspiration without raising the body temperature, thus helping the body to rid itself of toxins. The tea has also been used as a mild sedative in cases of insomnia.

Catnip is a classic herb for children, used for colic, the effects of overeating, and for emotional instability. The "catnip child" is one who feels things deeply on an emotional level and then typically holds those emotions inside, producing an upset stomach as a result.

Catnip is used in Europe as a remedy for bronchitis and diarrhea and as a soothing tea or a bath for menstrual tension and cramps. Pregnant women should probably avoid this plant as it has been said to bring on menstruation.

The ancient Romans added small portions of fresh catnip to salads. The tea is made by steeping one teaspoon of the herb in a cup of boiled water, and one or two cups a day are the recommended amounts.

Catnip tea is used in enemas for colic, restlessness, and insomnia. "Catnip fluff" is a children's cold remedy made by mixing powdered slippery elm bark with powdered catnip and honey and rolling it into ball form to be eaten as a candy.

Cayenne Pepper

Cayenne pepper, or African bird pepper, is known as *Capsicum annuum* in Latin. It is a native plant of South America, tropical India, and Africa, where it was a valued medicinal and culinary herb for thousands of years before its discovery by Europeans.

Cayenne pepper is a perennial plant in tropical areas and an annual in temperate zones. It is a beautiful plant, sometimes grown as an ornamental, with white or yellow blossoms and pods that range from yellow to red.

Despite its hot nature, cayenne is actually a soothing restorative for the digestive tract when taken in raw form. It is the cooked cayenne that can irritate the body. The best form in which to take this herb is powdered and packed in a gelatin capsule. Care must be taken to ingest it after a meal or to follow it with a large glass of water or a harmless burning sensation can occur.

Take cayenne pepper at the first sign of a cold or when flu is making the rounds in your neighborhood. It is also a classic remedy for diarrhea and cramps in the bowels. Oddly, it will also relieve constipation.

Cayenne has a fascinating effect on blood pressure. It can help lower the pressure when it is too high and raise it when it is too low. A daily dose of one capsule three times a day will benefit the heart and circulation and has been said to help prevent heart attack, colds, headache, indigestion, depression, and arthritis.

Studies with Kirlian photography, a technique developed in Russia that reveals an aura of light around living objects, have shown that the ingestion of cayenne pepper actually makes the light body, or "aura," grow. An Indian guru I once met told me that he always takes this herb before a speaking engagement as it increases his charisma with the audience. For those suffering with arthritis, a simple liniment can be made by mixing cayenne pepper and vegetable oil and rubbing it in to affected parts, after which the parts are covered with a flannel cloth.

Clover

Red clover, or *Trifolium pratense* in Latin, and white clover, or *Trifolium repens*, are valuable medicinals that most people think of as "weeds." Clovers are perennial plants found in grassy meadows all over the United States and Europe. They are a great favorite of bees and are often planted around gardens and orchards to attract the bees and ensure pollination of fruit trees and crops.

The leaves and flowers of the white clover can be taken as a tea to ease the pain of gout. Red clover blossoms are gathered when fresh and pink and dried for later use to make a tea that is cleansing to the blood and liver and that aids in constipation. To make the tea, steep four teaspoons of the flowers per cup of water for about twenty minutes and take up to one and a half cups per day.

Persons convalescing from stomach operations who have poor appetites will benefit from red clover tea. It is also anti-tussive, which means it is helpful in sedating a cough due to a cold, bronchitis, or whooping cough.

Externally, a red clover fomentation can be applied to rheumatism, gout, and cancerous tumors. To make the fomentation, steep four teaspoons of the flowers per cup of boiled water for about twenty minutes. Soak a cotton cloth in the resultant liquid and fold the blossoms inside. Apply the warm, tea-soaked cloth to the affected areas as a compress.

Red clover tea is said to be a cleanser of the blood and lymph systems, making it a valuable adjunct in cancer therapies. It also aids mumps, hardened glands, and sluggish menstruation.

Fresh red and white clover blossoms can be added to salads and eaten in sandwiches or used as a garnish for summertime dishes. The chopped flowers can be added to gelatin deserts along with other edible flowers such as white daisies, violets, and rose petals.

Echinacea

Echinacea is a perennial plant native to the American prairie that is now cultivated in gardens over most of the continental United States. It resembles a large pink daisy, with a bristly, raised center. This attractive ornamental now comes in shades from purple to white. It flowers from June to October, and should be a standard in any herb lover's garden.

Echinacea angustifolia is the variety of echinacea that has been found to be most effective in lab studies. The part used is the fleshy root, which is simmered in the usual proportions of two teaspoons of herb per cup of water for about twenty minutes, in a non-aluminum pot with a tight-fitting lid.

Another variety, called *Echinacea purpurea*, is also used medicinally. The parts used on this plant are the flower and the leaf. *Echinacea purpurea* has thin, thread-like roots, while the more desirable variety, the *Angustifolia*, has thick, fleshy ones, making them easy to distinguish.

Native American herbalists taught white settlers the uses of this plant, which is now recognized as one of our most important immune boosters and blood purifiers. Traditionally it was used for snake bite, scorpion stings, and the stings of centipedes, tarantulas, and sting rays. It is a useful plant for any septic condition of the blood, as well as for venereal infections, pneumonia, bronchitis, typhoid fever, and conditions involving glandular swelling. It is incredibly effective for sore throats, and a hot cup of the tea has been known to abort a cold in a matter of minutes.

The most effective way to use this plant is to take the tea every two hours until symptoms disappear. It can also be used as a preventative for times when flu and other communicable conditions are moving through the neighborhood. It has even been used as a preventative for malaria. A woman that I know once told me that on a trip to Africa she took one capsule of echinacea daily. She was the only member of the tour who did not develop malaria.

Echinacea is a classic remedy for eczema, acne, and boils. Good quality echinacea should leave a tingling sensation in the mouth and on the tongue.

Ginger

Known as *Zingiber officinale* in Latin, ginger is another "kitchen medicine" easily found on grocery store shelves. The wild variety, *Asarum canadense*, has distinctively heart-shaped leaves and a tiny maroon flower. It is usually found growing under the leaf cover in moist woods.

Ginger is known as an herb that moves internal secretions. It will break up a badly congested chest cold, improve digestive conditions of all kinds, and it is warming to the body, making it a classic wintertime tea.

To make the tea, simply chop up a root, using about two teaspoons of herb per cup of water, and simmer for twenty minutes in a non-aluminum pot with a tight-fitting lid. Adding honey and lemon to the brew will make it more palatable. Try adding a pinch of cayenne pepper for a really bad cold with tightly congested lungs. Take about three cups a day of the mixture.

Ginger root can be sliced and pressed with a spoon to expel the essential oils, which can then be rubbed into sore muscles and arthritic joints. Ginger tea with a little sage steeped into it will help to move lactic acid out of muscles that are sore from exercise.

Cold viruses have a very low tolerance for temperature variations in the human body. Ginger can be used to raise the body temperature to drive off a cold or a chill. At the onset of fever and chills, make a strong ginger tea to drink and use as a foot bath. You could also put a pot of strong ginger tea in the bathtub. Drink a cup of the tea while you soak in the tub, and after the bath get into a warm bed, making sure that you are well covered with mittens, a wool cap, and a sweater. The idea is to sweat as much as possible.

Ginger improves the digestion and is antinauseant. Try putting the powdered herb in gelatin capsules and take one when there is a problem with motion sickness. A capsule can be safely given to a child or even the family dog if car sickness, sea sickness, or air sickness is likely.

Powdered ginger can be inhaled as a form of snuff to open impacted sinuses, and a fresh piece of the raw root can be chewed to relieve a sore throat.

Ginseng

Ginseng, or *Panax quinquefolium* in Latin, is one of the most glamorous herbs on the market today. It is a perennial that favors rich, moist slopes in woodlands of the eastern United States. The wild American variety is considered the best in the world by Oriental herbalists, who have been using ginseng for at least five thousand years. Ginseng is becoming rare in the wild, however, so ecologically responsible herbalists will only buy the cultivated varieties.

Ginseng is an adaptogen, a general tonic that balances body systems, wards off stress, balances the metabolism, stimulates the mind, strengthens the body, and promotes longevity. Ginseng is said to protect the body from pollutants, poisons, disease, exhaustion, and the effects of exposure to the elements. Chinese herbalists use the root for fevers, inflammation, hemorrhage, and diseases of the blood. Women can use it to ease childbirth and to normalize excessive menstruation. It is used for heart weakness and general debility and has a reputation of being especially beneficial for the elderly.

Ginseng also has a reputation as an aphrodisiac. It is mildly stimulating to the nerves and to the glandular system, and has been recommended for alleviating feelings of lethargy in both the mind and the body.

Native American herbalists used the root for nausea and vomiting and included it in love potions. It also promotes appetite, improves the digestion, and has been used to soothe coughs, colds, and other lung complaints.

To make the tea, the root is collected after flowering and dried. The older roots, and especially those that resemble a human being in shape, are considered the best specimens. Use two teaspoons of herb per cup of water and simmer for about twenty minutes in a tightly covered, non-aluminum pot. The dose is a quarter cup taken four times a day, and not with meals. (*Editor's note:* People with hypertension should use ginseng with caution.)

Goldenseal

Goldenseal is known as *Hydrastis canadensis* in the Latin. This is an herb that grows in moist woods and meadows from the eastern to the central United States. It is a perennial with a hairy stem and two five-lobed serrated leaves. The flower is greenish white and the plant is sometimes called the "ground raspberry" because of the appearance of its fruit. The part used herbally is the yellow root, which must be used carefully because it stains the clothing and hands.

Goldenseal is becoming increasingly popular as a remedy for bacterial infections and colds, yet few people truly understand how to use it. It is an antibiotic, and like any antibiotic it has the property of killing off unwanted bacteria while at the same time wreaking havoc with friendly bacteria in the intestinal tract. Like all antibiotics it is useless against viral conditions.

This herb is valuable when used wisely for sinus infections, colds of bacterial origin, infection in the bladder and pancreas, as a douche, and as an antiseptic mouthwash. Gum infections such as pyorrhea can be helped by brushing the powdered root directly onto the gums. Goldenseal is sometimes mixed with powdered aloes, myrrh, and cayenne for an infection-fighting tooth powder. Try not to get the mixture on your tongue, as it is extremely bitter.

Powdered goldenseal can be inhaled as a snuff to relieve congested sinuses. It has been used in small amounts as an anti-nauseant in pregnancy. The tea, carefully strained through a clean cheesecloth or organic coffee filter, makes an excellent eye wash for conjunctivitis and other eye infections. Externally it can be applied to skin conditions of all kinds, including ringworm, wounds, and strep infection.

Keep in mind that caution must be used with this herb. As with any antibiotic, always follow a long course of goldenseal with bacteria-building foods such as miso, sauerkraut, yogurt, and garlic. People with high blood pressure should probably avoid it, and pregnant women should use it sparingly.

To make the tea use a half teaspoon of the root per cup of water and simmer for about twenty minutes in a non-aluminum pot with a tight-fitting lid. The tea can be taken in quarter cup doses, four times a day, and not with meals.

Lemon Balm

Lemon balm or melissa, known as *Melissa officinalis* in Latin, is a Mediterranean and Middle Eastern perennial that has become naturalized in the United States. It can be easily grown in gardens, where it reaches three feet in height and blooms in July or August. The leaves release a strong lemon scent when crushed.

Lemon balm is an excellent remedy for stress relief, depression, and insomnia. A classic mixture for melancholy is lemon balm, lavender, and spearmint, which will also be calming to the stomach, relieving colic, indigestion, and gas. Menstrual cramps are soothed by lemon balm, especially when mixed with catnip, as are headaches due to stress. Some forms of asthma are calmed by the use of this herb, and it has a beneficial effect on bronchitis.

Lemon balm can be added to herbal salves and ointments for sores and insect bites. Adding a strong brew of the tea to bathwater brings relaxation to adults and children, and it can be used as a tea or a bath to lower fevers.

Lemon balm is steeped to make a tea using the usual proportions of two teaspoons to a cup of water in a a non-aluminum pot. The most effective brew will be made with the fresh herb, and an easy way to ensure a good supply is to place the fresh leaves in the blender with just enough water to liquefy them. Freeze them in ice cubes for later use as needed.

Lemon balm tea can be placed on a compress and applied to the forhead for headache or applied externally to cankers and sores. Native American herbalists of the Cherokee Nation used this plant as a tonic for colds, typhus, fever, and chills. The Costanoan used it for stomach complaints and for colic in infants. Taken hot it raises the body temperature, taken cold it decreases it.

Lemon balm can be safely used in pregnancy for its relaxing effects on the nerves and its soothing effects on the stomach.

Milk Thistle

Milk thistle, called *Silybum marianum* in Latin, is a thistle that is indigenous to rocky, dry soils in Turkey and western and southern Europe, and which is now being grown in the western United States. It attains a height of three feet and has large purple flowers and shiny, dark green, spiny leaves.

Milk thistle's sphere of action is the liver, which it protects and rebuilds. The tea of the root and the alcohol tincture of the seed have been used to treat jaundice, pelvic congestion with menstrual difficulties, and spleen, liver, and kidney obstructions.

Milk thistle has a steroid-like action on liver cells. It actually seems to speed up protein synthesis leading to faster liver regeneration in cases of alcoholism, and poisoning from drug and chemical pollutants. No toxic effects have been noted.

Milk thistle has even been used to counter the effects of mushroom poisoning. People who had accidentally ingested *Amanita muscaria*, which normally causes death in 30–40 percent of those who consume it, experienced 100 percent recovery. Liver regeneration was increased by a factor of four.

Anyone who suspects that they have been poisoned by industrial pollutants or by heavy metals can benefit from milk thistle. It can also be used for cirrhosis of the liver, jaundice, hepatitis, and as part of a liver cleansing program to recover from the effects of long-term antibiotic therapy, alcoholism, or from the abuse of recreational drugs.

The most potent part of the milk thistle is the seed. Alcohol tinctures available from herbalists will often contain the extract of the seed and the root. Fifteen drops of the tincture is taken four times a day in a glass of water until relief is obtained. An alternate method is to simmer the roots gently for about twenty minutes using two teaspoons of root per cup of water. The root tea is taken in tablespoon doses, up to one-and-a-half cups per day. The seeds, being nearly insoluble in water, are best taken in an alcohol extract.

Mugwort

Mugwort is a common "weed" that can be found on roadsides and in fields from Europe to Asia and the Americas. Mugwort can grow to be about five feet tall, with a downy stem and alternate leaves that are green on top and downy underneath. *Artemisia vulgaris* is the Latin for this plant, which has tiny green to red flowers that grow on spikes from late summer to fall. The best way to identify it is by crushing the leaves between your fingers and by inhaling their aromatic scent. The above-ground portions are gathered when the plant is in flower and the roots are gathered in the fall.

Mugwort is a classic herb for premenstrual tension, especially when associated with moodiness and weeping. It can be taken as a tea or used in the bath. Mugwort is a mild remedy for the petit mal seizures of epilepsy, and has been used to relieve asthma. Mugwort baths have been effective for gout, rheumatic pains, and tired legs, and can hasten the delivery of a baby. The fresh juice is applied to poison ivy and poison oak to relieve itching.

Ointments can be made with this herb that will help to dissolve sebaceous cysts, especially those found on the neck. To make the ointment, take a few handfuls of the fresh chopped leaves and roots, place them in a non-aluminum pot, and just barely cover them with good quality olive oil. Simmer the herbs and olive oil for about twenty minutes, keeping a tight lid on the pot.

In a separate pot melt three tablespoons of beeswax for every cup of oil that you used. For example, if you poured three cups of olive oil over the herbs you will need to melt nine tablespoons of wax. When the oil and the wax are both simmering, pour the wax slowly into the herb mixture and stir. Next pour the hot liquid into very clean jars, straining the herbs through a cheese cloth or a strainer. Tightly sealed, the ointment should keep without refrigeration when stored in a cool, dark place.

If you are using the leaves to make a tea, steep about two teaspoons of herb per cup of boiled water for twenty minutes. When using the root for tea, chop it and simmer about two teaspoons per cup of water for twenty minutes. The dose is a quarter cup four times a day. For a bath, make about two quarts of the tea, strain, and add to your bath water.

The dried leaves can be sewn into sachets and placed with clothing to repel moths. (*Editor's note:* Do not ingest mugwort while pregnant.)

Mullein

Mullein is another common "weed" that everyone should learn to identify and use. It is called *Verbascum thapsus* in Latin, and it is found in Europe, North America, and in temperate regions of Asia.

Mullein is a tall biennial plant, meaning that it blooms in its second year. Its leaves and stalk are a pale shade of green and have a cloth-like, fuzzy texture. The yellow flowers grow on single or branched spiky stems and bloom from June to September.

The dried stalks were once used to make torches for outdoor uses such as funerals and processions. They were dipped in fat and then burned like candles.

The leaves and flowers make a tea that is a deep-acting lung tonic for bronchitis, coughs, and hoarseness of the voice. The tea of the leaves or flowers can also help with cramps in the digestive tract. To make the tea, steep one teaspoon of the herb per cup of boiled water for twenty minutes and take a quarter cup four times a day. An interesting use of the leaves is in smoking mixtures. The dried leaf can be smoked in a pipe or as a cigarette for asthma and for spasmotic coughs of any kind.

An oil that is a remedy for earaches can be made from the flowers, especially when there is a discharge from the ear, and for eczema that occurs around the ear. To make the oil, gather the fresh flowers as they come into bloom and place them in an amber glass jar. Just barely cover the flowers with good quality olive oil and allow the closed jar to sit in the hot sun or on a radiator or other heat source for three weeks.

The flowers will ferment in the jar, creating their own preservative and, after three weeks, the jar is opened and the flowers are strained out. The resulting oil should be kept in an amber glass jar or in a cool, dark cupboard.

Mullein oil has been found to have antibacterial properties. The usual dose is three drops of the oil, dropped into the ear, three times a day and packed into the ear with cotton at night. The oil can be rubbed directly onto the external ear for cases of eczema.

Crushed mullein flowers are applied to warts to remove them, and a poultice of the crushed leaves can be applied to wounds.

Myrrh

You have probably heard of myrrh because the Bible tells us that Jesus was presented with gold, frankincense, and myrrh by the three astrologers who came to visit him after they saw the Christmas star. Known as *Commiphora myrrha* in Latin, myrrh is actually a resin from a tree native to hot and dry regions of eastern Africa, the Arabian Peninsula, Somalia, and Ethiopia.

Myrrh trees grow to about nine feet tall with knotted branches that end in sharp spines. The bark develops cavities and sometimes wounds, into which pale yellow secretions accumulate. Over time these secretions turn into a hard, reddish-brown mass about the size of a walnut.

Myrrh is used today to make incense and perfume, and was used in ancient times as an embalming agent for corpses and as an important ingredient of the incense burned in ancient Jewish temples. The Bible relates that Moses used an oil that contained myrrh to anoint priests.

Medicinally, myrrh is aromatic and antiseptic and can be used as a mouthwash for sore gums, bad breath, and loose teeth, and as a gargle for sore throats. The tea is also taken as an expectorant for coughs, asthma, and for any chronic lung condition where there is no fever.

Myrrh tea acts to improve digestion and ease indigestion. It can also fight kidney and bladder infections. It is an immune enhancer as it stimulates white blood cell production, and is strengthening to the spleen and the lymphatic systems. To make the tea, steep one teaspoon of the powdered resin in a pint of boiled water for about five minutes. The dose is one teaspoon, six times a day, and not with meals. (*Editor's note:* Use myrrh in moderation—large doses may cause irritation to kidneys and diarrhea. Do not ingest myrrh while pregnant.)

Myrrh can be applied externally to sores as a wash. Since it has the tendency to seal a wound and prevent drainage, it should only be applied to wounds that are not yet infected and that have been carefully cleaned.

Nettles

Nettles are perennial plants found all over the world. They have opposite, heart-shaped leaves with saw-toothed edges. The leaves have tiny hairs covered with an irritating acid that produces a stinging rash when handled. The acid washes off easily in cold water and is harmless to the skin, even if it is painful. The leaves are gathered just before the plant begins to flower. You will definitely want to wear gloves when gathering this plant.

Ancient people used *Urtica dioica*, the Latin name for nettles, in the making of cloth. They also used it to slap paralyzed limbs because the stinging hairs of the plant increase blood circulation on the parts that are struck. Anglo-Saxon herbalists of the tenth century used it to counteract poisons and the bites of dogs and of bats. The seeds and flowers were taken in wine for fever and chill.

Nettle leaf tea is a classic spring tonic. It stimulates the kidneys, cures diarrhea, stops internal bleeding, cleans the blood, and is an important source of iron, calcium, and vitamin C, making it valuable in anemia. Nettle tea has been used to treat asthma, wheezing, and shortness of breath. The tea is also diuretic and has been used for cystitis and high blood pressure. To make the tea, steep two teaspoons of nettle leaves in a cup of boiled water for about ten minutes. The dose is a quarter cup four times a day, not with meals.

The decoction of the root is useful for diarrhea and dysentery, and can also be used as a scalp wash to stimulate hair growth. It is used as an external wash for old wounds, itching conditions, and for gangrene. To prepare the root, chop it and simmer about two teaspoons per cup of water for twenty minutes in a non-aluminum pot with a tight-fitting lid. Take about a quarter cup four times a day.

The fresh juice of nettles can be taken to improve digestion and to increase milk flow in nursing mothers. The dose is one teaspoon in a glass of water, three times a day. It can also be rubbed into the scalp to stimulate hair growth.

Nettles can be added to soups and quiches. The older plants must be cooked thoroughly, but the young plants gathered in spring can be eaten fresh in salads. Add nettles to wintertime teas to increase circulation and to warm the body.

Recent studies have shown that nettles are an effective anti-histamine when taken for seasonal allergies, and that they are also anti-inflammatory for arthritis.

Partridgeberry

Partridgeberry or beeberry is known as *Mitchella repens* in Latin. It is a common sight in woodlands from Canada to Florida and Texas. It has trailing stems that creep along the forest floor, bearing dark green opposite, oval leaves, tiny funnel-shaped flowers in June and July, and distinctive red berries that persist late into the fall and winter. Look for it near tree stumps in shady areas.

American herbalists learned the uses of partridgeberry from indigenous peoples, who made use of the leaf tea in the last weeks of pregnancy to make childbirth faster and easier. The tea was also taken for cramps, hives, fevers, and as a diuretic. The Cherokee even gave it to preganant cats and kittens, mixed with milk.

The Delaware used a strong tea of the roots or twigs of partridgeberry in the sweat lodge, a type of ceremonial steam bath, for rheumatic pain, and the Menominee used a tea of the leaf for insomnia.

Iroquois herbalists made a decoction of the root of partridgeberry for painful urination and used a tea of the roots for vomiting or back pains. The tea of the plant was given to children with convulsions and fevers and was taken as a blood cleanser in venereal diseases. Newborn infants would receive the tea via their mother's breast milk if they suffered from rashes or stomach cramps.

Externally, partridgeberry was made into poultices for wounds and to stop bleeding. A hot poultice was placed on the chest in the event of fever.

To prepare the herb for internal use, steep one teaspoon of the leaves per cup of water for about twenty minutes. One to three cups per day, taken at intervals, is the adult dose. Tincture of partridgeberry is available from herbalists, and fifteen drops are taken three times a day between meals.

Plantain

The plantains, called *Plantago major* and *Plantago lanceolata* in Latin, are plants that simply love people. I have never yet seen a yard or a lawn that didn't have some, somewhere. Plantain is perennial and can be found in grassy areas all over the United States and Europe. It has large, broad or thin, grooved leaves, depending upon the variety, and produces six to eighteen-inch tall flower stalks that resemble tiny cattails, and which are tipped by small white flowers from April to October and are later covered with brownish seeds.

Everyone needs to know this plant because it is one of mother nature's finest first aid remedies. If you happen to get a cut, insect bite, or sting while hiking or camping, simply chew the leaves of the fresh plantain and apply the chewed herb as a poultice to help with inflammation and pain. If you have a dirty wound that involves small, hard-to-discover slivers of glass or embedded dirt, add a little cayenne pepper to the plantain as a drawing agent. Adding cayenne will also help to stop the bleeding.

Plantain poultices can also be applied to poison ivy. To make the poultice, place the fresh leaves in a blender with just enough water to chop them. Add the powdered bark of the slippery elm tree, easily available from herbalists, or enough buckwheat flour to make a pie dough consistency. Roll out the poultice on a clean cotton cloth and apply to the affected area.

The fresh juice of plantain is taken in milk or soup to help in the healing of internal injuries and for kidney repair after repeated infections. It it is also good for for bladder conditions and for gastrointestinal ulcers. Chewing the roots can give temporary relief from toothache.

Plantain leaves are steeped in boiled water for about twenty minutes to make a tea that will benefit diarrhea, hemorrhoids, colitis, coughs, hoarseness, and conditions with mucous congestion.

Plantain seeds are high in protein and can be ground and added to muffins and breads. The tea of the seeds can also be given to children with thrush. To make the tea, simmer one ounce of the seeds in one-and-a-half pints of water until the liquid decreases to one pint. The dose is a tablespoon, taken several times a day. Plantain seeds can be ground or chewed and swallowed with water as a natural laxative.

Raspberry

Raspberry bushes are cultivated in most areas of the United States and can sometimes be found growing wild in loamy soils. The European raspberry, *Rubus idaeus*, is a native of the forests of Europe and has stems with few or no thorns. *Rubus strigosus* is the native North American variety that is often found at the edges of fields and thickets. Both varieties produce white, cup-shaped flowers in spring and summer, followed by edible, red fruits.

Raspberry leaves were used by Native American herbalists as a tonic for the female tract, especially for conditions involving the uterus. Raspberry leaf tea is a classic remedy for painful menstruation and can be taken daily throughout a pregnancy to help with morning sickness. It prepares the uterus for delivery by stimulating contractions while inducing relaxation between them, and later can be used as an after-birth tonic. It is said to reduce labor pains and helps to bring in breast milk. Raspberry leaf has also been shown to help prevent miscarriage, and is used to tone the uterus after abortions.

Raspberry leaf tea is slightly astringent, making it a good remedy for diarrhea. It makes a good gargle and mouthwash, as well as a wash for wounds and skin rashes. The infusion of the leaf is used to induce sweating in cases of fever.

To make the tea, steep four teaspoons of the leaves in a cup of freshly boiled water and allow them to steep for about half an hour in a tightly covered non-aluminum pot. The dose is one-quarter cup taken four times a day, not with meals. Raspberry leaves are also available in tablet form from herbalists, which may be a more convenient solution for busy mothers and those who work outside of the home.

According to the Doctrine of Signatures, a medieval system of plant classification, red fruits help to build the blood. The ancient Chinese system of medicine called the Five Element Theory also classifies red fruits and herbs as blood-building and regulating substances and as remedies for the heart. It should come as no surprise then that the red fruits of the raspberry are medicinal and can be used to fortify the blood, and when made into a syrup with red wine vinegar and a little honey or sugar they are said to strengthen the heart.

Saw Palmetto Berry

Saw palmetto, known as *Serenoa serrulata* in Latin, is a low, shrubby palm native to the east coast of North America, and is found growing in coastal areas of Georgia and Florida. The part used medicinally is the dark purple berry that matures in late fall and early winter.

Saw palmetto is useful for conditions affecting the testicles, ovaries, prostate gland, and urethra. It has the effect of increasing the sperm count in men and of ripening eggs in women, making it a useful herb for couples who are trying to get pregnant.

Saw palmetto is best known for its tonic effect on the prostate gland. It is an excellent herb for the prevention or management of prostate troubles to which older men are susceptible.

It tends to tone the mucous membranes of the body, especially those of the genito-urinary tract and the lungs, making it valuable as a follow-up to venereal diseases such as gonorrhea, as well as lung conditions from chronic bronchitis to asthma, and even tuberculosis. Some herbalists use saw palmetto as a remedy for impotence and frigidity in women and men. For an aphrodisiac effect it is best mixed with the herb damiana. Saw palmetto and damiana can be tinctured in brandy and honey for about a month, strained and then taken as a "nightcap" before bed.

To prepare the tea for prostate troubles or lung conditions, steep one teaspoon of the dried berries in a cup of boiled water for about half an hour. The usual adult dose is a quarter cup taken four times a day. When the tincture of the berries or the tea is used for inflammations of the prostate gland, it should be combined with an immune stimulant, such as echinacea, for the best results.

Saw palmetto is also mixed with *Pygeum africanum,* a powdered bark native to tropical Africa that has been shown to help reduce inflammation of the prostate gland. The usual dose for such tinctures is twenty drops taken three times a day, not with meals.

Yarrow

Yarrow, or *Achillea millefolium,* was known as "medicine plant" to the early European settlers of New England. Its foot-tall stalks with their feathery leaves and white flower clusters can be seen in meadows and fields and along roadsides from June to November.

Young yarrow leaves are picked and eaten in the spring as a general blood tonic. Add them to a salad of baby dandelion leaves, violet leaves and flowers, and wild onions.

Yarrow helps conditions where there is coagulation and stagnation of blood, such as in blood blisters, bruises, and menstrual problems. Yarrow is a remedy for fevers of sudden onset where the face and tongue are red. Yarrow is the great classic remedy for stomach flu and any condition where the intestines are infected, such as diverticulitis.

To make yarrow tea, take fresh or dried flowers and leaves and steep them for about twenty minutes in a non-aluminum pot with a tight-fitting lid. Use the usual proportions of two teaspoons of herb per cup of freshly boiled water. Up to cup a day is then taken at intervals, between meals. (*Editor's note:* Do not ingest yarrow while pregnant.)

High Desert Medicine Plants

⪼ By Bernyce Barlow ⪻

It's no secret that I spend a lot of time in the high basin range and desert regions of the West. It's the type of environment that grows on you after awhile. The big sky, boulder communities, hidden medicine springs, canyons, and petroglyph caves compliment the vast mystique of this high territory that some consider a wasteland. The lands are parched because in their past "lives" they endured the effects of oceans, volcanic activity, wind, and erosion. An inland sea left shells in some places. Dinosaur bones are layered into rock stratum, and other oddities abound. North America's oldest trees, the bristlecones, have chosen to reside in this barren environment, growing one inch every one hundred years for thousands of years. There are lessons taught in the high deserts and basins that can be found in no other place.

So it is with the medicine plants that grow here. Many can be found nowhere else. They seem to mimic their environment: sterile, dry, and purifying. There are a lot of cousin plants and cousins of cousins interrelated through genetic adaptation that grow in pockets throughout the West. The trick is knowing where those pockets are and the medicine purpose of the plant!

Sage is a good example. Not all sages smell the same. For example, the aroma of the California white sage and Dakota silver sage are both coveted for healing and ceremonial purposes. On the other hand, Great Basin sage has a distinct peppery smell to it and is usually not a first choice ritual sage. Nevertheless, Great Basin sage has a strong histamine affect, is an astringent, and has antimicrobial properties. Nursing mothers would best use sage tea while they are drying up their milk. As a matter of fact, sage tea is an old ranch trick used to dry up livestock. None of the above wild sages are good to cook with, although black sage works well, as do the cultivated sages for garden use.

When folks travel through the desert regions they think all they see is sage. This is an illusion we all fall for while driving seventy miles per hour down a two lane desert highway at noon! One plant blends into the next. Most are about the same color and height, bearing similar leaves from a distance. Once in a while, a stand of short trees breaks up the horizon, but once passed, the landscape quickly becomes familiar—more sage. The illusion dissolves once you get out of your car and walk among the shrubs and ground cover. The plants that looked the same are not the same. Some have tiny flowers, others have colored spikes and pink veins, and still others are tasselled, golden, or oat-like. As you explore you will find the desert floor is a magic carpet of low-lying plants, camouflaged by clinging to Mother Earth.

Listed below are a variety of plants you might find in a high desert or basin and range environment. Their practical and medicine uses vary, as do their harvest and preparation. The medicinal applications of these plants have been handed down through generations of healers.

California Mugwort

As far as healing plants go, mugwort is a front runner. It has been considered sacred by North American indigenous cultures for thousands of years. Used in ceremony, sometimes replacing sage, the mugwort is said to protect from evil. The Chinese used copious amounts of mugwort for herbal healing and moxa applications. Mugwort smudge is popular because of its ethereal earthy scent and medicinal properties. California mugwort grows in wet soil and can get five to seven feet high before seeding. It's found in pockets throughout the West and Pacific Northwest. The best time to harvest it is around Mother's Day. Used as a medicine tea, mugwort helps reduce rancid fats processed by the liver. It can induce sweating and help clear the sinus cavities. It should not be used by pregnant women due to its energetic effects on the uterus. Applied as an external tea or poultice, mugwort is said to reduce swelling. A standard tea, one part herb to thirty-two parts liquid, works fine with mugwort. If you want a stronger tea try one part herb to twenty parts liquid. You can let the tea sit overnight or boil it for ten to fifteen minutes.

Indian Snake Root

I carry this little root in my medicine bag. It's a powerful root that has been used by Native American Sundancers for centuries. The plant is ancient in terms of genetics and began as a tropical plant that adapted to a desert environment. It grows in washes in the deserts of Arizona, New Mexico, Mexico, and Texas. I have seen it as far north as Nevada and in a few desert sites in Southern California. It is best harvested in the late summer. Snakeroot medicine aids in digestion by stimulating secretions in the stomach. It helps the liver through metabolic stimulations, brings on a sweat to break a fever, aids in the function of white blood cells to fight infections in the body, and increases blood suppy. Not bad for a scrubby little root. Do not use this root if you are pregnant or are using other drugs that have to do with metabolic stimulation. You can make a tea by using the stronger tea proportions above or make a tincture. For a tincture I use one part herb to two parts 190 proof alcohol (God bless Everclear). Fill the jar or container to the top with herbs for best results. Let the jar sit two weeks covered and untouched. After the two weeks are up, squeeze out the herbs into the container, keeping as much liquid as possible. The alcohol draws the medical constituents out of the plant into the liquid. The remaining liquid is your tincture. Twenty drops of tincture morning, noon, and night perscribed for one week, then tea once a week for a month or two is the standard dose according to Apache medicine. *Ah Ho!*

Juniper

In some tribal systems juniper berries are carried in personal medicine bags for protection. The Pueblo women string juniper berries as necklaces to bring good luck. Worldwide, juniper has been used to ward off evil spirits. It's just one of those kinds of trees! Juniper grows throughout the West. Juniper tea is taken for urinary tract aggravation, but its oils are irritating and it should not be consumed when liver or kidney problems are present. As a spice, grind up the berries and use them as a game marinade (ten berries per pound). It takes the bite out of the wild meat. I use the powdered berries for tea and to sprinkle on sweat lodge rocks. The tea is easy to make. Use a teaspoon of powdered leaves or berries to a cup of water, but do not use during pregnancy due to the oils found in the plant. Trees like juniper that have a heavy oil concentrate in their tea make the liver and kidney work harder when they are trying to break down and excrete the oils. That is why folks with liver or kidney ailments or women who are pregnant should avoid all teas with a heavy oil concentrate. As a smoke, juniper makes a good loose smudge or can be powdered into incense. It is also the flavoring used in making gin. Harvest when the berries are green and full, usually mid-summer.

Matarique

Also known as buffalo root or Indian plaintain, this plant has been used to help control blood sugar levels in the early treatment of adult diabetics. It grows in Apache country and was widely used by the tribal nations of the Southwest not only for diabetes, but for internal cramping. Matarique is not an herb to use on a daily basis. Two weeks is enough to control the occasional elevated sugar level. Thirty drops a day of tincture is the standard dose, to be administered three times a day. This herb should not be used with prescribed insulin treatments. For cramps the treatment is much shorter—just a day or two. As an external tea poultice, matarique helps heal bruises and sprains. The standard tincture method uses the root only. Try to keep the root whole as long as possible. If you chop it up or grate it, it will stay potent for only half the time of the whole root. Stored in an airtight dark jar in a dry environment, a whole root lasts about two years, while the cut-up plant lasts just a year. The best time to harvest matarique is summer through fall.

Prodigiosa

This is the companion herb to matarique in the control of high blood sugar levels brought on with the onset of insulin-resistant adult diabetes. Unlike matarique, this herb can be taken daily as a tea or as a tincture to control blood sugar levels where insulin programs have not been initiated. Prodigiosa also aids in digestion if taken as a cup of tea an hour or two before the heaviest meal of the day. If you have gallstones, this is not your cup of tea, but if you have a healthy gallbladder, a daily cup of prodigiosa will help keep it that way by making sure bile doesn't build up into stones. The tea twice a day has also been used to help those who suffer from acute arthritis. Harvest the flowering branches in the spring. They are good for about a year. Standard tea and tincture prescriptions apply to prodigiosa. Use the whole branch and flowers too!

Yerba Mansa

This is another wonderful medicine plant that is used world-wide. Found in pockets around the West in damp, wet ground, yerba mansa offers itself in a variety of ways. Diuretic evacuation of uric acids, anti-inflammatory effects, and repairing tissues are all a part of this plant's medicine. Its root tea is antiseptic and makes for a good external wash or mouthwash, especially on hard-to-heal sores. Use the strong tea formula for this and leave the root intact until you are ready to use it, otherwise it may spoil. For internal medicine, the root is best served as a tincture made and administered in the standard way. Yerba mansa smells pleasant, and the vapors from a steamed grated root are said to loosen congestion in the chest. Yerba mansa can be harvested year round and will last six to eight months with appropriate storage.

Vim and Vigor Without Viagra

⇝ By Leeda Alleyn Pacotti ⇝

A warm twilight breeze plays through your hair, tickling your skin. Heavy scents of rose, lavender, and jasmine entice your nostrils, one breath as intoxicating as candle-warmed brandy. The evening Moon glows through billowy clouds, casting pale prismatic shimmers over the dewy grass. Within the dark recess behind you, the poignant, straining urgency of violins, expressing Scheherazade's love for her captor, draws at your heart and more.

Then, you remember—this used to be arousing! What happened? Did you grow old? Did you become bored? Or worse, are you simply out of practice? Although these may be your first thoughts about an escaping sexual fervor, chances are age, boredom, or celibacy have nothing to with it.

Despite exhaustive research to explode sexual myths and discover all

manner of scientific possibility about human reproduction, one cherished thought rivets the attention of every sexually expressive man and woman: the healthy, human, deliberate act of fiery, passionate, orgasmic copulation. When you find yourself losing interest or barely taking notice, panic sets in. Your most basic human instinct, previously ever-present, seems to have left you. Or has it?

In 1998, the pharmaceutical prescription, Viagra, hit the spring marketplace, enjoying unprecedented sales and commotion, later garnering the Nobel Prize for its discoverers. By the end of summer, reports of heart-related deaths among Viagra users began to mount, culminating in lost sales and income for Viagra's manufacturer, Pfizer. An easy way to regain male sexual prowess became a living nightmare to some and a confusion to others.

However, the introduction of Viagra hinted at a primary cause of sexual decline. Unless you scrupulously study the abundance of allopathic pharmaceuticals, you are unlikely to know how many carry insidious side effects that depress or seriously limit sexual arousal and physical expression. Whether one damaging prescription is taken over a long period of time or several are taken simultaneously, the general physical effect is the same: your bodily tissues are altered, and, when altered, they act differently than you expect. The effect of alteration causes men and women to experience sexual indifference or disinterest, with men lapsing into impotence and women into frigidity.

This is not a hopeless situation, though. An important reality about your body is that it responds to remedy. Specific herbs enhance sexual drive and ability. Specific vitamins, minerals, and other nutrients help your body reconstruct damaged tissue.

What may seem an inevitable decline through the years is a fallacy. Upon reaching adulthood, your body is designed to perpetuate its state of maturity. This means it does not perpetuate the break-neck, bumbling intensity of teenage growth. Instead, your body naturally functions with measured, deliberate energy, keeping a reserve for that blood-boiling, turbulently desirous, tension-piercing moment.

Sexual Ills and Causes

Interestingly, beliefs throughout this century have been that women's sexual difficulties are predominately psychological, while men's are physical. If these beliefs were true, women would be as erotic as harem girls after a few insightful discussions, and men would be raging dynamos after an appropriate operation. The difficulties, though, are more twistedly complex than the beliefs.

A woman primarily experiences an inhibited sexual desire, unfortunately referred to as frigidity. It is not that she is necessarily cold in emotion, but that one or more influences have caused her to relinquish her belief in satisfying sex. Inadequate stimulation before intercourse will leave her feeling uninvolved. Hormonal changes, resulting from the menstrual cycle, menopause, or a hysterectomy, can cause profound physical discomfort during intercourse, especially if her body cannot produce sufficient lubrication for the vagina.

A man's difficulties include inhibited sexual desire, but the physical effect is impotence, or the inability to raise or sustain an erection for intercourse or ejaculation. Because brain stimuli is an important part of male arousal, an inhibited sexual desire can promote impotence. Poor blood circulation to the penis, disrupted neural transmission to the surrounding musculature to sustain the erection, and disordered hormonal release are physical contributors that impede an erection. Ultimately, a man is left feeling inadequate, reticent, and angry.

For either sex, a recurring cycle of emotional and physical distress emerges. The difficulty in lovemaking creates a belief of undesirability; the belief of undesirability further inhibits physical response; and the inhibition of physical response creates further reticence to enter into sexual encounters—all denying the end result of intercourse.

Compounding the personal dynamic of internal stress, both sexes can be victims of the unknown side effects of prescriptions, which take a toll on emotional and physical stamina. Without a litany of pharmaceutical tradenames, generic types of medications, both prescription and over-the-counter, are known to deplete physical performance and bodily nutrients. These include amphetamines, antidepressants, antihistamines, antihypertensives, diuretics, muscle relaxants, sedatives, stomach acid inhibitors, tranquilizers, and ulcer medicines. Indulgence in caffeine and nicotine stimulants, alcohol, and illegal drugs also robs the body of its ability to perform.

The relief from antihistamines to control allergy and cold symptoms is a trade-off for sexual enjoyment, which is enhanced by proper histamine levels in the body. Several studies have disclosed that low histamine levels in women prevent orgasm and high histamine levels in men quicken ejaculation. Regular use of antihistamines produces delayed sexual desire in both sexes.

Besides internal stress, external circumstances can equally affect men and women. Pressures from death, divorce, depression, family problems, frustration, home moves, overwork, and interpersonal tension hinder the emotional and mental frames of mind, conducive to sexual interest. Inadequate diet, through overconsumption or underconsumption, leaves the body lethargic and unable to release its energies. Stress management techniques, lifestyle changes, and assessment of personal perspective go a long way toward remedying what seems uncontrollable or unbearable.

When "something wrong" is sensed as the cause for sexual difficulty but nothing is attributable in the environment, internal physical stress can arise from a glandular dysfunction. Hypothyroidism or an underactive thyroid can cause low sexual desire. Exhaustion of the adrenal glands, which are critical to sexual development and desire, occurs through increased flow of adrenaline throughout the body, the increased flow stimulated by stress. Adrenaline responses also continually excited by food sensitivities or a high consumption of sugar, fat, coffee, and alcohol leave the mind exhausted for desire and the body unprepared for performance.

Correcting lack of desire and impotence takes more than a simple pill. There is no magic bullet that ends these problems forever. Prescriptions such as Viagra taken within hours of love-making provide a fleeting, physical enhancement. Some have powerful, degenerative effects on other organs of the body. Addressing the cause of the problems by examining medications, diet, lifestyle, and environment lets you take control to effect a permanent change toward sexual enjoyment and fulfillment.

Sexual Herbs and Spices

Herbs and spices are principally enhancements, although they must be ingested over a longer period of time than drug remedies. Like prescriptions, which frequently have their basis in herbal extractions and concentrations, the effects of herbs and spices on the body and mind will gradually wear off. Treat them as short-term, transient remedies. In all cases, check with your health-care provider for dosage quantities tailored to your physical health.

Herbal teas and capsules in pure forms are readily available in health food stores, with directions indicated. When using spices, choose naturally harvested seeds, roots, and leaves when possible, rather than the irradiated culinary spices in grocery stores.

Herbs and Spices for Women

DONG QUAI (*Angelica sinensis*), considered the queen of women's herbs, is an all-purpose tonic for reproductive organs. It rejuvenates and normalizes ovaries and strengthens the uterus. During hormonal irregularities, it stimulates increased production, which diminishes hot flashes and can stop the growth of ovarian cysts. Take dong quai root tea or capsules in the late afternoon and evenings. Caution: Do not use this herb during pregnancy.

FENNEL (*Foeniculum vulgare*) promotes natural estrogen. Take it as a tea or munch a few seeds in the late afternoon or evening.

FENUGREEK (*Trigonella foenum-graecum*), also a promoter of natural estrogen, helps combat vaginal dryness and the associated painful discomfort. Chew seeds or take fenugreek as a tea before each meal. (*Editor's note:* Do not ingest while pregnant.)

LICORICE ROOT (*Glycyrrhiz glabra*) acts similarly to cortisone and estrogen, stimulating the endocrine system. Consume licorice seeds or herbal capsules in the evening for one week at a time. Caution: Licorice must not be used by pregnant women, diabetics, or those with glaucoma, high blood pressure, severe menstrual problems, heart disease, or a history of stroke.

PARSLEY (*Petroselinum crispum*) is estrogenic and increases the feminine libido, warding off disinterest. Parsley may be consumed any time except during pregnancy.

RED CLOVER (*Trifolium pratense*) carries the plant-estrogen coumerol, which is a helpful hormonal replacement. Red clover tea should be consumed from early to late morning.

SAGE (*Salvia officinalis*) alleviates mental exhaustion and reinvigorates the brain, and is helpful in neural messaging to the sexual organs. Drink sage tea or take the capsules from late morning to late afternoon. Caution: Do not use sage if you have a history or presence of a seizure disorder, are lactating milk, or have been diagnosed as iron anemic.

SUMA *(Pfaffia paniculata),* sometimes called Brazilian ginseng, helps alleviate fatigue, stress, and the effects of anemia. Suma promotes the production of natural estrogen. Take suma as a tea or in capsule form.

Herbs and Spices for Men

CARDAMOM (*Elettaria cardamomum*) contains androgenic compounds that assist or promote male hormone production. It is the best source of cineole, which is stimulant for the central nervous system, consequently increasing neural messaging to organs and muscles.

CINNAMON (*cinnamomum*) has been found to increase blood flow, which helps in sustaining erections.

GINGKO (*Gingko biloba*) aids erections by increasing blood flow into the penis. It also combats atherosclerosis, which clogs blood vessels supplying the heart and other parts of the body. The effect of the tea is negligible, so it should be taken in capsule form. Expect the effects of gingko biloba to show after about six months' use. Caution: Large doses can cause diarrhea, irritability, and restlessness.

GOTU KOLA (*Hydrocotyle asiatica*) is considered a brain food and a rejuvenator, increasing both mental and physical power, and strengthens the pituitary gland. It energizes the brain, warding off mental fatigue, depression, and senility. Gotu kola does not contain any caffeine. Drink the tea or take capsules with meals and at bedtime.

HYDRANGEA ROOT (*Hydrangea arborescens*) helps alleviate arthritis, gout, and rheumatism, making ease of movement more pleasurable. Hydrangea is best taken in the evening and is not for long-term use.

QUEBRACHO (*Aspidosperma quebracho-blanco*) is considered a male aphrodisiac in South America, and the bark contains the compound yohimbe (see yohimbe below). Caution: Do not use quebracho if you have high blood pressure or experience dizziness.

SAW PALMETTO (*Serenoa repens*) is a nutritional aid for any wasting disease. It feeds the endocrine system to rebuild atrophied flesh and can help in rebuilding organs, such as atrophied testicles. Saw palmetto helps shrink prostate tissue. Although an enlarged prostate has no effect on sexual function, some men may feel more reassured and confident to sustain an erection when using saw palmetto. Saw palmetto may be taken at any time.

YOHIMBE (*Pausinystalia yohimbe*) is an African tree bark and a powerful sexual stimulant for men, with equally powerful side effects. In about 40 percent of cases, it produces partial or full erections. Unlike most herbs that are extracted for pharmaceuticals, yohimbe is safer in prescription form and has FDA approval. Before purchasing an over-the-counter extract or capsule, consider the disadvantages carefully and talk with your health-care provider about prescription forms, such as Yocon and Yohimex. Caution: Side effects from raw yohimbe include anxiety, elevated blood pressure, dizziness, hallucinations, headache, increased heart rate, panic attacks, and skin flushing. Do not use yohimbe if you have kidney disease or psychological disorders. (*Editor's note:* yohimbe can potentiate MAO inhibitors and hypertensive drugs. Do not ingest while pregnant.)

Herbs and Spices for Both Sexes

ANISE (*Pimpinella anisum*) contains several estrogenic compounds, which in some people produce an androgenic (male hormonal) effect. It also has been known to increase the male libido. Anise oil, seeds, tea, and extracts can be taken when needed.

DAMIANA (*Turnera aphrodisiaca*) is considered a sexuality herb, containing alkaloids to stimulate nerves and organs. It rejuvenates sexual organs and the genital area by increasing blood flow, which assists erections, and balances hormones to restore natural sexual functioning, which is especially helpful during menopausal phases. Take damiana as a tea in the afternoons or as an extract about one or two hours before lovemaking; results will be apparent in several days. Caution: If you are a diagnosed anemic, damiana interferes internally with iron absorption.

GINSENG is usually recommended for men. However, it comes in three varieties: American (*Panax quinquefolium*), Korean (*Panax shin-seng*), and Siberian (*Eleutherococcus senticosus*). Of the three, the American is considered the most potent, and the Korean, the weakest, although the Korean variety has the greatest content of the mineral germanium, which normalizes malignant blood cells. Ginseng revitalizes the endocrine system, earning a reputation as an anti-aging herb. Its content of panaxin stimulates the brain, improves muscle tone, and strengthens the cardiovascular system.

Panquilon, a glycoside, further activates the endocrine system by increasing hormonal levels, leading to rejuvenation. Ginseng will increase the sex drive, but it increases the appetite for food, as well. Whether taken as a tea or in capsule form, use ginseng in the morning and midday. Caution: Do not use ginseng in the presence of heart disorders, high blood pressure, or hypoglycemia.

SARSAPARILLA ROOT (*Smilax ornata*) has the sapogenin diosgenin, a precursor of progesterone and DHEA (see the section on nutrition, below). This sapogenin stimulates production of female progesterone and male testosterone. In men, the testosterone content helps regrow hair. Sarsaparilla influences the individual genetic pattern, by forcing DNA (the genetic coding) and RNA (the transmitter of genetic coding to cells) to function properly, causing the body's cells to return to normal behavior, resulting in a gradual rejuvenation effect. Take tea or capsules from the late morning to late afternoon.

WILD YAM ROOT (*Diocorea villosa*) also contains the steroids dioscin and diosgenin and true estrogen precursors. (For more discussion of diosgenin, see DHEA in the nutrition section). The steroids increase vigor for both sexes during lovemaking. Capsule, extract, or tea may be taken any time, when needed. As a regular therapy, however, take wild yam root for two weeks; stop for two weeks; then continue repeating the four-week cycle.

Sexual Nutrition

Ultimately, the best remedy for sexual difficulties is returning the body and mind to a robust adult state. After reducing or eliminating stress with proper management, adopt a regular diet containing 50 percent to 75 percent fruits and vegetables, with proteins from cereals, beans, dairy, eggs, nuts, and meat limited to thirty-five grams daily (the equivalent of a quarter pound of beef and three eggs). Cook your own meals, and eliminate regular ingestion of refined, processed, or pre-prepared (fast) foods to avoid body- and mind-altering additives, preservatives, and excess salt. The overall effect will be a well-nourished body at natural weight, with all systems working in healthy concert.

However, some important vitamins, minerals, and other nutrients needed by the body and mind can't be fully supplied through the regular diet, especially when hormonal changes, illness, or unusual stresses occur. When these are depleted or seriously low the result is a gradual sexual indifference or physical inability. Your health-care provider can suggest dosage quantities to suit your physical or remedial needs.

Nutrients for Women

VITAMIN B-3, or niacin, is used daily by the body and lost through sweat and urine, as are all B vitamins. Vitamin B-3 assists in the release of histamines, which increases the level in the blood and promotes a woman's ability to achieve orgasm easily.

Nutrients for Men

FAVA BEANS (*Vicia faba*) are an extraordinary source of L-dopa, an intermediate amino acid in the formation cycle of melanins. A six- to eight-ounce serving will help maintain an erection. If fava beans help, consider sprouting them for salads to eat a smaller quantity, resulting in an equal concentration of L-dopa. Caution: Too much L-dopa in a man's body will cause priapism, a persistent erection, unrelated to sexual arousal.

VELVET BEANS (*Mucuna*) or ox-eye beans (*ojo de buey*) are an esteemed aphrodisiac. These beans also contain L-dopa at least equivalent to that in fava beans, and possibly more. Caution: Too much L-dopa in a man's body will cause priapism, a persistent erection, unrelated to sexual arousal.

Nutrients for Women and Men

BEE POLLEN contains gonadotropin, a hormone that is similar to that released by the pituitary gland, which activates, stimulates, and nourishes the reproductive system. One teaspoon of bee pollen in water or juice prior to lovemaking overcomes fatigue and gives an extra energy boost. Bee pollen is high in pantothenic acid or Vitamin B-5, an anti-stress vitamin that corrects adrenal exhaustion.

DHEA, or dehydroepiandrosterone, is the most abundant hormone in the bloodstream, produced by the adrenal glands. Production of DHEA is greatest until about age twenty-five, diminishing gradually to a 10 percent or 20 percent production at age eighty. DHEA helps the body generate estrogen and testosterone. Most DHEA is extracted from wild yams, using the hormonal precursor diosgenin. Diosgenin, found in wild yam extracts, is converted by the body into sexual hormones. Potentially, therapy with wild yam root over the long-term is less hazardous than DHEA therapy. When DHEA therapy is chosen, do so with care. Caution: DHEA therapy can cause oxidative damage to the liver, which is offset by antioxidant supplements of Vitamin C, Vitamin E, and the mineral selenium.

L-HISTIDINE, an amino acid, restores sexual power, reducing impotence and improving orgasm. Available in free-form capsule, L-Histidine should be taken with a capsule of free-form amino acid full complex, separately from other protein foods. As a regular therapy, take L-Histidine and the amino acid complex for one week; stop for one week; then continue repeating the two-week cycle, until you realize physical improvement.

MANGANESE is an important trace mineral. When it is deficient in the body, this condition manifests as sexual indifference, including impotence in men and male and female sterility. Manganese can be taken in pill form or obtained from beans, whole grains, nuts, and sunflower seeds.

ROYAL JELLY is a highly concentrated food made by nurse bees to feed the queen. It reestablishes the normal function of disturbed adrenal glands by acting on the adrenal cortex. Royal jelly should be consumed after an experience of emotional or physical trauma or during a period of stress. Royal jelly is high in niacin, or Vitamin B-3, and pantothenic acid, Vitamin B-5.

IODINE. Thyroid nutrition keeps the gland from going into underactivity, which decreases the sex drive. Feed the thyroid with iodine in the form of kelp, the trace minerals copper and zinc, and the amino acid L-Tyrosine. Certain foods will also deplete nutrition to the thyroid. Reduce or avoid consumption of cabbage, kale, turnips, and soybeans.

VITAMIN E is essential for the production of sexual hormones and may be taken in capsule form or obtained through nuts and seeds.

ZINC, a trace mineral, assists in achieving orgasm and is necessary for normal function of the prostate gland. High concentrations of zinc are found in sperm. It is depleted when refined, processed foods are eaten or when antihistamines are used. Obtain zinc in caplet form or by eating beef liver, nuts, seeds, and seafood.

As you can see, sexual function and expression is more than an occasional instant or a fleeting effect from a magic pill. With understanding and tender care of your body's needs, you can anticipate and participate in luxuriant episodes of sensuously sultry, sensually erotic, tempestuously climactic copulation.

Bibliography

Balch and Balch. *Prescription for Nutritional Healing, 2nd Ed.* Garden City Park, NY: Avery Publishing Group, 1997.

Duke, James A. *The Green Pharmacy*. Emmaus, PA: Rodale Press, 1997.

Lepore, Donald. *The Ultimate Healing System, the Illustrated Guide to Muscle Testing and Nutrition*. Woodland Publishing, Inc., 1985.

Ojeda, Linda. *Menopause Without Medicine*. Claremont, CA: Hunter House, 1989.

Herbal Essence

≈ By Harry MacCormack ≈

For years I have grown more than thirty types of "herbs." I have taken "herbs" prescribed by Dr. Cheung of Far East Trading Company in Portland, Oregon, many of which most of us in the West have never heard of. While thinking about this article I began to wonder just what constitutes an herb. What makes an herb different from other plants? Why are some plants seen as herbs by some while they are not listed that way by others?

While entertaining these questions I stumbled across the term *essence*. This word is often used in describing herbs. I looked up essence in *Webster's College Edition Dictionary*. It says, "That which makes something what it is; intrinsic, fundamental nature (of something); essential being: a substance that keeps, in concentrated from, the flavor, fragrance, or other properties of the plant, drug,

food, etc. from which it is extracted; essential oil."[1] Then I began to wonder if anyone knew what constituted an herb's essence.

I began looking to two of my favorite horticultural/agricultural gurus, Dr. Alan Kapuler of Peace Seeds/Seeds of Change and Dr. James Duke, now retired from the U.S. Department of Agriculture. Dr. Duke has written an amazing book based on his extensive database. The database allows him to cross-reference all kinds of "essential" big chemical information he has collected over the years as he has worked with hundreds of plants. *The Green Pharmacy*, published by Rodale, is definitely worth owning. Dr. Kapuler has, among all his other accomplishments, published data on amino acids as essential genetic foods. Some of his work includes revelations about what are traditionally called "herbs."

What Is An Herb?

Webster's Dictionary defines an "herb" as any seed plant whose stem withers away to the ground after each season's growth, as distinguished from a tree or shrub, whose woody stem lives from year to year. The second definition is: "any such plant used as medicine, seasoning or food; mint, thyme, basil, and sage are herbs." No wonder I'm confused. The *Dictionary* gives a third definition: "vegetative growth; grass; herbage." This leaves me wondering if anyone can tell me what an "herb" is. These definitions eliminate hundreds of "herbs" in the jars at the Far East Trading Company, or even willow bark and certain mushrooms from the realm of "herbs." Have you ever grown sage in the Pacific Northwest? It does not die back to the ground. Its woody stem produces new growth from year to year. In our maritime climate, modulated by ocean currents, mints often produce until they are cut, slowed only by low light levels. Many "herbs" that grow as annuals in the northern zones of our hemisphere are perennials in places like Italy, Southern China, and South America.

So what is an "herb?" We humans value herbs because of their intensity. Unlike other plants we ingest, herbs seem extreme in some fashion. They are strong, and their intensities do not manifest always in the same way. Some herbs, especially those valued for culinary usage, smell as intense as they taste. Their flavor overpowers other flavors and usually lasts a long time. Some herbs, such as the barks from China that Dr. Cheung has me take for balancing, have no smell until boiled. They stink up the whole house and taste terrible. Their intensity is valued because of what they do in human biological systems.

Both medicinal and culinary plants called herbs usually come with long cultural histories associated with healing—overpowering disease and sickness. Generally speaking, the term "herb" usually refers to plants from within some cultural tradition of healing.

In my years of work with Native American teachers I was taught that all plants are in relationship with the two-legged people. Where there is lack of balance you can open yourself to receive information from plants. They will "show" you how they can help you, and be partners with you in your particular condition. You can feel their intensity. This feeling is far different from the experience of buying boxed herbs from a shelf at the store. Yet in both cases we call intense plant products herbs.

Enough. All plants, including trees, fruits, seed pods, and nuts might be herbs, depending upon the use humans find for them.

Essential Amino Acids

Doctor Alan Kapuler and Doctor S. Gurusiddiah have worked for years utilizing the equipment of the Bioanalytical Laboratory of Washington State University to look at the occurrence of twenty basic amino acids in vegetables and herbs.[2] Twenty amino acids are needed to build proteins, which are essential human foods. Kapuler and Gurusiddiah have shown that high levels of various amino acids make certain foods, like potatoes (which turn out to have all the amino acids in a relatively good balance, and are therefore survival foods in several cultures), keys to human sustenance. In Volume Six of the *Peace Seeds Research Journal*, these two researchers released their data about essential amino acids in medicinal herbs. They found that in the herbs they investigated there appeared "spikes" of certain amino acids. These spikes are larger-than-expected amounts of one or more amino acid. This leads them to hypothesize that "a major part of the medicinal properties associated with herbs rests with free amino acids and not with rare, unusual, obscure toxic molecules as is commonly believed."[3]

These findings, along with the rest of the amino acid work, earned Kapuler a standing ovation at a national meeting of biologists. Herbal essence might not be what most have thought it was. For instance, echinacea and arugula both showed high amounts of proline. High cysteine in burdock and black salsify might be why these food "herbs" have a medicinal history. Licorice mint had high amounts of alanine, as did the red clover formula often used in cancer therapy. Gotukola and dwarf ginseng showed small amounts of several amino acids and higher amounts of glutaminic acid and glutamine. Unexpected amounts or proline, valine, phenylalanine, and isoleucine were found in hyssop, the biblical herb. St. John's wort was high in asparagine, glutamic acid, and proline, possibly accounting for its valued antidepressant qualities.

Why is it important to realize that high levels of particular amino acids may signify an herb's essential healing power? We are a society that thinks it gets lots of protein. Some have said we get way too much protein because it is not really usable. Proteins are basic macromolecules that make up our cells. Proteins keep all kinds of biochemical "electrical" interactive functions running in our bodies. Each protein is one of several polymers, each hundreds of amino acids long. Each amino acid is one of twenty specified by the genetic code. Knowing that ample amounts of free amino acids are in vegetables, fruits, and herbs, Kapuler states "we will need at most only 25–35 percent of our current 80–100 gram estimated RDA for protein."

Many healers and spiritual teachers have linked heavy protein intake, usually from meat or flesh sources, to all kinds of disease, including cancer. Amino acids are simpler foods, readily assimilated by our bodies. They are, therefore, the basis for a healing diet. Some amino acids are known to calm nerve endings. Others are known to stimulate enzymatic processes. That herbs show peaks of these substances is a clue to their historic uses.

Phytochemicals

Phyto (from the Greek *phyton*, a plant) chemicals are often credited with an herb's success in dietary healing. Dr. Duke's *The Green Pharmacy* is loaded with stories of how chemistry in certain plants brings about prescriptions for possible alleviation or at least prevention of disease. Among my favorites of all Duke's achievements is his Cancer-Prevention Herbal Salad. Duke credits Jonathan Hartwell's ethnobotanical classic *Plants Used Against Cancer* for pointing the direction. He states that more than half of Hartwell's citings of medical folk literature contained at least one phytochemical useful in the treatment of cancer.[4] Dr. Duke's salad now includes garlic, onions, red peppers, tomatoes, red clover flowers, celery, fresh chicory flowers, chopped cooked beets, fresh calendula flowers, chives, cucumbers, cumin, peanuts, pokesalad, purslane, and sage. His cancer prevention dressing includes flaxseed oil, evening primrose oil, garlic, rosemary, a dash of lemon juice, and hot peppers (to taste).

What is the cancer-fighting phytochemical base in some of these herbs? It includes the sulfides in garlic, capsaicin in red peppers, limonene in citrus fruits, and lycopene in tomatoes.

Everywhere scientists look in the plant world they find intensified levels of chemicals that can be used by humans to generate health. With aid of computerized databases we can now know why many "herbs" that are legendary in all cultures have the effects they have in a particular human big chemical system. It is important to note that not all human biochemistry is the same. Herbs do not necessarily bio-activate in the same ways from person to person, hence Dr. Duke's salad prescription, which works on the principle of "the more you've got in there, the better the chances for health."

Plants and humans are really not all that different. We're all made of the same life-producing substances. The intensity in plants or "herbs" is often related to growing conditions. Soil nutrient levels, mineralization, and climate allow a plant to thrive easily or force it to fight for its life. Scientists have found that plants under stress for various reasons, including insect attacks, often produce more of the chemicals that actively help a human whose bio-chemistry is out of whack. In other words, herbs are not all the same. Some of the most potent herbs may be those that are not pampered in our gardens.

Thinking along these same lines, Dr. Duke points out what many of us have said for years; some of the most healthful herbs in our gardens are ripped out and thrown away because we see them as weeds. Several of my favorite cases in point are purslane, lamb's quarters, and pigweed.

Purslane tastes great. It can be used in salads or steamed and used in place of spinach or other less nutritious greens that are more popular cultivars. What purslane has going for it is the beneficial oils called omega-3 fatty acids. You might be paying big bucks for these compounds as they have be popularized by the health industry. We need them because omega-3 fatty acids help prevent cardiovascular disease. Purslane is our best green source of these fatty acids. Purslane is also loaded with antioxidants, which are also sold in pill form for a high price. Antioxidants are "mops" for free radicals, those reactive oxygen molecules that damage the body cells and contribute to all kinds of degenerative problems, including heart disease. Purslane is also an excellent source of magnesium, which helps boost stamina and energy.

There is a lot of advertising around the notion that we need more calcium in our diets. Two of the best sources for usable calcium are lamb's quarters and pigweed. Pigweed leaves are about 5.3 percent calcium on a dry weight. Both of these weeds taste great in a salad, and I use them in all kinds of other dishes, including pesto. We even sell our weeds with accompanying nutritional information at the farmers markets.

Another weed herb, which is native to the wilds of the Ohio River valley, is black cohosh. I have a few women friends using this herb instead of commercial estrogen to relieve the symptoms of menopause. Tests have shown that women taking black cohosh root extract have stimulated estrogenic activity, offsetting hot flashes and vaginal dryness.

This leads to the question: are the active ingredients in an herb that are extracted and put in pills doing the same work as the herb itself does when fully ingested? This is a troubling question. Some of us wonder if freshness of the vegetables doesn't offer another level of vitality.

The Power

Scott Cunningham continued the ancient folk tradition of magical herbalism. In his books published by Llewellyn, another level of herbal essence abounds. He wrote in the *Encyclopedia of Magical Herbs:* "The basis of herb magic—and all magic—is the power." Scott saw this power as all shamanistic cultures have seen it. "It is the life force, the essence of the universe, that from which all beings manifest, and into which we resolve."[5] Elsewhere I have discussed a possible scientific explanation for this theory, based on the physics of Dr. O. Ed Wagner as revealed in his *Waves In Dark Matter.*[6] Here let us simply remember that humans and all plants are resonators—transmitters of basic wave energies. Some of us concentrate wave energies in a manner peculiar to our individual or species design. The design (genetic and wave-adapted) of plants can be seen and understood by humans who have a vibrational affinity with plants. My Native American spiritual teachers taught me to interact with plants in this way. To find out if a plant is "good" for you to ingest, you must first be in touch with your own power, your sense of place and purpose. Then plants can communicate with you.

Scott Cunningham defined magic as "the practice of causing change through the use of powers as yet not defined or accepted by science." Much of the folklore surrounding herbal usage falls in this category. For instance, the listing of gender, planet, element, and historic powers for an herb is not explainable totally by knowing amino acid or phytochemical contents of that herb. How do we know that basil is masculine, is ruled by Mars, is of the fire element, is associated with the deities Vishnu and Erzulie, and has the powers of love, exorcism, wealth, flying, and protection? We now know that basil has six compounds that can lower high blood pressure. It also contains compounds that act as expectorants, but the magic of basil, one of my favorite herbs, is in its legendary powers and tastes. Tradition dictates why herbs seem intense enough to bring about well-being. When used magically to intervene in out-of-balance big-chemical-psychological conditions, the essence of herbs is stronger than the science, and the essence is usually the reason a particular herb is chosen to interact with a particular human. Both the phytochemicals and the belief may be significant in the efficacy of the herb.

Endnotes

1   *Websters Dictionary College Edition.* New York: World Publishing Company.

2   Kapuler, Alan. "The Twenty Protein Amino Acids Are Primary Human Food" in *Peace Seeds Research Journal Vol. 6.* Corvallis, OR, 1991.

3   *ibid.* page 13.

4   Duke, James. *The Green Pharmacy.* Emmaus, PA: Rodale Press, 1997, pg. 113 and elsewhere.

5   Cunnigham, Scott. *Cunningham's Encyclopedia of Magical Herbs.* St. Paul, MN: Llewellyn, 1985.

6   MacCormack, Harry. "Waves In Dark Matter" in *Llewellyn's 2000 Moon Sign Book.* St. Paul, MN: Llewellyn Publications, 1999.

The Humble Castor Oil Pack

⇝ By Penny Kelly ⇜

When it comes to healing, nothing sounds more old-fashioned than talk of packs and poultices, yet few practices offer as much healing power for the time, energy, and price as the humble castor oil pack. In use for hundreds of years, but really made famous by Edgar Cayce, the castor oil pack is a wonderful way to take care of yourself as well as find relief for serious physical problems. I first used one at the direction of my M.D. who said it "might be helpful" in easing my arthritis. What an understatement! Within a couple of days, the consistent pain in my arm faded away to almost nothing.

When that worked so well, we tried it next on my husband, who suffers from asthma and bouts of bronchitis that can last from November to May. It may have been pure

coincidence, but his struggle to breathe disappeared overnight. His lungs weren't completely cleared—that took a few more weeks—but he was up and moving and able to work for long periods of time without the fatigue caused by never getting enough oxygen. Since then, we have used it to help heal everything from ovarian cysts to sprained ankles, from staph infections to colds and flu, from gall bladder problems to headaches and backaches.

Castor oil comes from the bean of the castor oil plant, whose Latin name is *Ricinus communis.* The plant is native to Africa and the Middle East, and has been used for thousands of years, starting with the Egyptians, through the Greeks, and right down to the present day. The castor oil bean plant is a tall, graceful plant that grows to a height of about sixteen feet. The bean itself is extremely poisonous and there is no known antidote. One bean will kill a child, and the poisonous substance, ricin, was used by the Russians during the cold war to "dispose" of people they believed were a threat to their national security. Using umbrellas fitted with needles, they "accidently" injected tiny amounts of ricin into the leg or arm of the supposed enemy, who then suffered a long, slow illness that led to death weeks or months later.

In spite of the danger lurking in the whole bean, when it is pressed, the poison remains in the bean and the oil that is extracted is marvelously restorative to the human immune system, especially when it is absorbed through the skin. Castor oil used to be given by mouth, but is extremely hard on the gastrointestinal system, causing nausea and sometimes diarrhea. Since the vitamins that are essential for any kind of healing and rebuilding efforts in the body are oil-soluble vitamins, the assumption is, that along with its own healing properties, castor oil provides a balanced, oil-based environment for dissolving vitamins A, D, E, and K. Absolutely no healing or cell rebuilding goes on without vitamin A, many minerals cannot be utilized without vitamin D, the body's defense system is handicapped without vitamin E, and absorption of nutrients that stabilize the nervous system cannot take place without vitamin K. Unless the body has plenty of fats and oils available, it will be unable to utilize these important vitamins.

To put together a castor oil pack requires a half-dozen things: the oil, some wool flannel (use cotton flannel if you are allergic to wool), a piece of plastic or a plastic bag, a heating pad or hot water bottle, a couple of towels (one large, one small), and two hours of your time.

You can get a sixteen-ounce bottle of cold-pressed castor oil from your local health food or natural health store for about $9.00. If they don't have it on hand, ask them to order it for you. The drug store may also have it, but make sure what they have is "cold-pressed" or it won't have much healing ability left in it.

Once you have the oil, get a large square of wool flannel and fold it so it is four layers thick and just covers your abdomen. Lay the folded cloth on the piece of plastic and make sure the cloth is at least an inch smaller than the plastic all the way around. I use a "two-gallon size" plastic baggie that can be purchased at any grocery store and this covers me from side to side. If you can't find the two-gallon size, just cut a one-gallon size along the bottom and one side, then unfold it to make it twice as wide as it originally was.

Now drizzle the oil over the cloth, working it in slowly until all four layers are saturated, but not dripping. The idea is to have a supply of oil available for your body to absorb right through your skin without the oil running all over once it gets warm. When the cloth is full of oil, the pack is ready to use.

Next get your hot water bottle and fill it with very hot water. If you don't have a hot water bottle, you can use a heating pad. There are pros and cons to each. If you had surgery and your abdomen or wherever you're putting the pack is extremely tender, the hot water bottle may feel ungodly heavy, unstable, and uncomfortable at first. The heating pad will usually be much lighter and more comfortable, but it has electricity and anomalous electromagnetic fields running through and around it, many of which are not good for the body. The bed or chair where you want to lie or sit while you do the pack for may not have an electrical outlet nearby, which makes the hot water bottle a handy portable heat source, but the hot water bottle may cool off before you're done. Of course, you can always get up to refill it, or maybe put another towel or small pillow over it to keep it warm longer. In the end it comes down to personal preference.

Once you've decided where you're going to sit or lie down for the two-hour time period, it's time to heat the pack. You can take the plastic off and put the pack in the oven on a cookie sheet for a few minutes, or you can leave the plastic on, turn the heating pad on, and set the pack on it to warm up a bit. Just don't put the pack in a microwave. The high, quick heat generated will break down the molecular structure of the oil and it will not be able to generate the healing energies you want.

While the pack is heating, gather anything you might like to drink, to read, your favorite crossword puzzle, or paper and pen to make notes or capture thoughts and put these by the bed or chair where you will be resting. Finally, remove any good clothing and put a robe on. It's also a good idea to put a towel under you just in case you fall asleep, move, or roll and a corner of the oil-soaked cloth gets out from under the plastic and onto the sofa, chair, or mattress. Once this happens, the oil is almost impossible to remove.

When you are ready and the pack is warm, sit or lie down and get yourself comfortable. Put the pack over your abdomen. Put the plastic bag over the pack, and put a small hand towel over both of these. Settle the heating pad or hot water bottle comfortably over the pack, then relax for a couple of hours. Sleep if you can. If not, then daydreaming is the next best choice. Read, do phone work, or other paperwork only if you think you absolutely have to.

I often do a castor oil pack at night and will sleep with it in place for five or six hours. When I absolutely have to roll over, I set aside the hot water bottle or heating pad, remove the hand towel, fold the pack in half so that it is covered by the plastic, and go wash my abdomen with warm water and soap. This is a good idea so you don't give the oil a chance to cause a rash or dermatitis. No one in our family of six has ever gotten a skin irritation from using a pack, but washing the oil off is a good precaution.

You can use a castor oil pack anywhere on the body where there is a problem. Put it on your chest if you have congested lungs, on your back if you have had back problems or surgery. Wrap it around your leg, arm, or foot if you've broken or sprained anything, put smaller-sized packs on your neck, face, or fingers. Putting it on your abdomen will stimulate the function of your immune system if you are looking for a general tonic.

Packs are usually done in a series. For instance, with gall bladder troubles, use the pack five nights in a row, then skip two nights, then use it again for three more nights. For a staphylococcus infection in a limb, use it six nights in a row, break for two nights, and finish with up to six more nights if necessary. You can repeat any sequence as many times as you need to. Our experience has taught us to use a couple rules of thumb that say, when you're not sure what to do, use the pack for one week, skip three nights, then use it for a second week. Usually there is an obvious change in the condition you are trying to heal. If this change is obvious after, say, only two days, then use the pack for one day longer than the day you notice the change, making a total of three days. Skip two days, then use the pack again for three more days. Discontinue the pack once healing is completed.

Everyone in our family has their own individual packs, cut to fit several different body areas. A pack can be reused or reoiled for somewhere between six months and a year. If you use it often, six months will be the maximum. When we are not using ours, the packs are simply folded in half with the plastic on the outside, then put in one of those small, square, metal cake pans that you buy at the grocery store. The pans are disposable, often come three to a package, and are quite cheap.

We tend to use the packs more heavily in the winter, and by the time summer rolls around, the pack is ready to be replaced. If someone needs a new pack made in the middle of summer for a serious infection or a sprained ankle, the pack will be kept in the refrigerator so it won't become moldy in the humid weather.

When we first started using castor oil packs, the quick, dramatic healings were truly gratifying. When other healings took longer, I became impatient. I wanted the quick, decisive turnaround that antibiotics once offered. Anything that took time away from family and financial survival made me feel anxious, even guilty.

As my sensitivity to antibiotics grew more dangerous, they became less and less of an option, but I still wanted the quick-fix they offered. Slowly I had to face the fact that they hadn't offered me real healing at all. They had only rescued me for a moment. I merely fooled myself into thinking I was better when I hadn't done a single thing to correct the real sources of the problem. These sources were found in things like the nutritional quality of the food I ate, my stressed life, an emotion or decision I'd been avoiding, or a crisis of the sprit in which my life suddenly appeared to have no meaning. It became clear that real healing takes time, and that relaxing is a necessary part of healing. True healing is a luxury we rarely allow ourselves any more, and yet only when we take the time to relax will we be able to address the emotional, mental, and spiritual aspects of our illness. The castor oil pack, long used for deep physical healing via correction of imbalances in the body, lends itself beautifully to the kind of introspection that promotes healing at all levels, leaving you whole, firm, and secure.

Sacred Healing Plants of Hawaii

～ By Bernyce Barlow ～

T hroughout the Hawaiian Islands are found *heiaus,* or temples, where the priests and kahunas served the royal family lines. The temples were the hub for religious activities where Hawaiian rituals and ceremonies regularly took place. Since the Hawaiians used the plants of the islands to their fullest extent, the heiau's medicine gardens were full of sacred plants used to represent, honor, and evoke the many gods of the Hawaiian people. The plants were also used to heal the islanders by the *Kahuna La'au Lapa'au,* or herbal specialist among the healing kahunas.

It was the duty of the La'au Lapa'au to know the healing properties of each plant and the gods they represented. One of the meanings of kahuna is "keeper of the secrets," and if a La'au Lapa'au gave out herbal secrets he/she would have been out of a job.

Therefore, the medicine gardens of the La'au Lapa'au were kept in strict confidence as were the prescriptions of administration and rituals within the boundaries of the heiaus.

Fortunately, the plants of Hawaii have given up many of their secrets under the scrutiny of modern medicine and science, validating the ancient wisdom of the kahunas. Many of these plants we know and use, while others are less recognized. Certain Hawaiian plants even grace our mainland gardens with their Dawn Star magic! Listed below are some of the most popular herbs and plants used by the Hawaiian culture. This is by no means a complete list, but it is a showcase of Hawaii's tropical variety and enchantment, which has not lost its traditional application through the years.

Hawaiian Healing Plants

Arrowroot

Arrowroot, known as *pia*, is part of the tacca family. Its tubers are used as food and in medicine. A carbohydrate, arrowroot is used as an ingredient in a coconut milk drink or steamed and used in the dessert called *haupia*. The tuber is usually grated. As medicine, the starchy tubers are pounded with iron-enriched red clay, then eaten raw for dysentery symptoms.

Awa

Awa is part of the pepper family. Its root was used by Hawaiians in medicine, offering, and ceremony. Its effects are said to be pain relieving and relaxing. Abuse of awa caused poor eyesight and scales on the skin, as well as a general decline in health. Captain Cook's journals likened the root drink to a potent liquor whose unhealthy effects disappeared with the cessation of its regular use. Awa's best use was in ceremony and controlled medicine. Many of the Hawaiian gods accepted traditional offerings of awa in exchange for their favor, as did the priests and kahunas. Awa is also known as kava kava.

Banana

Although the islands were loaded with at least seventy different types of bananas, many were tabu, especially to women, who could only partake of two or three varieties. Other types of bananas were tabu to all but the priesthood and royal family. You could be sacrificed to an angry god because you ate the wrong banana! Thank goodness the tabu has been lifted, because this plant carries a lot of good medicine! Other than the wonderful nutrients of its fruit, the root of the banana was used in curing thrush in an infant's mouth. From the flower tips a nectar was harvested to be given to infants as a vitamin supplement. The nectar was also used as a sweetener for bitter medicine concoctions. The juice from the flowers was used as a dye. Due to tabus, only the men harvested the sacred banana tree, utilizing each trunk, leaf, and frond. However, the goddess Hina favored that particular tree, so its harvest often included the recognition of her.

Breadfruit

Known as *ulu*, breadfruit is a member of the mulberry family. All parts of the tree are useful, but it is the sap and fruit that are regularly used in cooking and medicine. The breadfruit is a carbohydrate that can be made into poi, puddings, and dried snacks after the rind is removed. As a medicine, the fruit is used as an absorbing starch. The wood of the tree is light, so everything from drums and hunt tools to boats can be made from it. For some, it is the wood of choice because when the ulu leaf is dried out it can be used like sandpaper to polish up the handiwork. For the hard-working Hawaiian, this meant only one trip to the tropical hardware store! The sap of the breadfruit is sweet and very sticky. It is harvested where the leaf stem meets the mother branch. The gummy substance can be used like fly paper or as a glue. It can be chewed like gum or applied as a waterproof sealer. The sap is also used in medicine and for capturing small birds (like flypaper) to pluck for ceremonial robes and regalia. Yes, they let the little birdies go afterward.

Candlenut

Known as *kukui*, candlenut belongs to the spurge family. The tree bears a nut that has a multitude of uses in medicine. The juice of the green candlenut was coveted as a cathartic, a cure for thrush, and an external medicine for deep cuts. When burnt, the ashes of the nut were added to medicine teas or used as tattoo dye. All kinds of dyes came from the kukui tree, with colors ranging from copper to black, with tones of brown in between. Black dyes came from the roots, and burnt reds and brown dyes were harvested from the bark. Inside the candlenut is a kernel that contains oil. The kernels were strung and burned like candles by the islanders and were a main source of light on the islands. Fisherman used candlenut oil to clear and calm the waters to see their prey. They would chew up a few kernels and spit them out onto the sea! The fishermen also dipped their nets in the inner bark slime of the tree three to four times a year. The slime tea kept the nets from falling apart from decay. The meat of the kukui nut is sweet, and in medicine is used for urinary disorders. Mix thirty to forty nut meats with tea water, then drink. A weaker solution was made into an eyewash and weaker still, a mixture of five roasted nut kernels pounded together with hau blossoms was prescribed as a lower purgative tea.

Coconut

Known as *nui*, coconut is a member of the palm family. The tree is obviously not an herb, but its Moon-white meat makes for a truly delicious spice. Pass the macaroons, please. As it is with Hawaiian plants, the coconut tree yields more than gigantic nuts. Like the breadfruit, every part of the coconut can be used for something practical like shampoo, drums, roof coverings, support beams, ropes, brooms, or a light source oil. Medical kahunas often used coconut milk and grated coconut meat to ease the bite of a bitter medicine or as a children's drink. The milk was also used in diabetic treatments. The oil of the coconut is found in the kernels and was used by the kahunas on the skin. Ceremonial awa bowls were made from polished nui shells, as were the spirit bowls of the traditional kahunas.

Gourd

In Hawaii, gourds are known as *ipu*. Internationally, gourds have been used for containers, musical instruments, ritual rattles, whistles, and practical utensils. The Hawaiians were no exception and they used the gourd to its fullest potential. In medicine, green gourd pulp tea was used as a purgative colonic, and gourd pulp as a cleansing suppository, A big part of ancient Hawaiian medicine had to do with purging above and below, so many of the medicine plants had to do with one or the other, as well as curing purge effects.

Hibiscus, Milo, and Hau

Hibiscus, milo, and hau are cousins that belong to the hibiscus family. These three plants were frequently used by kahunas in women's and children's medicine. The slime of each is harvested where the leaf meets the mother stem. Hau slime was used to reduce fevers and the bark was made into a tea for women in labor. Babies were given hibiscus slime as a vitamin supplement, and the young flower buds were chewed then given to small children as a food supplement. Boils were drawn by chewing the bottoms of a few hibiscus flowers then applying them over the boil. Hibiscus tea was popular, especially when mixed with a little sugar cane juice. It has lots of vitamin C! The plants afforded cordage and light weight wood for the Hawaiians, too. The milo was used in a similar fashion as hau and hibiscus. It also yielded oil, dye, and gum to the islanders, who liked the taste of its sap. Because the hau was a tabu plant, milo was often used in its place.

Indian Mulberry

Known as *noni*, Indian mulberry is a member of the coffee family. The fruit of the noni is bitter, but its medicinal applications have merit and were wisely used by the kahunas of the islands. Intestinal worms and body lice were driven out by the fruit of the ripe noni, and it was used as a tea for high blood pressure over a period of days. The juice from a ripe noni was sometimes squeezed into a deep cut to pucker the inner layers of skin to hasten healing (ouch). Poultices of noni brought boils to a head, and the flowers and fruit of the noni were used to cure bladder disorders over a short period of time. Because of its unpleasant taste and odor, the noni fruit was not the food of choice among the islanders, but the inner bark of its roots was favored as a yellow dye, and when coral (lime) is added, the dye turns red!

Mountain Apple

Known as *'ohi'a-'ai*, mountain apple is a member of the myrtle family. Its size varies depending on where it is growing. Large trees can be forty to sixty feet tall. The 'ohi'a-'ai bears a pleasant fruit after seven or eight years of growth. The Hawaiians made steamed puddings from the fruit or ate it raw, but the preferred way to eat the mountain apple was dried. The apple pulp could be pounded and dried in sheets, then added later as a spice or supplement to a meal. Too much mountain apple fruit could upset the digestive system, so it was eaten in small amounts, usually with other foods. The inner bark and the top leaf buds of the mountain apple mixed with sugarcane juice were used as an internal medicine tea to treat venereal disease. The awikiwki plant, mixed with mountain apple bark, was the external tea for skin disorders.

A Healing Landscape

~ By Penny Kelly ~

*I*f the world fell down tomorrow and your medicine cupboard was bare, what options would you have if an emergency arose? It's easy to grab a bottle of echinacea from the health food store, or pop vitamins and minerals to supply you with the nutrients that are no longer present in the food you eat, but what if these conveniences were not there, either temporarily or permanently? You needn't be a doomsday fan, yet it's a wise practice to keep one foot in the pool of common sense. Maintaining a sense of responsibility for yourself instead of throwing that responsibility to the winds generated by the economic and political jet stream will keep you feeling safe and secure, even if the prevailing winds become chaotic.

Chances are you live in a suburb today, surrounded by a few flowers, bushes, and trees that are part of the

decorative landscape. You probably come and go every day without giving these flowers and bushes a second thought except when they have to be trimmed, or when mother nature decorates them with snow or ice. Yet many of these decorative plants are useful, powerful healing agents that could be used in a pinch, even given the facts that, one, you might be an amateur, and two, some are strong enough to be considered poisonous if taken to extremes.

Arborvitae

One of the most common trees for landscaping use is a slim evergreen called arborvitae. It can grow to sixty-five feet and still be only five or six feet in diameter. The branches are short, compact, and rather than leaves or needles, they have these sort of green, overlapping scales. Also known as white cedar, whose Latin name is *Thuja occidentalis*, this common "foundation tree," so called because it can be planted close to the foundation of your house, is quite useful in clearing the lungs in cases of colds, bronchitis, and respiratory congestion. It will bring on menstruation, so should not be used during pregnancy, yet a standard infusion made from one ounce of the green branches and twigs in a quart of boiling water and steeped for ten minutes will bring relief from headaches, and even from the pains of angina, if sipped a tablespoon at a time, four or five times over the day. This same infusion can also be used as a hot compress to ease muscle aches and the pains of arthritis, and it can be used to clear up all sorts of skin problems and infections because of its antiviral and anti-fungal properties. Because of the toxicity of its main volatile oil, thujone, it should be not be used for more than seven to ten days at a time, just in case it starts to build up in your system. It goes without saying that desperate times can require desperate measures, and if you are ever in a situation in which you have to use something that is more potent than you're used to, keep in mind that common sense and caution make a wonderful couple!

In fact, make it a rule never to take anything endlessly whether you're taking vitamins, minerals, herbs, or some other healing supplement. The rules of thumb are several: for minor problems, take the substance for five days on, then take two days off; for mediocre problems, seven days on, three days off; and for serious problems, (or for long-term supplementation with vitamins) fifteen days on, five days off. Repeat the cycle as needed if you're taking vitamins, but if you're using an herbal remedy and haven't had relief or healing after three cycles, then you either have the wrong diagnosis or the wrong medicine. Perhaps its time to reevaluate your healing program and return to the yard to see what else you might have available—perhaps something just a powerful but with a slightly different set of effects.

Forsythia

Another decorative plant with powerful medicinal properties is your forsythia bush. Forsythia is multitalented, and research in China has shown that it has potent antitumor properties. A decoction made from the leaves and twigs is used to cure breast cancer.[1] For your own uses, you can pound or macerate the leaves and apply their juices to the skin to heal rashes and minor infections. You can make an infusion using the root to reduce fevers, and the outer covering of the seeds can be infused to create an antibacterial tea that detoxifies infections, reduces swelling, and helps drainage. If you have had a stroke, the same seed capsule tea can be used to help reduce or control other strokes, and even in the case of children's diseases like measles and chicken pox, it will help clear the skin and reduce fever at the same time, clearing the body of toxins gently. It's an all-over body detoxifier, can be used in a compress to clear away boils, will fight colds and flu, and to top it all off, it's a brilliant spring beauty with its bright yellow flowers. (*Editor's note:* Do not ingest while pregnant.)

Roses

Do you have roses in your yard? If so, you have another source of both beauty and health. While not every species of rose is medicinal, quite a few are, and about a dozen are especially useful.

Taking the petals off a common red rose before the flower opens fully and infusing them in water is an old remedy for headaches and dizziness. This also works as a blood cleaner, stabilizes the nerves, and strengthens the heart. Rose hips are an excellent source of Vitamin C at a time of year when you need it most—the winter. Pick them only after it has gotten cold and stayed cold as they will taste much better after frost. Rose petal infusions can be used as a tonic for your whole system, a rejuvenating wash for your eyes and gums, or to ease cramps during your period. You can crush the rose petals in a small amount of boiling water, then strain and add this water to a jar of honey. You can steep the petals directly in a bottle of vinegar, a flask of wine, or a bottle of oil to energy, and reduce fatigue. Finally, you can dip the petals in sugar water, freeze them, and add them to drinks, salads, and desserts for a delightful treat that seems to touch your soul. (*Editor's note:* Do not ingest rose leaves.)

The most common species of *Rosa* used for medicine listed by John Lust in his reference, *The Herb Book*, are the species *californica*, *centifolia*, *damascena*, *eglanteria*, *gallica*, *laevigata*, and *roxburghii*. Those listed as medicinal by Lesley Bremness in *Herbs* are *canina*, *damascena*, *rubiginosa*, *galica versicolor*, *gallica officinalis*, and *rugosa*. If you already have these in your yard, enjoy them! If you've been thinking of planting roses, you might consider some of these species so you have the double benefit of beauty and health.

Periwinkle

Many people find a common ground cover growing in their yard that is known as "periwinkle," or "sorcerer's violet." Known by landscapers as *Vinca major*, this low-growing evergreen with shiny leaves and bluish-purple flowers can be made into a tea that not only lowers blood pressure, it reduces menstrual flow, and guards against migraine headaches. *Vinca minor* looks just like *Vinca major*, except that it will produce blue, pink, and white flowers rather than just the bluish-purple ones, and it is basically the same in terms of medicinal effects. The infusion is a standard one: one ounce of herb to one quart of boiling water steeped ten minutes, and the parts to be used are the flowers and leaves. This is another plant that tends to be highly toxic if used in large doses so always go slowly, and do not take for more than a week or two at a time. Start with a tablespoon, less if you are a small adult, and note any effects, reducing to a half-tablespoon if necessary. Do not ingest if you are pregnant.

Vinca has been used since the days of the ancient Greeks and is known to have excellent ability to stop internal bleeding when the tea is taken by mouth, and to stop external bleeding when it is used as a compress. It has the unusual capability of stimulating the heart to beat strongly and evenly while at the same time relaxing the individual and reducing nervous tension. It contains a variety of active compounds, some of which will help eliminate insomnia and reduce leg or foot cramps. It increases the flow of blood to the brain, calms those who have bouts of hysteria, and is a potent antiseptic whether taken internally or used externally. Because it is astringent in nature, it aids in cases of diarrhea and helps relieve hemorrhoids. Among its numerous other uses are quieting coughing spasms, as digestive agent, as diuretic, and in clearing eczema. *Vinca* also contains a compound called reserpine, an effective cancer-fighting agent in certain kinds of cancers. (*Editor's note:* Do not use *Vinca* if you have low blood pressure or constipation.)

Hawthorn

The last few items you might find in your front yard are all trees with powerful healing abilities. They are the hawthorn tree, the white willow, the elderberry, and white birch. Uses of these trees span the gamut of almost anything you might need, from aspirin and laxatives to lymph circulation and heart trouble.

The hawthorne tree is the heart specialist in the group. The leaves, the flowers, and the berries are all useful in strengthening a heart that has been worn out by kidney troubles and poor circulation. Hawthorn berries are a specific remedy for a good, strong heartbeat that is not too fast. They lower high blood pressure, raise low blood pressure to normal levels, improve digestion by stimulating stomach juices, and prevent diarrhea. A tea made from just the flowers works wonders on heart valve troubles, but you can make a standard infusion of tea from the flowers, the leaves, and/or the berries to get the remaining medicinal effects noted. This tree has been used around the world for hundreds of years, is basically nontoxic, and is truly one of nature's gifts to mankind. It grows to just over thirty feet high, is thorny, has white flowers in spring, and goes by the Latin name *Cratoegus laevigata*, or *Cratoegus monogyna* (the English species), or *Cratnegus cuneata* (the Chinese species).

White Willow

White willow is the painkiller in the group, and it is from this tree that Bayer Company extracted the ingredients for aspirin. A little of the bark from the branches of the white willow (or black willow, pussy willow, and weeping willow) can be made into a decoction to create an aspirin-like tea that will ease the pain of nearly everything from sore throats to arthritis to sore muscles. The bark tea is powerful when there is a need to reduce a fever, and there are a half-dozen other uses, among them relief from kidney stone troubles, laryngitis, colitis, and anemia. An infusion made using the buds of the tree will clean and purify the blood, thus fighting inflammation and infections. Using the leaves instead of bark from the branches will bring about a calmness that induces sleep, and in fact, almost any of the willow species whose Latin name begins with *Salix* will have the same sedative effect.

Elderberry Tree

If you have an elderberry tree in your yard, you can rest assured that your medicine cupboard is half-filled even if you don't have any of the other flowers, shrubs, or trees already mentioned. The flowers, the berries, the leaves, the bark, the inner wood, and the roots are all useful and have been relied on by people around the world for thousands of years. As a source of vitamins, you can count on elderberry to supply you with Vitamin A, the B Vitamins, copious amounts of Vitamin C, plus the flavonoids rutin and quercitin, as well as both linoleic and linolenic acids.

If you are coming down with a cold, an infusion of the leaves and flowers will provoke a good healing sweat, bringing the cold to a quick end. Using just the flowers in a tea will relax and calm you when you have serious decisions to make, or you can put a handful of elderflowers in a small cloth bag then into your bathtub, fill with hot water, and soak in it. Not only will you sleep well, you'll wake up calm and with a good deal of mental clarity.

As for the berries, they can be made into jams, jellies, or pies, all of which are quite tasty. If you want a healing effect from them, you have to eat them raw, but not too many at once! They will cure constipation in short order yet without violence, and a tea made from the berries will ward off migraines, and eliminate gas and end stomach upsets. Eating them raw will also help reduce the pain and inflammation of arthritis, rheumatism, and sore muscles. You can make them into wine and sip it when you have a cold, or steep them in a standard infusion to relieve respiratory congestion. An infusion made from the bark of the elderberry tree can be used to induce vomiting if needed, and a decoction of the bark can be used to relieve toothache. (*Editor's note:* Raw elderberry contains the cyanogenic glycoside called sambringigrin. It can cause vomiting and diarrhea if ingested.)

Birch Tree

Last, but certainly just as important in the healing landscape, is the birch tree. You may know it as white birch (*Betula alba*), silver birch (*Betula pendula*), river birch (*Betula allegheniensis*), or the paper birch (*Betula cerrucosa*), but all quite similar in their amazing healing effects. Birch leaves have a sap in them that is highly antibacterial; they can be mashed and placed on a cut or wound to prevent infections. The leaves can also be made into a tea that not only works as a diuretic, research has shown that it literally dissolves kidney and bladder stones! It will also lower blood cholesterol, induce relaxation, and relieve the pain of sore throats. We have used a decoction made from the leaves to wet a compress for strained muscles, and this can also be used to speed the healing of many skin rashes, including allergic reactions to plants such as poison ivy.

You may not be an experienced herbalist who could step out into the yard and grab the makings of a miracle potion. Few of us start that way. Far more common are the stories of someone who either couldn't tolerate the side effects or couldn't get the healing effects they needed desperately from the commercial prescriptions available, so they went looking in the world of nature's plants and found the relief there. That often opens the door to what quickly becomes the astounding array medicinal options, some of which you have growing right in your own yard, others that you recognize as "weeds."

Skill grows slowly, one plant, one problem at a time, but few skills are as useful and comforting as being familiar with the plants you meet every day, knowing that they offer pleasure for your eye, your nose, and perhaps your tongue, and healing for your body and mind if you should ever need it.

Endnotes

1   Bremness, Leslie. *Herbs.* An Eyewitness Handbook. New York: Dorling Kindersley Publishing, 1994. This book is great not only for its scope, but for the well-done photography of over 700 herb species from around the world.

Herbs and Homeopathy

❧ By Joan Hinkley ❧

Homeopathy and herbs are often confused in their action and usage. I will seek to illuminate on these similarities and differences in this section. Since I am both a homeopath and an herbalist, I am often asked the questions such as: "Should I take herbs or homeopathy?" "How does this remedy work?" "What is the difference between homeopathy and herbs?" "Will the herbs interfere with the homeopathic remedy?" To effectively answer these questions one must understand both systems and how they interact with each other, as well as how to use both systems together and when not to do so.

While homeopathic remedies and herbs are often confused with each other, both in terminology and usage, they differ distinctively in their systems of healing. They share some similarities in their origin, but their

preparations are very different, as are their actions on the systems of the body. So what is the difference between herbs and homeopathy? So many people ask this question that it is worthy of our attention. Let us begin by exploring these systems separately.

Herbs

Herbs have different meanings to different people. In times past an herb was a plant, and an herbalist was one who utilized the plant material to bring about the alleviation of suffering on several levels of one's being. There are so many thoughts and ideas as to what an herb constitutes that it is impossible to define herbs for all. Some believe herbs are the relationship the plant has with the human population itself; thus herbalism is the exploration of humanity's relationship with the plant kingdom. It could then be said that herbalism is the relationship between man and plant. The profession of herbalism was regarded very highly until the advent of our culture's desire to be technologically based. Because of our desire for technological capability, a great deal has been lost concerning our relationship with plants, as well as our whole environment and identity.

To a botanist, herbs are plants that are non-woody. An ecologist views herbalism as the relationship between plants, animals, and the environment, as well as the description of communities of plants and their life cycles. The culinary arts restrict their definition of herbs to those used to prepare food. To a modern person who is ailing from a discomfort, an herb is a capsule, tablet, or pellet that cures.

An herbalist is one who uses herbs to support and bring about a healthier balance in the human body. To an herbalist, an herb is any plant material that is growing, whether it is a shrub, tree, or non-woody plant material, etc. An herbalist studies plants from growing to harvesting and prepares them into acceptable modalities of healing. This system of supporting and healing the body is the most similar to pharmaceuticals, yet different in its action. A very large percentage of pharmaceuticals are made from plant material either directly or indirectly. The chemistry of the pharmaceutical is made to mimic a constituent of the plant that was originally used to bring about the healing desired. Herbs in their raw, pure form have many wonderful constituents in them that make up the chemical components to give each plant its own personality. Since the emotional and physical needs are so closely interwoven, it behooves us to listen to them all at the same time. Plants are physical, yet, due to their composition, they may bring about an emotional adjustment while acting on the physical.

Homeopathy

Homeopathy is a scientific medical system developed by Dr. Christian Friedrich Samuel Hahnemann. This medical system utilizes various substances such as herbs, minerals, and animals, which are never destroyed to obtain a homeopathic remedy. These may be found in the *Homeopathic Pharmacopoeia of the United States*. Homeopathy encourages the healing process through homeopathic remedies used to stimulate and encourage the body's natural healing forces of recovery. Homeopathy has a significant role in both curative and preventive medicine. The homeopathic medical system seeks to bring about a healthy state for the whole person, as an individual, rather than treating disease alone. For this reason, people with the same disease may often be given different homeopathic remedies.

Homeopathy is derived from the Greek word *homoios*, meaning "like" or "similar." This describes the homeopathic principle of stimulating like with like. Conventional medicine believes that symptoms are caused by the illness, whereas homeopathy sees the symptoms as the body's natural reaction in fighting the illness. It seeks to stimulate them rather than suppress them, thereby increasing the body's natural response to illness. Homeopathy deals indirectly with the chemistry and structure of the physical body by dealing directly with substance and energies at a more subtle level. It may be thought of as a subjective medicine because it deals with energies that are strongly affected by the mental and emotional activity of the individual. More than 2,000 homeopathic remedies exist. They usually come in the form of granules, tablets, or liquids, which are prepared in scientific laboratories

Many people find the terminology of these two systems confusing. So before we continue, let us define what a remedy is in each system. Herbal remedies are: the actual plant material in capsules or tablets; the actual plant material in bulk (raw fresh or dried material ready to be used to make a tea); and/or the actual plant material prepared into a liquid tincture. These are the most common forms of herbal remedies.

Homeopathic remedies, on the other hand, are not the actual plant material at all but the action (often referred to as the spirit) of the mineral, animal, or plant material. In homeopathic remedies the material has been succussed many times until the original plant material no longer exists as it was. Succussion is the action of shaking the remedy up or the condition of the remedy being shaken up vigorously. In both cases the homeopathic medicine is prepared into a liquid form and successed in a vial or bottle. Each shaking stroke ends with a jolt, usually by pounding the hand engaged in the shaking action against the other palm or a book.

The homeopathic remedy is diluted as well as being successed. This act of reducing the concentration of a solution produces various levels of potencies. Homeopathic remedies are diluted to the point where they no longer actually have the substance of the original material in the remedy. These levels include from 1X to 50M or more. These numbers represent the number of times succussion and dilution has occurred.

The herbs act more directly on specific systems, while homeopathic remedies tend to strengthen the core energy of the person taking them. This indirectly affects all systems of the body. When the physical is well, the emotional will reflect that and vice versa. This is a delicate balance that nature plays in our need for well being and understanding of life.

Another difference is that herbs tend to be more supportive than corrective, whereas homeopathic remedies tend to be more corrective than supportive. Herbs strengthen the body while it corrects itself. Homeopathy corrects while the body supports the self-correcting process. Both can be very gentle, yet at the same time effective in bringing about change. The degree to which aggressive therapy or gentle therapy occurs tends to be more in the hands of the practitioner and a factor of any time limitations that may be imposed by an impending disease state.

Digitalis: An Example

To continue to understand the differences of herbs and homeopathy let us use the plant foxglove (*Digitalis*) as an example for this comparison.

First of all, while homeopathy always takes the Latin term for the primary names of the remedies, the common names are most often used with the herbs. You may, however have as many as ten different names for one herb, including the common names, the Latin names, and several regional names. For example foxglove (Latin name: *Digitalis purpurea*) has many country names such as: witches' gloves, dead men's bells, fairy's glove, gloves of our lady, bloody fingers, virgin's glove, fairy caps, folk's glove, and fairy thimbles. The Norwegian name is *revbielde*. The German name is *fingerhut*.

Never use digitalis in its raw herbal state except under the guidance of a qualified herbalist. Digitalis contains four compounds, known as glycosides, of which three are cardiac stimulants. The most powerful of the three glycosides is digitoxin. This glucoside is an extremely poisonous and cumulative drug that is insoluble in water. The other glycosides are digitalein, which is amorphous, but readily soluble in water; and digitonin, a cardiac depressant. Each of these compounds differs in their action, but when combined in the foxglove plant itself they make a balanced, complex form of medicine. In the third edition (copyright 1917) of *A Manual of Pharmacology and its Applications* to *Therapeutics and Toxicology*, by Torald Sollmann, M.D., is a clear picture of the usage of earlier pharmacy applications of digitalis. It states "*Digitalis* (Digit.) U.S.P.; *Digitalis Folia* (Digit. Fol.) B.P.; *Digitalis* (Foxglove Leaves). The dried leaves of *Digitalis purpurea*. The B.P. specifies that they must be collected when the plant is beginning to flower. Dose, 0.1 Gm., 1½ gr., U.S.P.; 0.03 to 0.12 Gm., ½ to 2 gr., B.P.; as pills. Maximum dose, 0.2 Gm., 3 gr." It becomes obvious that digitalis was used in its raw state, but only by those who were knowledgeable. We may also determine that much knowledge existed about the herb, and that studies had been conducted to determine the correct quantity of herbs to use in various cases.

Digitalis, which has been used in natural forms for years by the medical field, acts strongly and directly on the heart. Digitalis has been used since early times for heart cases. It increases the activity of all forms of muscle tissue, but more especially that of the heart and arterioles. When the herb is absorbed into the bloodstream its action contracts the heart and arteries, thus causing a dramatic increase in blood pressure. After taking a moderate dose the pulse slows markedly. It also has a correcting effect on irregular pulse in that it will cause an irregular pulse to become regular. It can reduce internal capacity of the heart by contracting the heart. This benefits cases of cardiac dilatation. It will increase the amount of blood in the heart and thus improve the nutrition of the heart. It also has an action on the kidneys. In small doses it serves as a powerful diuretic and may be used appropriately in cases of dropsy. This is not a safe herb to casually experiment with, but rather to respect and to use only under the guidance of a qualified herbalist. Dosage will vary with age and body mass.

While this herb may tend to support the heart, it may not make the actual correction to eliminate the difficulty. Homeopathy, on the other hand, may make the actual correction. Digitalis in homeopathic form might be utilized when the pulse is abnormally slow, or where palpitations occur after grief. It may also be effective where there is a fear of death from cardiac symptoms, such as fear of the heart stopping, or remorse or guilty feelings. To sufficiently understand a case and properly suggest a homeopathic remedy the homeopath must understand every aspect: emotional, mental, physical, and psychological. I can speak of having had heart difficulty that is now gone after using homeopathy.

When we examine the use of the same herb in homeopathic form we see that there are many mental symptoms that accompany potential physical discomforts of the heart. Some of the more prominent mental symptoms are anguish with nausea, anxiety in the evening, anxiety as if guilty of a crime, anxiety from motion, anxious about the future, fear, apprehension, dread, especially during heart symptoms. Other mental symptoms may be a sense of suspicion or mistrustfulness, unsympathetic and unscrupulous activities or thoughts, or sadness with sleeplessness from unhappy love. These symptoms may express themselves on the mental level with lascivious thoughts in old men with enlarged prostate. There is also a sense of feeling as if they would fly to pieces. These types may experience a fear of death from cardiac symptoms, fear of the heart stopping, remorse, and guilty feelings. They may also exhibit palpitations after grief. Physically they are worse from exertion, raising up, lying on their left side, the smell of food, cold drinks, food or weather, from music, or from sexual abuse or excess. They may feel better from rest, cool air, lying flat on their backs, empty stomach, sitting erect, or from weeping.

People experience what they consider to be "side effects" with herbs. Let us examine this a little deeper. Pharmaceuticals may have side effects when used according to instructions. Herbs will not have side effects when used according to instructions. Therefore we may determine that it is not the herb causing the side effects but rather the human taking the herb incorrectly, thus causing difficulties. Herbs primarily support the physical system without side effects. In turn, they also bring about a more balanced emotional/mental state. Homeopathy primarily affects the emotional/mental state of the person's inner being while balancing the physical. The two different approaches compare to one entering a house through two different doors. The inside of the house has the same floor plan, but if the back door has debris against it you must enter through the front door, and vice versa. We must enter through the avenue that our body will allow us to, then continue to work with all the rooms. If we look at the body as a house that contains various rooms, we would not clean only one room and never pay any attention to the other rooms. It wouldn't be a comfortable way to live. So it is that we must understand the different health modalities to make a good decision as to which approach is best for our body and as to how to continue with the healing process. Deciding which way to begin should be left up to an experienced homeopath/herbalist.

To make a final comparison, often both modalities fall under the categories of alternative, complementary, or holistic medicine. Once again we become entangled in terminology. What is alternative medicine? Complementary medicine complements what? One statement that is true is that both herbs and homeopathy are holistic medicines that encompass the healing of the entire person, thus the need to take into account all of the aspects of a human being who is ill. The sum of the person includes environment, culture, economic conditions, social needs, current emotional state of being, physical status—literally everything about the human as well as his or her relation with the surroundings. The studies of herbs and homeopathy are similar in that they enhance the whole person to encourage wholeness. They differ in their preparations and how each modality approaches the disease housed in the human body, as well as in their usage by the practitioner. Neither modality is right or wrong, but rather a matter of choice. The preferred modality is to be administered considering current conditions such as environment, economic status, social needs, current emotional state, capability, etc. as well as the ability of the ill person to follow instructions.

Magical Herbal Immunotherapy

~ By Marguerite Elsbeth ~

The human body is an integrated circuit. The mind, the central nervous system that protects and defends us against potential disease, and all other parts of the body, are in constant communication. Every cell in the body is a living, conscious organism that can send messages as well as recognize and fight disease-producing intruders.

Our bodies are continuously invaded by viruses, bacteria, and toxins that are impossible to avoid, as they are in the air, water, soil, and the food we eat. We generate harmful cells every day, but most of the time we are safe from harm's way, and life goes on without our ever realizing we were in danger. Our bodies hold off disease because they are defended by the immune system and the healing system or DNA, the macromolecule that defines life.

Each of us has about a trillion cells called lymphocytes, or messenger cells, at the core of the immune system. We also have about a hundred million trillion molecules, called antibodies or warrior cells, which are produced by the lymphocytes. The lymphatic system, a maze-like network of tiny tubes that carry life-sustaining sustenance, brings the messenger and warrior cells where they need to go to keep us healthy, whole, and moving.

However, the actual healing system is a functional system. It is not a collection of structures that can be neatly slotted and labeled like other bodily systems. Function supercedes structure when it comes to healing because the human body has a defensive orb of ability that can be stimulated to action. Healing is an inherent dimension of life. The healing system always works and is always on call. It has a diagnostic capacity that can identify and eliminate damaged structures and replace them with healthy, normal structures.

The Mental/Emotional Connection

There are three kinds of influences that weaken the immune system: persistent infections, toxic injury, and unhealthy mental and emotional states. Our mental and emotional habit patterns comprise the root of all physical imbalance.

We don't get sick because germs cause illness, even though we may harbor disease-causing organisms from time to time. Our immune system takes care of that through defenses that are part of the web that connects the central nervous system and the endocrine system. This suggests that our resistance to infection varies according to our state of mind and emotions. Therefore, becoming ill actually depends upon how we respond to germs emotionally! If we feel depressed and miserable, we are more likely to get sick because depression blocks the immune response, as does stress, which usually stems from an unhealthy diet, lack of exercise, nicotine, alcohol, caffeine, drug addiction, a dissatisfying work situation, or the loss of a lover, spouse, child, or friend.

However, we can also enhance and strengthen the immune response via our habitual thoughts and emotions. Our spiritual beliefs, meditation and prayer practices, feelings of love, hope, and faith, the active use of creative imagination, proper diet and exercise, vitamin and mineral supplements, and especially our relationship with and use of medicinal herbs, are perhaps the most powerful tools we have to maintain wholeness within ourselves.

Sympathetic Healing

Various cultures around the world have a long-standing tradition of herbal medicine that is closely intertwined with spiritual beliefs and customs. Thus plants have been used for centuries in conjunction with magic to heal, purify, and strengthen the body, mind, and emotions.

Plants respond to our thoughts and feelings just as our immune systems do. This is because plants are sentient beings, animated by the same universal life-giving spirit found in all creatures and things. Known by many names—Great Spirit, Great Mystery, God or Goddess—this innate spirit-energy is both the healer and the medicine. This makes plants sympathetic to our bodies just as we are sensitive to their healing properties. Sympathetic is the operative word when it comes to stimulating the healing system with medicinal herbs.

Physically speaking, we may associate the word sympathetic with that part of the autonomic (self-governing or primal) nervous system, originating in both the lumbar region (or the small of the back), and the thoracic region (or chest area), of the spinal cord. The functions of these two regions include the arrangement and disposition of smooth muscles, the heart muscle, and glands. It is also affiliated with a particular nerve of the sympathetic nervous system that is a part of the autonomic nervous system mentioned above. This nerve is one of two cords connecting a series of ganglia along the spinal column, and is the body's headquarters for both ordinary and non-ordinary vibratory perception.

Consequently, feelings of sympathy are physical reactions caused by vibrations we can instinctually sense from a neighboring vibrating object, and will usually denote a person, place, or thing that is in natural harmony with our tastes, moods, and disposition. Our intuitive understanding of how the body operates on physical, emotional, mental, and spiritual levels eventually led humankind to develop the art and practice of sympathetic magic, which is based on the following two principles: (1) like attracts and produces like, or an effect resembles its cause, and (2) things that have once been in contact with each other continue to act on each other at a distance even after physical contact has been severed.

The first idea is self-explanatory: if we can absorb it, we can inherit its essential energy. The second thought intimates that whatever we do to a material object will equally affect the person with whom the object comes in contact. Simply expressed, sickness begets sickness, and health begets health. This makes the application of sympathetic magic as a healing tool a no-brainer. Therefore, we need not concern ourselves regarding the mental or physical processes involved regarding why herbal medicines work to keep us well any more than we need give our attention to how we breathe, blink our eyes, or digest our food. Whether by synchronicity, cosmic flow, or a state of grace, healing happens.

Healing System Herbs

While there are many valuable medicinal herbs on the alternative health market, the following are specific herbal medicines that can directly assist the immune and healing systems in maintaining optimum health and well being.

ASTRAGALUS is a true tonic containing polysaccharides, large molecules composed of chains of sugar subunits that can strengthen against immune debilitation and increase resistance to disease in general via enhanced production of white blood cells, antibodies, and interferon. It promotes other herbs known to increase energy, assists digestion, and stimulates circulation. This herb is especially helpful for people with bronchitis, sinusitis, cancer, and AIDS, or those lacking vitality or feeling weakened by stress.

BURDOCK ROOT contains two polyacetylene compounds that inhibit the growth of bacteria and fungi in the body. Therefore, this herb is administered mainly as a blood purifier. Some herbalists also consider it to be both a diuretic and diaphoretic. When applied as a poultice, burdock may be used to treat psoriasis, acne, and other skin conditions, as well as bruises, burns, knee-swellings, and gout.

ECHINACEA ROOT carries a substance called caffeic acid glycoside, which reacts with the immunity cells to facilitate the wound-healing process, making it an immune stimulant, a blood purifier, and an effective antibiotic. Use this herb to treat rheumatism, streptococcus infections, bee stings, poisonous snake bites, tumors, syphilis, gangrene, eczema, hemorrhoids, and wounds.

GARLIC has been traditionally associated with strength, speed, and endurance. It destroys and represses various bacteria, fungi, and yeast due to its primary component, allicin. This substance, which forms when the cloves are crushed, has an antibacterial action equivalent to 1 percent penicillin. Cooking may reduce its healing potency. Garlic is effective against influenza, typhus, worms and parasites, respiratory ailments, high blood pressure, cardiac and circulatory dysfunction, and stomach cancer.

GINGER ROOT (actually a rhizome) contains enzymes and antioxidants, and affects the production and deployment of eicosanoids, which mediate healing and immunity by reducing abnormal inflammation and clotting. It is a leading stimulant and anti-inflammatory that promotes good circulation and digestion, settles upset stomachs, nausea, and motion sickness, and relieves aches and pains. Ginger also has strong anti-cancer causing agents that block carcinogens that mutate in DNA. (*Editor's note:* Do not use medicinally if you have gallstones.)

GINGKO BILOBA directly affects the metabolism—the energy stores of the body. It may be used to treat fatigue, lack of motivation, low blood pressure, depression, poor circulation, and especially, brain "fog." (*Editor's note:* Ginko may potentiate MAO inhibitors.)

GINSENG is reputed to help every human ailment. It is a powerful "adaptogen" that protects against physical and mental stress, and helps the healing system functions return to normal more quickly than usual. This herb also increases longevity, defends cells against radiation, prevents heart disease, and is useful in treating anemia, atherosclerosis, depression, diabetes, edema, hypertension, and ulcers. (*Editor's note:* Do not use if you have hypertension.)

GOLDENSEAL has an active ingredient called hydrastine, a mild antiseptic that influences circulation, muscle tone and smoothness, as well as uterine contractions and bleeding. It may also be used as an eyewash to treat eye irritation, and to lower blood sugar levels, thereby reducing stress and anxiety. (*Editor's note:* Do not ingest while pregnant.)

LICORICE contains a medicinal terpene component that has a structure similar to a steroid. It is a tremendous energy booster due to its high sugar-like content. This herb is commonly found in cough syrups and drops because it soothes the chest and helps bring up phlegm. Licorice is also highly effective in treating ulcers, relieving rheumatism and arthritis, and inducing menstruation. (*Editor's note:* Do not ingest while pregnant. Not for long-term use. Avoid medicinal doses of licorice if you have diabetes, hypertension, liver disorders, or kidney problems.)

MILK THISTLE seeds include a healing substance called silymarin which enhances the metabolism of the liver cells and protects them from toxic injury. This herb is beneficial for alcohol users and individuals taking pharmaceutical drugs that are hard on the liver, including cancer patients receiving chemotherapy. It is an excellent tonic for toxic chemical contamination, chronic hepatitis, and abnormal liver function in general, as this herb will help the body to recover from any injury.

RED CLOVER is a powerful blood purifier and immune stimulant. It has been used effectively in treating ulcers, stomach cancers, whooping cough, and various muscle and bronchial spasms. Combined with equal parts of blue violet, burdock, yellow dock, dandelion root, rock rose, and goldenseal, it is a strong remedy for cancerous growths and leprosy. This herb is also very quieting to the nervous system in general.

Dowsing for Sympathetic Herbs

Dowsing is a way of working with our instincts, feelings, intellect, memory, and creative imagination. It usually requires the use of a pendulum, which can be any relatively balanced object hanging from a string, although most people prefer to use a polished crystal or gemstone point. The following method may be used to discern illness in the body as well as to determine which immune-enhancing herbs are most sympathetic to the body's needs:

- Obtain a pendulum.

- Gather the herbs in question, place a small sample of each herb around a large, round plate so they are not touching, and have this before you.

- Draw an outline of the body, and below it write the name of the person to be dowsed. Keep the pen handy.

- Take a moment or two to think about what you are about to do, and pray to the powers that be, as well as to the herb spirits for guidance and assistance.

- When you feel ready, hold the pendulum in the search position, suspended between the thumb and index fingers of your left hand.

- Ask the pendulum which way is yes. It will move either clockwise, counterclockwise, or back and forth. Usually clockwise is yes, but whichever way it goes is yes for that particular pendulum, and you may consider the opposite direction as a no. Back and forth indicates maybe.

- Begin at the head area and wait for a response, noting whether the pendulum says yes, no, or maybe. Note your findings directly on the figure. Continue by slowly running the pendulum down the figure and stopping at strategic areas, making notes as you go. The yes answers indicate there may be a problem in a given area. Maybe responses show that there may be the potential for difficulty in the area. No means no problem. The yes and maybe responses may require herbal treatment.

- Next, hold the pendulum over the plate of herbal remedies. If, for example, the pendulum said yes to the head area, then focus on the head area as you allow the pendulum to swing around the plate until it points to or settles over one (or more) herbs in particular. Or, hold the pendulum over each herb, and again wait for a yes, no, or maybe response. Yes to the head area and yes to a particular herb is a sympathetic match.

Revering the Herb Spirits

It may be necessary to establish an initial familial rapport with the herbs we intend to use for medicinal purposes. The living spirit inhabiting plants and herbs is invisible to us unless we are willing to open up our senses to it. When we start to become intimately aware of this source of energy and let it enter into our lives, we can then communicate with it mentally, emotionally, and physically, through talk, prayer, and action. Only then do we gain a deeper respect for the inner and outer workings of nature, and especially the plant kingdom.

If we are aware of and emotionally connected to the spirit dwelling within a particular medicinal herb, it may become our guardian, friend, and ally, and assist us to help ourselves to resist the cellular intrusions that seek to break down the immune system. In fact, this clarisentient link with the herb-spirits that are to become our longevity-producing medicine is absolutely essential to our continued good health. Therefore, it is wise to develop an attitude toward plants that is free of preconceptions.

Shamans, medicine people, traditional peoples, and healers have always recognized the spirit power in plants and herbs, and consequently have sought to revere this energy while simultaneously bonding with the herbs being considered for use. Once you have established which immune-boosting herbs are sympathetically compatible with your specific requirements, you may wish to secure your relationship with them in the following manner.

Try wearing a medicine bag on your person that contains the plants or herbs to be used for treatment, or keep pictures of the herbs on your altar, desk, or kitchen table.

Plant the living herb in your garden, or in a pot to be kept inside the house, and feed it every evening with a food offering of your choice or tradition (for example, sprinkle the plant very lightly with cornmeal or natural tobacco if you happen to follow a Native American path). You may also wish to offer an herbal incense such as sage, cedar, sweetgrass, or pine to the herb spirit on a regular basis. This is done by lighting the incense and allowing the smoke to gently drift around the herb while expressing your gratitude and praying for it to acknowledge and help you.

The Ritual Preparation of Herbs

Natives of the Seminole nation in Oklahoma infuse the medicinal plant in water, singing a prayer, and bubbling the infusion by blowing into it through a reed or cane pipe. They believe that the song or prayer enters the medicine this way, and that the way the air bubbles through the medicine predicts how well it will work.

The Huichol Indians of Mexico treat a certain species of cactus as a god due to the ecstacy it produces when eaten. The hunter-gatherers of this holy cactus impose a severe restriction upon themselves and their mates. Until the cactus is gathered and a festival is held in its honor, they only wash their hands on special occasions, and only with water brought in from the distant land where the sacred cactus grows.

All of these rituals connect the people who practice them to the plants that will serve as food or medicine, as well as to the earth that brings them forth. The food or medicinal plants are then harvested with the object of bringing nourishment to the body.

Today, when we seek an alternative treatment or herbal remedy for what ails us, we usually access the information in a book, on a web site, or over-the-counter at our favorite natural food store. Then we struggle with protective plastic wrapping, pop open a bottle, maybe wrestle with cotton stuffing for a minute or two, down a capsule, and forget all about it until it is time to take another pill. This arrangement is a poorly planned ritual indeed, because it does nothing to connect us to the vital livingness of the herb itself, save the fact that we have ingested the substance.

Those who are more adventurous may buy loose herbs and take the time to make an infusion or tea to gulp down. This method is a more positive form of ritual, due to the specific purpose of the preparation involved as well as to the satisfaction received when we are soothed by the herb's fragrant aroma, and the hot, steaming liquid flowing into our systems.

Both of these methods may work, due to the awareness of the subconscious mind to our actions. However, if we were to add a prayer of acknowledgment, state our intention, imagine that the herb medicine or tea is healing what ails us right now, and thank the herb spirit for coming to our assistance, we would have performed a complete ritual, short of actually sowing and harvesting the plant ourselves! Better living through plastic notwithstanding, we may not be gaining full advantage of the healing herbs unless we add some form of ceremonial preparation to the mix, because ritual is prayer in motion.

Medicine–Making by the Moon

⤜ By Gretchen Lawlor ⤛

The Moon holds dominion over the plant kingdom. This is old wisdom. Many traditions, including homeopathic pharmacy, biodynamic farming, most indigenous farming practice, as well as that of our own magical herbalism, use the influence of the Moon to profoundly affect the available life force of plants. To make potent, effective medicines, align your efforts with the force and current of the Moon.

Many herbalists believe that plants that grow naturally in one's own environment are 1,000 times more medicinally potent that anything that is commercially grown and processed. There is also a strongly held feeling that plants that grow naturally in a region are the most effective healers for ailments common to that region.

With this in mind, consider what you could accomplish in preparing

medicines using potent local plants and timing your efforts to coincide with their peak vitality. This is what medicine-making by the Moon is all about. Align yourself with the laws and force of nature to maximize the power of your product.

Making your own medicines gives you the opportunity to pick and prepare medicines while the plant is still fresh and full of life force. In the process of making the remedy you gather information through all your senses, which adds significantly to your knowledge of the plant.

In discovering and harvesting a plant, you receive information about shape and smell, the color, the strength of the stalk, or the delicacy of the leaves and flowers. You have information gleaned from where it was growing, what conditions it was thriving in. The knowledge you gain from books, from herbalists who have gone before you, is made personal by your own experience in the field.

How do you start making your own medicines? Get a good plant identification book, and get out walking in your own wilds. Watch for plants that you are particularly attracted to, or stand out in some way, and get to know them better. They will be your first teachers.

One of my most profound plant experiences happened after I had graduated as a naturopathic doctor and was doing advanced studies in the field. I was walking through a grassy open place and heard, or sensed, a plant actually yelling at me.

"Hey you!" it said. Stunned, I looked down. There stood a beautiful white yarrow plant in full bloom, demanding that I stop and pay attention to it. I didn't hear anything more in that moment, I just stood and took in that plant. My every sense was acute as I tried to figure out what was going on. You can believe that I went home and researched everything I could find about that plant. It continues to reveal more of itself to me with every contact, even now, years later. I consider it one of my most potent pharmaceutical tools or allies, and a very dear friend.

When I started making flower essences (a form of herbal medicine that uses the vibrational energetics of the plant as its healing constituent), I remember a teacher who sent us off one day to fall in love with a flower. These days I don't make a medicine unless I have that passion in my connection with a plant. That's the kind of relationship with a plant you need to make very potent medicine.

It is most important in good medicine-making that one respects the wild nature of plants. Really strong medicine, the best, is made from wild plants growing where they will, rather than cultivated or constrained.

Plants are wild, and we cannot truly treat them as tame. Cultivated plants just don't have the same ferocity and raw energy, and frequently feel much more subdued that the "weeds" of the wild. It's not to say one should never make medicine from a cultivated plant. There are situations where that is our only option (with even more of a need to use the lunar tides to do our work with them).

Wild plants do not conform to our man-made rules or cultural expectations, so we must find ways to meet them, to listen to their language. When you are in a foreign culture, if you are a good traveler you watch, listen, and learn the language of the territory.

So it is with the plants that surround you. You want to meet, to relate to these wild beings. To make truly passionate wild medicine, you must be with the wild, must find your own wild to do it well.

One of the ways to do this is to honor and act in accordance with the phases and cycles of nature. The most obvious and simple way to do this is to work with the light and dark of the Moon.

This is old knowledge, accumulated over the centuries. Anything that has endured for so long must surely have had a reason for coming into being, and must hold truth in it. I am not going to spend time explaining why or in justifying the knowledge, but will just tell you what works.

Simply put, during the increasing light of the Moon, from New Moon to Full, the energy of the plant is rising, being pulled up and out of the plant. During the decreasing light, from Full Moon to New Moon, the energy of the plant is being drawn back down, into the roots.

Let me give you some rules of timing by the Moon that can be immediately applied for both harvesting plants and for medicine-making.

Medicine-Making in the Waxing Moon

In this two-week period the life force is increasing and rising through the plant. The sap is being pulled upward and outward to the extremities of the plant, especially to the leaf and the flower. The sap is rising, and the plant is willing to give off its power.

This period is excellent for all harvesting, except for roots, which may be better harvested at last quarter. (Some magical practitioners feel there is a very potent short period for harvesting roots in the two days immediately after New Moon, though most avoid the day of the New Moon itself).

The waxing Moon is also a good time to draw the energy out of the plant into the alcoholic base of a tincture, into an oil, or even to pick to dry the plant, except if it is the root which contains the most active ingredients (such as dandelions). Put the plant in alcohol at New Moon, and strain it out two weeks later at Full. The drawing power of the waxing Moon will significantly increase the extraction of the medicinal force of the plant.

Collect herbs that build health—the tonics and stimulants—during the waxing Moon, with the increased light.

Medicine-Making with the Waning Moon

In this two-week period, from the New Moon to the Full, the vital forces of nature are going down into the roots of the plant and extending down into the earth. The life force is below the surface. It is a good time for feeding roots, and a good wet rain during the wane of the Moon will be absorbed more swiftly and be more nourishing to the plant. The wane is considered to be the best time for harvesting roots for maximum potency.

Gather those herbs used to remove disease, for example, the expectorants, astringents, and antiseptics, during the wane of the Moon. Obviously there is some contradiction here, as the general rule of using the waxing Moon for harvesting is not being applied.

Do your best. Remember that it is intent that is most critical to potency, and sometimes it is just not possible to harvest at the right time. For example, it is not wise to harvest in extremely wet conditions because the tendency to mold or rot is increased. The wise herbalist may have several rules to consider, and choose them to best support circumstances.

Medicines that are difficult to absorb are more easily assimilated when taken in the waning cycle, particularly with older people, where assimilation may be an issue.

Take medicines whose intent is to decrease, sedate, or eliminate in the wane of Moon. This is particularly noticeable of sedatives, which have less resistance to overcome during this waning phase.

Using the Quarters of the Moon for Medicine-Making

New Moon/First Quarter

The first few days of the New Moon are considered best for harvesting roots, as well as for harvesting anything that is fully ripe, i.e. the fruit or seeds of plants. Picked in this phase the herb will dry well and retain its flavor, smell, and life force. Do not harvest leaves right at New Moon, as they carry an ongoing life force, and are best picked from a few days after New Moon all the way to Full Moon, a window of approximately twelve days.

Second Quarter Moon

The second quarter moon begins approximately seven days after the New Moon. It is good for harvesting, and for routine projects that require some organization and energy. Some herbalists consider it to be one of the optimum times to harvest plants when you want to use the twigs and stems, such as ephedra or sweetgrass. This is because the plant energy is in movement through the plant, but not quite as concentrated yet in the extremities of leaf or flower.

In drying a plant to make a tea, the essence is concentrated in the leaf, and is best harvested just before the Full Moon, then dried in the waning cycle. Drying takes generally two weeks to complete. By timing most of the drying in the waning cycle but commencing the process just before, the essence is conserved in the plant as it dries.

Full Moon/Third Quarter

At Full Moon and for the day and a half to either side of the Full Moon itself, the Sun and Moon are opposing each other. This is a time of peak emotional energy, which can be overwhelming if not contained. This is why ceremonies to dedicate energy are often performed here. Medicine-making for profound magical intent can be made now, but requires skill in focusing the energy or it is easy to spoil a medicine. Medicines made at Full Moon by someone who cannot hold the disciplined focus tend to go bad quickly, or have an undesirable stimulating effect on the patient.

Harvest flowers right after the Full Moon itself. The flower is the ultimate manifestation, the energetic peak of the plant.

Most Full Moon medicine-making is done after the Full Moon energy has stabilized, several days past Full. Then it becomes better for medicines whose intent is to eliminate, shrink, or detoxify. Fasts are best started in the Full Moon quarter, two days after the Moon is Full.

Fourth Quarter Moon

This seven-day phase begins about halfway between the Full Moon and the New Moon. This is the best time for weed elimination—for clearing out tenacious and invasive plants with bad boundaries, such as blackberries or scotch broom. For really difficult clearing, both cut down plants and apply topical poison (preferably organic) to the stumps because they are pulling down the energy.

Things are more willing to let go in the fourth quarter, whether this is to die or to release. It is easier now to let go of anything that isn't critical. Many herbalists recommend harvesting roots at this fourth quarter, when the life force is bound deeply in the root. However, there is controversy here, with some herbalists raising the possibility that the sap or volatile oils are not yet as available as they soon will be in a short window of opportunity just after the New Moon.

Harvesting Potent Root, Leaf, Flower, and Seed

Many gardeners use not only the phases and quarters of the Moon for optimum production, but also the sign of the Moon. The sign of the Moon, by element (fire, earth, air, and water) concentrates moisture and life force into different parts of the plant. Medicine makers also use this knowledge to gather or prepare at times of maximum concentration of the life force.

EARTH SIGNS (Taurus, Virgo, and Capricorn) concentrate the life force in the root of the plant.

WATER SIGNS (Cancer, Scorpio, and Pisces) concentrate the life force in the leaf of the plant.

AIR SIGNS (Gemini, Libra, and Aquarius) concentrate the life force in the flower of the plant.

FIRE SIGNS (Aries, Leo, and Sagittarius) concentrate the life force in the fruit/seed of the plant.

Administering Medicines with the Moon

Just as there are better times for harvesting and preparing medicines, there are times for the application of these medicines that will achieve far greater success. It is important to keep the functions of building up and tonifying separate from the functions of breaking down and dispersing. Timely application of the right medicine will require less time and materials to make a positive effect because it is working with nature's instinctive energetic tides.

Waxing Moon

In the waxing cycle, the spirit of a plant is more willing to go out into the world to give off its vital force. Medicines administered now encourage more vitality and are more stimulating to the system. Tonics are best given in the turning seasons of the year, spring and fall, and always in the waxing Moon phase.

Treatment for depression commenced in the waxing Moon catalyzes increased life force, flooding the system with light. St. John's wort, or hypericum, is an excellent antidepressant that helps the body to take in more light. It is best prepared on its own day—St. John's Day or Midsummer's Day, the Summer Solstice—when the forces of light are at their maximum.

Waning Moon

At this time the life force is going inward, spiraling inward. This is the best time to eliminate anything that you wish to get rid of. Purgatives and vermifuges (worm medicines) are most effective. If you have an infestation of fleas in a house or on an animal or plant, or are dealing with resistant internal parasites, this is the optimum time to apply appropriate medications.

This is the time for fasting to lose weight. Waning Moon is the time to begin efforts to break a habit. Magical tradition believes it takes twenty-one days (three cycles of seven) to break a habit. Set the intent at New Moon and begin your preparations, but start the regime itself with the decreasing light.

Waning Moon is also the time to commence treatment to get rid of warts, to reduce tumors, and to detoxify from drug or alcohol abuse.

Preparing Yourself for Medicine Taking

The lunar cycle dictates the intent of the medicine maker as well as providing signs as to plant vitality and activity. Remember, it is the wholehearted and dedicated focus of your intent that makes for the success of magical medicine-making.

If you consider the waning cycle to be one of downward, inward energy, you can understand why this is the time for the practitioner to feed his or her own roots and essence. This is the time to gather in your own resources, to take your supplements, especially minerals (vitamins are more effective administered in the waxing Moon).

Care for yourself and clear yourself of anything that would get in the way of being a perfect vessel of powerful medicines. It is your responsibility to tend to yourself, clear and ready yourself. This is not the best time go out and bother the plant world, which is preoccupied with aligning itself with life force turning inward. Both you and the plant are instinctively less involved with the outer world.

In the wane, nourish your own essence in order to be prepared and in peak form, ready to take advantage of the fresh impulse and enthusiasm of the next waxing cycle.

Using the In-Between Times

There are times in the year when the magical worlds are closest, when the forces of nature are peaking. For intuitive contact with the plant world, these are the most significant moments. These are the times to still yourself and listen to what the plant beings have to share. These points are the solstices (December 21–23 and June 21–23), the equinoxes (March 21–23 and September 21–23), and the cross quarter days of Candlemas (February 2), Beltane (May 1), Lammas (August 1–2), and Samhain or Halloween (October 31).

In these in-between, turning times there is more access to the other worlds. Magic is afoot and close. Listen and learn at these pivotal moments. It is true also that circumstances can change more easily when the tides of life are also changing. The whole energetic field of nature is unsettled. There is less inertia to overcome.

Dawn and dusk are two other significant turning times There are occasions when we cannot make our medicines with the larger cycles of Moon phase or sign, and may have to make do with a minor cycle, such as dawn or dusk.

St. Michael's Day, September 29, is a magical day for harvesting roots. In the Celtic countries of Scotland and Ireland there used to be elaborate fertility rituals on this day when the women would harvest the carrot crop, then present any particularly fine specimens to their men.

Magical medicine-making requires creating a special relationship with the plant beings. You are asking the plant for its help—asking it to share its life force with you.

For most, maybe all of us, there are only a few true plant allies we will discover in our lives. In Ireland and Scotland, the Celtic lands from whence most of our western mystery tradition stems, often a healer was know for a specific gift, or for a specific remedy. In our times, we are used to having the choice of hundreds of remedies at our local store. They do not have the potency—the magic—of a medicine produced locally by someone who has a deep and passionate relationship with the plant world.

To find your allies, get out into the wild and listen. Consider the plants around you in your childhood. Often they are your first friends, and hold something special for you.

Good magical medicine-making is very much a two-way relationship, like being a good traveler in a foreign country. Make an effort to learn the language. Allow yourself to be touched by the culture. Honor their unique ways and live by them when you are around them. Be respectful and say thank you, return energy for what you take. Watch for the aspects of the culture that excite you or resonate with your deep self. Surrender to changing from the contact with this foreign culture. Be willing to embrace your own wild self. It will emerge, I guarantee you, from contact with these vital green beings with which we share this planet.

Another Look at Kava Kava

By Deborah Duchon

When anthropologist Martha Ward went to Polynesia more than twenty years ago, she already knew about an unusual plant that she would find: kava kava. She knew that the people whom she would live with conducted nightly rituals where they pounded the whole plant into a mucky, slimy pulp that they would drink from a communal cup made of a hollowed-out coconut shell. She couldn't wait.

Her very first night in the village, she followed the sound of rhythmic pounding to the town center, where the men had already started the nightly event. When the cup was passed to her, she raised it to her lips (against the advice of her colleague, a public health doctor) and sipped. She felt her lips and tongue go numb. She felt herself starting to drool like those around her. She felt calm, serene, and contented.

During her long sojourn in the South Seas, she would spend many evenings in the same surroundings, watching the town's social, political, and religious life unfold around her, partaking of the shared cup of kava. She saw that when there were tensions between people, they would work out their differences during the nightly kava ritual. In fact, the people had a saying to the effect that nobody can stay mad if they drink kava. During the inevitable frustrations that she experienced, she found kava and the ritual that surrounded it to be a source of strength and clarity. The answers to the most difficult challenges she met came to her during these evenings.

At the end of her fieldwork, when she left the islands to return to the U.S.A., she knew that it was kava that she would miss the most. As she returned to her homeland, a place where drugs are abused, she wondered what would happen if kava kava were to be discovered by the West. She hoped it would never happen, because she expected that Americans would use it just for the "high" and it wouldn't be used in the same context, as a part of the society where problems were worked out, but for the thrill of it.

One wonders what Martha Ward must be feeling now as kava kava has become the new darling of American devotees of herbal cures, in the wake of echinacea and St. John's wort before it. She might be pleased that it has not become another marijuana or heroin, but she might also be dismayed that it is used only like any other pill, and not with the same reverence as it is in the South Seas. She wouldn't be alone. Kava kava has been well known to anthropologists for years, and archeologists have found evidence of its use in the South Pacific region for up to 3,000 years. Perhaps, if this secret was destined to escape into the modern world, it has found itself in the best possible niche. Modern herbalists use plant remedies with their own kind of reverence, and, although their rituals may not be as elaborate, they have figured out how to tease the active ingredient out in ways that match the American lifestyle and health demands.

Kava kava, also known simply as "kava," is known to botanists as *Piper methysticum*, and is closely related to black pepper. It is an erect shrub that can grow to more than twelve feet in height, with smooth, heart-shaped leaves and jointed stems. The mature plant, at least two to three years old, is used for medicinal purposes. Younger plants simply lack the necessary potency. It was first discovered by the Western world in the 1700s by Captain Cook, who told the world about it in his writings. For many years, missionaries discouraged its use, thinking it a pagan ceremony, and, indeed, it was used for some religious occasions. Compare it to wine in our own culture. We use wine for occasions ranging from holy communion to a variety of other social (and antisocial) occasions. Even though many Polynesians converted to Christianity, use of kava remained widespread by native peoples from Hawaii to New Guinea. It is interesting that as recently as 1992, on the island of Oahu in Hawaii, Hillary Clinton (on the campaign trail) was greeted by native Hawaiians holding a kava ceremony in her honor.

Kava first entered the mainstream in the United States in 1980, when a small shipment was received at a health food store in Brookline, Massachusetts. A store employee, Mr. Chris Kilham, tried it. He later wrote of the experience, "A sensuous wave of muscular relaxation washed slowly through my body like India ink spreading on white paper." Mr. Kilham became kava's champion. He visited the Republic of Vanuatu (formerly New Hebrides) to line up suppliers and eventually was named an honorary chief. He gives radio interviews, and even wrote a popular book about it called *Kava: Medicine Hunting in Paradise*.

Kava has been proven to have four pharmacological effects. It is: (1) sedative and hypnotic; (2) muscle relaxing; (3) analgesic and anesthetic; and (4) anti-fungal.

The active ingredients are a cluster of chemicals called "kavalactones" that act especially on the hippocampus and amygdala areas of the brain. Studies in Germany have proven that it is effective and safe, although too much at one time can have an intoxicating effect. German doctors are now regularly sending their patients to the pharmacy to purchase kava instead of Valium or Xanax for anxiety. Experts are saying that anyone who has stress in their life can benefit from a little kava. A recent survey suggests that sixty-five percent of the American population is under stress. That's a big potential market. No wonder that the herb and vitamin companies are excited about kava!

If you are interested in using herbal medicines, it is important to look at kava from other points of view. Remember the list above of its effects. It is a muscle relaxant, for instance, and analgesic. In the South Seas, women traditionally used it to ease painful menstrual cramps. It relieves tension in the muscles without causing drowsiness as so many Western medicines do. This is potentially very important. In traditional Chinese medicine it is considered beneficial for the heart because it increases blood flow without increasing the heart rate. Chinese healers see this as a form of increasing the force of ch'i, or one's own life force. This corresponds to the Fijian healers' belief that drinking kava helps one gain access to the Vu, a spirit force. Fijian spiritual healers, incidentally, are called *dauvagunu*, which translates literally as "expert at drinking kava." The Fijian word for kava is "yaqona."

In *Pharmaceutical Biology* by Wagner, a German textbook, kava is discussed at length. Wagner reports that fifteen psychoactive kavalactones have been isolated so far, and that they have different effects, explaining the variety of effects that this plant is claimed to provide. Wagner states that the lactone kawain and dihydrokawain are muscle relaxants, analgesics, and desatives. On the other hand, the yangonins help with concentration and memory loss. Some kavalactones are concentrated in certain areas of the plant. This is important to know, because the herbal capsules that you can buy in a health food store are not necessarily made from the whole plant, as a shaman would prepare it. European-produced standardized kava is made only from top cuttings, eliminating the root, where most of the psychoactive kavalactones reside. In fact, there are many varieties of the plant living in different parts of the South Pacific. They can have different properties. Experts suggest that if you are interested that you try more than one brand from more than one part of the world until you find the formulation that works best for you.

Kava was introduced to the Hawaiian Islands by the earliest Polynesian voyagers who settled the South Pacific by traveling in large sailing canoes. It is cultivated and grows in the wild, as well, throughout the island chain. In the Hawaiian language, it is called awa. In Hawaiian medicine, it is used for general debility, sore muscles, fever and chills, colds and asthma, congestion of the urinary tract, and rheumatism. It is also used to help young children get to sleep. Usually, the child's mother chews a few leaf buds, and then gives them to her child.

Hawaii is also the source of kava plants themselves. Should you be an adventurous gardener in an area with a mild winter or an inside conservatory, you can purchase sprouted nodules with started roots packed in coconut fiber from the Nuka Hiva Trading Company, which sells its plants and other prepared kava products on the internet. They sell varieties that grow to five to eighteen feet in height. Some are listed as more potent, some as pleasant tasting, and others are vigorous growers or just interesting to look at. The growers claim that in their environment the temperatures go down into the fifties. The kava plants like lots of water and shade as well as well-drained soil.

Kava growers are a unique breed who seem to thrive on the adventure of living in the tropics and growing a plant that has somewhat narcotic properties for a living. Yes, it is considered narcotic, and people have been known to develop a "habit." Interestingly, though, the habit seems to be more psychological than physiological. When they leave the islands and are cut off from their source, they seem to suffer no ill effects. The most serious effect on the islands seems to be with young, unmarried men who stop off for kava on their way home in the evening. They forget to eat dinner and get emaciated. Sounds like a weight-loss idea to me.

There is much too much information about kava to fit into a short article like this. After all, entire books have been written about it. If you want to know more about this fascinating plant and its physiological effects, here is a list of further resources, both on the internet and available on traditional paper.

Resources

Books

Cass, Hyla and Terrence McNally. *Kava: Nature's Answer to Stress, Anxiety, and Insomnia.*

Challem, Jack. *FAQs All about Kava.*

Connor, Kathryn M. *Kava: Nature's Stress Relief.*

Elkins, Rita. *Kava Kava, Valerian, Nervine Herbs.*

Grands, Connie. *Kava and Anxiety.*

Hasnian, Walji, Ph.D. *Kava: Nature's Relaxant for Anxiety, Stress, and Pain.*

Kilham, Chris. *Kava: Medicine Hunting in Paradise.*

Lebot, Vincent. *Kava: The Pacific Drug.*

Lebot, Vincent. *Kava: The Pacific Elixir: the Definitive Guide to its Ethnobotany, History, and Chemistry.*

Reichert, Ronald. *Kava Kava: The Anti-Anxiety Herb That Relaxes and Sharpens the Mind.*

Sahelian, Ray. *Kava: The Miracle Antianxiety Herb.*

Singh, Y. N. *Kava: A Bibliography.*

Internet Resources

WWW.KAVAKING.COM. This is a large website of the Kava King Company. It contains articles, drawings, photographs, and other kava-related paraphernalia. In case you are not internet active, their phone number is 1-800-638-0082.

WWW.NUTRITIONWORLD.COM/NEWSLETTER/KAVATROL.HTML. This website is operated by Natrol, the largest mainstream herb company to become involved with kava early on. At this time, they are the largest producers and distributors of kava products in the United States. Their phone number is 1-800-881-3598.

WWW.NUTRITIONSCIENCENEWS.COM/NSN_BACKS/APR_96/KAVA.HTML. This is an interesting article from a back issue of the *Nutrition Science News,* and it comes complete with references. This is one of the few websites that is not trying to sell you anything.

WWW.HAWAII-NATION.ORG/CANOE/AWA.HTML. This is a large website on the "canoe plants" of Hawaii, including awa (the Hawaiian word for kava) and other exotic tropicals.

WWW.ALOHA-HAWAII.COM/4ISSUE/AWA.SHTML. This is another interesting article.

WWW.MAUIGATEWAY.COM/~KAVA/. This is a Hawaiian source for kava. There's something very appealing about getting a plant like kava directly from the source instead of going through a big vitamin company.

WWW.TRIBALSITE.COM/NUKA/INDEX.HTML. This is a fascinating site operated by kava growers and collectors in Hawaii. The sell their products mainly to the big companies, but you can buy smaller quantities direct on the internet, or call them at 808-965-7766. This is the only source for real kava plants, should you want to try growing your own. The company owner includes some stories of his own life and experience, which are fun to read.

WWW.COCONUT.COM/FEATURES/KAVA.HTML. This is a very large website (sixteen pages long) devoted to kava, its history, its usage, and the new markets that seem to be opening for it. The best way to read this web site is to print it out and then read it with a cup of herbal tea. It's excellent—informative and entertaining.

WWW.PRAIRIENET.ORG/~KAGAN/WELCOM1.HTM. This is a personal web page devoted to kava. It looks like it was written by a college student who really cares. Not bad at all.

WWW.HEALTHY.NET/LIBRARY/ARTICLES/HOBBS/KAVA2.HTM. This is an informational, and rather technical fact sheet. The site contains references.

WWW.HEALTHY.NET/HSLIBRARYARTICLES/HFH/KAVA.HTM. This is an accessible article written for people who work in health food stores.

Herbs
for
Beauty

Aromatic Essences for Beauty

~ By Judy Griffin, Ph.D. ~

romatic herbs have been used for over 5,000 years to link the physical to the spiritual world. Their ability to produce scent and oils to improve health, beauty, and moods initiated alchemical transmutation. The belief that aromatic substances are linked to the divine led to the practice of distilling essential oils.

The first essential oil still was made over 5,000 years ago from terra cotta. It was discovered in the Indus Valley of Pakistan with remmants of medicinal and skincare herbal medicines. Herbal medicine and aromatic oils were chosen for their ability to uplift and transform the personality as the body healed itself. Medicines and essential oils were applied to the skin to achieve the deepest levels of healing. Scents worn on the head and face uplifted the whole body. Aromatherapy and the use of aromatic plants remains the essence of

wholistic medicine and spiritual transformation. Practical use of aromatic herbs for health and beauty brings about true healing through the creative transformation of the psyche.

An ancient Chinese proverb states: "We have the face we inherit for thirty years; then, we get the face we deserve!" So, let's get started on a head-to-toe aromatic herbal makeover.

First, remember: the skin, hair, and nails are the largest organ of the body. The skin is also the largest immune organ. Healthy skin reflects a healthy body. Herbs and essential oils will beautify all skin types as well as protect the skin from viral, fungal, and bacterial invasion. Aromatic herbs penetrate and regenerate the deepest layers of skin, renewing radiant skin and health.

The skin's surface contains dead cells. Children can quickly regenerate new cells and replace the dead skin. Over the years, regeneration slows down, old cells build up and unwelcome lines and wrinkles appear on lusterless skin.

The face, hands, and feet are first to tell a history of abuse, aging, and stress. A basic makeover accents these three areas with the wisdom of simple herbs and flowers.

Gentle Facial Cleanser

This mild soap substitute is kind to all skin types, and an effective cleanser. It is reminescent of the pleasure of cottage gardens.

- 2 cups water
- 2 tablespoons fresh or dried soapwort stems (*Saponaria officinalis*)
- 2 tablespoons rose petals or lavender leaves and flowers or, for oily skin, lemon verbena or lemon grass

In a covered glass pan, simmer water, soapwort, and rose petals for 10 minutes. Steep 15 minutes and strain to remove all plant particles. Cool mixture and use one or more tablespoons to cleanse the face before bedtime. Refrigerate leftovers for up to three days. Bottle in a clean screw-top jar. Pure essential oils may be added to the mixture as it cools. To two cups of cleanser, add two drops of rose or lavender for normal to dry skin. For very sensitive skin, add two drops of carrot seed oil. For oily skin, add two drops of lemon verbena, lemongrass, or lemon balm oil.

Herbal Facial

Following a thorough cleansing, an invigorating facial will improve circulation, deep cleanse, and reduce large pores. Steam before bedtime or upon arising.

2   cups water

2   tablespoons freshly crushed fennel seeds

4   tablespoons fresh or dried peppermint, spearmint, or lemon balm

Simmer water in a glass pan. Add fennel seeds and peppermint. Cover and continue to simmer 5 minutes. Cover your head with a towel. Uncover the pan; turn off the heat; bend over to within a foot of the pan and allow the steam to touch your face and neck for up to 10 minutes. (Approach the pan carefully to avoid steam burns.) Pat dry with a clean towel.

Optional herbs may include sage, thyme, and basil to reduce sinus congestion, or chamomile flowers and/or rosemary leaves to reduce headaches and tension.

Quick Herbal Toner

For normal and oily skin, apply with a cotton ball after cleansing.

6   tablespoons rose water

2   tablespoons witch hazel

Mix together rose water and witch hazel. Store in an airtight glass bottle. Shake gently before using. Store up to six months.

Rosewater Clarifier for Delicate Skin

For delicate skin, try vegetable glycerin in an herbal water for protection. Apply with a cotton ball after cleansing.

6   tablespoons rosewater or an herbal infusion of
     your choice

1   tablespoon vegetable glycerin (available at health
     food stores)

Combine rosewater with vegetable glycerin. Bottle in an air-tight glass jar. Shake before using. Store up to six months.

T-zone Scrub for Oily Skin

Following a facial steam, a gentle oatmeal scrub will thoroughly cleanse and correct oily skin. Apply to the t-zone around the nose and any areas where blackheads or congested pores occur.

3   tablespoons milk

1   tablespoon chamomile flowers or lemon thyme
     leaves, fresh or dried, or a mixture of both

⅓   cup oatmeal, finely ground

In a small pan, heat milk. Add chamomile flowers. Remove from heat; cover, and allow to steep 10 minutes. Strain. Add oatmeal to herb infusion to form a paste. Smooth the paste on your face and allow to dry for 10 minutes. Rinse with warm water. Refrigerate any leftovers for up to two days before discarding.

Cleansing Milk for Sensitve Skin

For those with delicate skin, a mild cleansing milk follows the herbal facial steam, leaving the skin radiant.

1   cup milk

3   tablespoons one or combination of the following:
     fresh violet flowers; fresh cornflowers; lavender
     flower and leaves; or fresh or dried fresh marigold
     mint flowers and leaves (*Tagetes lucida foeniculum*)

In a small saucepan, heat milk to a simmer. Remove from heat. Add herb(s). Cover and steep for 15 minutes. Strain into a glass screw-top bottle or container. Apply to face and neck with a cotton ball. Refrigerate leftovers up to three days.

Soothing Eye Pillows

To soothe inflammed, strained eyes or reduce puffiness, brew an herbal tea to relax your eyes and your body.

1½ cups water

2 chamomile tea bags

1 tablespoon ground dried lady's mantle leaves

In a small saucepan, bring water to a boil. Remove from heat and add tea bags. Add lady's mantle if desired. Cover and steep for 10 minutes. Strain. Lie down. Place a tea bag on each eye for 10 minutes. Remove and enjoy the remaining tea to reduce stress.

VARIATION: For quick relief, lie down with a slice of cucumber over each eye for 10 minutes. Rinse with cold water.

Fine Wrinkle Masque

Here's a quick remedy to reduce large pores and erase fine lines.

1 egg white

1 drop carrot seed oil or lavender essential oil

Add carrot seed oil to egg white. Apply to the face and neck, avoiding the eyes. Allow to dry. Rinse with cold water.

Freckle Lotion

Use this lotion to fade brown spots and freckles. Apply morning and night. Allow to dry before applying a moisturizer.

1 cup water

2 tablespoons fresh parsley leaves

2 tablespoons fresh dandelion leaves

2 tablespoons cocoabutter or beeswax

1 vitamin E 400 I.U. capsule

3 drops lemongrass essential oil

Boil water in a small sauce pan. Remove from heat. Add parsley leaves and dandelion leaves. Steep 15 minutes, covered. Strain to remove all particles. Melt cocoabutter or beeswax in a double boiler or microwave. Squeeze the vitamin capsule into the cocobutter. Blend the herbal infusion into the cocoabutter. Blend at high speed for 1 minute with a hand blender. Add essential oil. Spoon into a wide-mouth jar with a screw-top lid. Store at room temperature.

VARIATION: Substitute 2 tablespoons of marigold or evening primrose flowers for 2 tablespoons of dandelion leaves.

Skin-Softening Lotion

Marshmallow root is an excellent demulcent to soften and soothe sensitive or irritated skin. Use it on the face, hands, and body.

3   tablespoons marshmallow root, *Alathea officinalis*

1½   cups water

In a small saucepan, simmer marshmallow root in water for 15 minutes. Refrigerate overnight and allow to infuse into the consistency of a lotion. Strain into a wide-mouth glass jar. Apply to skin morning and evening. Refrigerate up to five days.

VARIATION: Add 2 drops of rose, lavender, ylang ylang, or sandalwood essential oil and squeeze the contents of 1 capsule of vitamin E 400 I.U. into the lotion for extra protection.

Lip Salve

Wear this salve on chapped lips or use it to protect your lips during the winter and summer months.

4   drops carrot seed oil or lavender essential oil

6   tablespoons jojoba oil, divided

4   tablespoons beeswax or cocoabutter

Add carrot seed oil to 2 tablespoons of jojoba oil. Set aside. In a double boiler, melt beeswax. Remove from heat. Beat in remaining jojoba oil. Add the carrot oil mixture, beating to mix thoroughly. Spoon into a wide mouth jar with a screw-top lid. Apply daily as needed to avoid dryness. Store at room temperature.

Moisturizer for Damaged Skin

This moisturizing cream protects and corrects chapped and dry skin. It is especially beneficial for the face, hands, and feet.

Basic Cream

⅓   cup water

2   tablespoons fresh marigold blossoms (my preference is marigold mint, *Tagetes lucida foeniculum*)

⅓   cup beeswax or cocoabutter

⅓   cup jojoba or almond oil

1   vitamin E 400 I.U. capsule

1   betacarotine 25,000 I.U. capsule

Essential Oils (as desired)

5   drops carrot seed oil

6   drops lavender essential

3   drops rose essential oil

3   drops sandalwood essential oil

3   drops sage essential oil

3   drops lavender essential oil

3   drops chamomile essential oil

3   drops carrot seed oil

5   drops marigold mint

Boil water in a small sauce pan. Remove from heat and add marigold blossoms. Cover and steep 10 minutes. Strain, squeezing the liquid from the flowers. In a double boiler, melt beeswax. Remove from heat. Add jojoba oil and the contents of vitamin E capsule and beta-carotine capsule. Using a hand mixer, beat in the marigold water at medium speed for 1 minute. Pour into sterile, wide-mouth jars with screw-top lids. Cool and add oils.

Herbal Manicure

Here's a manicure that strengthens brittle nails.

- 2   cups boiling water
- 6   tablespoons horsetail herb, *Equisetum*
- 1   tablespoon warm sesame or olive oil
- 1   drop sandalwood, patchouli, or lavender essential oil

Add horsetail herb to water. Simmer, covered, for 20 minutes. Remove from heat and allow to steep 30 minutes. Strain. Soak nails in this infusion for 10 minutes in a soup or cereal bowl. Refrigerate leftover infusion in a closed container. It will keep for up to five days. If you do not use the infusion often, freeze it in a plastic container for up to six months. Defrost and refreeze as needed.

After soaking for 10 minutes in the infusion, mix warm oil with essential oil and rub the nails and cuticles with the mixture.

Relaxing Herbal Footbath

Footcare is important for reducing stress. Use a simple herbal infusion to relax the feet and refresh the soul after a day at work.

- 8   cups water
- 8   heaping tablespoons fresh rosemary, thyme, sage, lemongrass, or marigold mint

In a large pan, bring water to a simmer. Add the herb(s) of your choice from the list above. Cover and remove from heat. Steep 20 minutes. Strain and pour into a bathtub or footbath. Soak for 15–20 minutes. Apply an herbal oil or lotion to tired feet.

VARIATION: 8 drops of an essential oil or blend can substitute for the herbs in an infusion.

Bath Salts

For those who desire an all-over body relaxation therapy, an herbal bath will remedy even the most distressing day. There are several ways to create therapeutic atmosphere for an herbal bath.

The easiest way is to prepare an herbal bath salt with epsom salt, to relax the muscles and detoxify the skin.

Aromatic Bath Salt

4   cups epsom salt

1   cup baking soda

4   ounces herb of your choice or 10 drops essential oil

In a large bowl, combine epsom salts, baking soda, and herbs. Store in a glass Mason jar with a screw-top lid for 10–14 days before using 1 cup in a bath. Strain out leaves if desired. Below is a list of a few herbs to choose from.

LAVENDER leaves and flowers will reduce insomnia, anxiety, nausea, and tension headaches. It is one of the essential oils I use to help cancer patients during chemotherapy.

PEPPERMINT will reduce muscle pain, spasms, and headaches from muscle pain. A bath is both invigorating and analgesic.

MARJORAM AND OREGANO will reduce muscle pain, headaches from muscle spasm, and rheumatic pain that travels throughout the body. Marjoram has been successfully used to reduce high blood pressure and menstrual cramps.

GERANIUM calms heart palpitations, heat flashes, restlessness, gastrointestinal distress, cystitis, ulcer pain, neuralgia, and pain from shingles. Geranium balances sebum oil secretion for oily and dry skin.

PATCHOULI reduces athlete's foot and fungal infections, and regenerates skin tissue, improving scars and stretch marks. For those who appreciate the aroma, patchouli has an antidepressant and aphrodisiac effect.

ROSE decreases sympathetic stress-related nervousness. A natural antidepressant, rose increases confidence and helps us feel attractive. It strengthens female reproductive organs, reducing miscarriage, heavy menses, clotting, and painful menopause and menses symptoms. Rose is soothing to dry, itchy, and inflamed skin. I used it to alleviate eczema symptoms for my children.

ROSEMARY will lift depression, increase circulation and lymphatic drainage, reduce cluster headaches and rheumatic aches, and help with colitis and colic.

SAGE is a decongestant muscle relaxer. It reduces hot flashes, oily skin, and symptoms of sinus congestion. Combined with thyme, sage reduces chronic lung, flu, and cold symptoms.

CLARY SAGE essential oil is effective as an antidepressant and muscle relaxer. It reduces insomnia and spasmodic, asthmatic coughs.

GINGER AND CINNAMON, known as heating herbs, are best used in massage oils because they may irritate sensitive skin. However, they are sometimes employed in a bath for arthritic complaints, chills, poor circulation, and general debility. Avoid if you are pregnant or hypertensive.

THYME is a powerful germicide. Use it in baths for colds, flu, cystitis, bronchitis, and spasmodic coughs.

FENNEL is beneficial in a therapeutic bath for those who suffer from nervous indigestion, bloating, and constipation. It has an estrogenic effect increases breast milk and relieves swollen breasts.

LEMONGRASS deep cleanses, astringes, tonifies, and deodorizes skin. It relieves stress and nervous exhaustion.

LEMON BALM reduces depression, insomnia, headaches, nervousness, and inflamed skin. The essentail oil is marketed as melissa, from the Latin name *Melissa officinalis.* True melissa is very expensive since the yield is low. Make sure your source is unadulterated.

BASIL reduces mental fatigue, nervous anxiety, and restores the psyche. In India, the holy basil *Ocimum basilicum sacredum* is used to alleviate mental and emotion imbalances and disorders such as paranoia.

SANDALWOOD essential oil is a very relaxing antiflammatory. It reduces inflamed mucosa in the lungs and as an antiseptic, clears infection from the genito-urinary tract. Sandalwood is especially beneficial for inflamed, itchy skin. It has the unique ability to calm the mind for meditation and enhance physical enjoyment as an aphrodesiac. The highest grade is "mysore;"

the best common grade is "agmarked," guaranteed to conform to Indian government standards.

Herbal infusions and essential oils may be directly added to a bath also. Use the recipe for the footbath, doubling the recipe to make two quarts of herbal infusion.

Essential oils are best added to a warm bath after it has been drawn. The oils are volatile and evaporate easily. Therefore, aromatherapists often blend ten to fifteen drops in two tablespoons of honey, milk, or cream before adding the oil or oil blends to the bath.

Essential oils and aromatic herbal infusions are generally safe and nontoxic when used in the amounts previously suggested. More is not better and can be dangerous to certain health conditions, such as hypertension and epilepsy. Pregnant women should consult with their midwife or health care provider before using essential oils in bath therapy.

Aromatherapy for Pets

Herbal infusions and essential oils are enjoyed by pets as well as people. They are best used diluted on unbroken skin. Reduce the amount of essential oils to three to five drops in a bath. If the pet weighs more than you do, ten to fifteen drops is acceptable.

Here are some general guidelines for choosing an aromatic bath for your pets. Always dilute essential oils in a bath or carrier oil before application except for lavender. Dilutions may be directly applied or sprayed onto your pet. Do not let your pet ingest essential oil. Do not use essential oils on or near pet birds or fish.

EUCALYPTUS repels fleas and unwelcome pests. It is also successful in treating lice.

GERANIUM is used successfully as an insect repellent. Owners find it very calming for their pets.

LAVENDER is very sedative for itchy or hyperactive pets. It can be applied undiluted to burns, bites, and skin with allergic dermatitis. Lavender is also beneficial in repelling fleas and mosquitoes.

LEMON GRASS repels mosquitoes and fleas. It is also successful in removing ticks and lice.

PEPPERMINT repels fleas and may be used to remove ringworm. It is often combined with eucalyptus and tea tree. As a deodorant, peppermint allowed us to give up my dog's nickname, Stinky.

TEA TREE, *Leptospermum scoparium*, treats ringworm and insect bites. It is beneficial as a general repellent combined with lavender, eucalyptus, and peppermint.

Comfrey-Yarrow Bath for Whatever Ails You

There are some herbs that are not highly aromatic, yet are very effective in bath therapy for people and pets. Since ancient times, comfrey and yarrow have been used to soothe, cleanse, and regenerate skin. Yarrow is also an excellent hemostatic that stops bleeding and often heals wounds without scarring. Comfrey was so popular in medieval times that it was believed to restore virginity with only one bath. So, if you want to follow an herbal tradition you must try at least one comfrey-yarrow bath. It is an excellent treatment for varicosities and spider veins.

- 2 quarts water
- 2 cups each comfrey and yarrow leaves

In a large pan, simmer water. Add comfrey and yarrow leaves. I prefer fresh, but dried also work well. Two ounces of comfrey root can be substituted for comfrey leaves. Cover and simmer at the lowest heat for 30 minutes. Remove from heat and allow to steep 30 more minutes. Strain and add to a warm bath or footbath. Relax and allow the ancient echoes of centuries past to float through your memory.

Aromatic Massage Oils

Herbs can be infused in therapeutic oils to reduce stress and nurture the skin. Aromatic herbs and their essential oils also affect moods and the electromagnetic field of energy that sparks vitality and the life force itself. In a massage, these herbs increase lymphatic drainage, increase circulation, and reduce cellulite. Since the skin is a sensitive, dynamic organ regenerating as the Moon cycles, aromatic massages also enhance rejuvenation and the glow of radiant healthy skin.

Fragrant Massage Oil

Apply this warm herbal oil after a bath or during a massage for maximum relaxation.

4 ounces sesame oil

4 tablespoons fresh rosemary, peppermint, lemon thyme, sage, rose petals, orange flowers, or lavender

In a saucepan, heat sesame oil to simmer. Add herbs. Remove from heat. Cover and allow to steep 15 minutes. Strain and apply warm. Sesame oil will also reduce anxiety, insomnia, and nervousness when used regularly. It is very sedative to the nervous system. For a quick massage oil, use essential oils to replace the herbal infusion. Store in dark glass bottles or refrigerate.

Variations

Try one of these essential oil blends in 4 ounces of sesame oil:

- 15 drops sandalwood, sage, lavender, rosemary, or lemongrass essential oil.

- 10 drops of lavender, 5 drops of sage, and 2 drops of sandalwood enhances relaxation.

- 10 drops of rosemary, 4 drops of spearmint, and 4 drops of lemon grass or lemon verbena is uplifting.

- 8 drops of peppermint, 4 drops of sage, and 4 drops of lavender is excellent for pain and rheumatism.

Carrier Oils

There are several carrier oils to use as mediums for herbal infusions and essential oil dilutions. Each have unique therapeutic properties. Vegetable, nut, seed, and emu oils are preferred. Mineral oils block the skin's pores and prevent absorption of the herbal properties. Cold-pressed, organically-produced oils have the best effect. Here are several you can make at home or purchase from a grocer or health store.

Sweet Almond

Sweet almond is a very popular oil due to its soothing affect on many skin types. The oil is light and readily absorbed. Purchase cold-pressed oil and use it on delicate skin, such as the face.

Arnica

Arnica is a macerated oil from the herb *Arnica montana*. It is best applied to unbroken skin for sports injuries, sprains, bumps, and bruises. The flowers, which are toxic if used internally, contain immune stimulants that increase circulation and reduce inflammation. The dried or fresh flowers can be steeped in hot oil to produce a remedy for bumps and bruises. Do not use if pregnant.

- 6 tablespoons heated vegetable oil
- 2 tablespoons fresh or dried arnica flowers

Steep arnica in vegetable oil 20 minutes, covered. Strain and bottle in a clean glass jar. Apply topically or add a third of the amount to a carrier oil blend to use for massage.

Calendula Oil

Calendula oil is macerated from the flowers and used to heal external ulcers, sores, eczema, and cracked skin. It may be applied to sore nipples during lactation and worn to prevent stretch marks. An oil of *Calendula officinalis* is antiseptic and antifungal, containing betacarotenes that soothe damaged skin. To make an oil, gather fresh flowers or purchase them dried.

- 4 tablespoons heated vegetable or nut oil
- 2 tablespoons calendula flowers

Steep flowers in oil for minutes. Strain and bottle in a clean, dark glass jar.

Carrot Seed Oil

Carrot seed oil is a odorous, orange-colored oil extracted from *Daucus carota* seed and often blended in a vegetable oil. It is high in beta carotene and nourishing to the skin. Use it for aging, damaged, and scarred skin in an oil or lotion. The color stains, so be sure to let it absorb before dressing. A homemade oil can be made if you obtain organic seed or grow carrots to produce seeds from the flowering heads.

1   tablespoon carrot seed

1   tablespoon vegetable oil

Crush carrot seed in a mortar and pestle. Heat carrot seed in vegetable oil for 15 minutes. Steep, covered, for 20 minutes. Strain and refrigerate in a dark glass bottle.

Comfrey Oil

Comfrey oil is obtained from the macerated herb. Use the fresh leaves or dried root. *Symphytum officinale* soothes pain, broken bones, bruises, and burns.

1   cup vegetable oil

4   tablespoons chopped, fresh comfrey leaves or 1 ounce of chopped root

1   vitamin E 400 I.U. capsule

Heat leaves in oil for 20 minutes. Keep the heat low to avoid rancidity of the vegetable oil. Steep covered for 20 minutes and strain well. Add the contents of the vitamin E capsule and refrigerate.

Evening Primrose or Borage Oil

Evening primrose or borage oil is rich in essential fatty acids that soothe eczema, psoriasis, and aging skin. They are usually diluted in another carrier oil. Ten to twenty-five percent is recommended. These oils are best purchased. The seeds of evening primrose are very tiny and it is difficult to express the therapeutic properties, but borage seeds are larger.

2   tablespoons heated vegetable oil

1   tablespoon borage seeds

Add borage seeds to vegetable oil. Simmer on low heat for 10 minutes. Strain and bottle in a dark glass. Refrigerate.

Grape Seed Oil

Grape seed oil is antiseptic and antifungal. It has a balancing effect on oily skin. Blend with another massage oil or use undiluted topically on oily skin.

Hazelnut Oil

Hazelnut oil is also rich in essential fatty acids. It benefits aging, scarred skin and reduces acne. The aroma is very pleasant.

Jojoba Oil

Jojoba oil is a stable liquid wax that easily penetrates and balances both dry and oily skin and hair. It has anti-inflammatory properties that soothe wounds, eczema, and psoriasis. Blend with other oils or use directly on the skin and hair.

Olive Oil

Olive oil is an ancient healer beneficial for arthritis pain and red, itchy skin. Use only extra virgin cold-pressed oil. Dilute it 50 percent with a less viscous oil, such as almond oil.

St. John's Wort Oil

St. John's wort oil is extracted from the flowers of *Hypernicum perforatum*. The oil treats wounds, burns, backaches, hemorrhoids, and varicose veins. The shrub blooms in the spring. Gather the flowers and immediately steep them in heated oil.

2   cups heated vegetable oil

1   cup macerated fresh St. John's wort flowers

Add flowers to oil. Cover and simmer 1 minute. Remove from heat and steep 20 minutes. Strain and bottle in a wide-mouth jar.

Oregano Oil

2   cups vegetable oil

1   cup fresh or dried oregano leaves

Heat vegetable oil in a sauce pan. Add oregano leaves. Simmer on low heat for 10 minutes. Remove from heat. Steep 10 minutes and strain into a glass jar.

Emu Oil

Emu oil is an animal product available commercially. It is very effective in treating arthritis and rheumatism locally. Add essential oils for best results or blend the emu oil with an herbal oil.

Arthritis Oil

½   cup oregano herbal oil (see above)

½   cup emu oil

6   drops eucalyptus oil

10   drops peppermint essential oil

4   drops oregano essential oil (optional)

Combine oregano oil, emu oil, eucalyptus oil, and essential oils. Apply topically to painful joints.

Massage Oil Blends

Here are a few ideas for massage oil blends. Use four to seven essential oils for a blend in an odorless carrier oil. Twenty drops of essential oil equals one teaspoon. Make the blend in an easy-to-pour cup, such as a measuring cup. Store the blend in a dark glass bottle. Use within six months.

Decongestant Immune Blend

4   tablespoons comfrey oil

4   drops thyme essential oil or tea tree oil

2   drops lavender essential oil

1   drop lemon grass or eucalyptus oil

Repel Insect Blend for People and Pets

3   tablespoons comfrey oil

2   tablespoons olive oil

1   tablespoon grapeseed or St. John's wort oil

4   drops lemongrass essential oil

3   drops eucalyptus essential oil

2   drops lavender essential oil

Cellulite Blend

2   tablespoons each jojoba oil, almond oil, and grapeseed oil.

6   drops ginger essential oil

2   drops cinnamon essential oil

1   drop lemongrass essential oil

Cellulite Blend Version Two

6   tablespoons canola, grapeseed, or almond oil, or a combination

1   (2-inch) cinnamon stick

1   (2-inch) slice of fresh ginger

1   tablespoon lemongrass

Heat oil. Simmer cinnamon, ginger, and lemongrass in oil for 10 minutes, uncovered. Remove from heat. Steep for 15 minutes. Strain and use to stimulate lymphatic drainage from cellulite.

Beauty Blend

1   tablespoon each calendula and jojoba oil

1   teaspoon carrot seed oil.

4   drops rose essential oil

2   drops lavender essential oil

1   drop sandalwood essential oil

Blend all ingredients together. Apply on fine wrinkles at night. Comb several drops through the hair and dab on scars or stretch marks.

Sports Massage Blend

2   tablespoons each arnica, St. John's wort, and comfrey oil

4   drops peppermint essential oil

4   drops lemongrass essential oil

4   drops sage essential oil

1   drop ginger essential oil

Less Stress Blend

2   tablespoons almond, hazelnut, canola, or olive oil

4   drops lavender essential oil

2   drops basil essential oil

2   drops sadalwood essential oil

1   drop clary sage essential oil, optional

Shampoo and Conditioner Blends

Castille Shampoo Blend

½   cup unscented liquid castille shampoo

1   tablespoon jojoba, comfrey, or grapeseed oil.

Blend castille shampoo and jojoba together. Blend in your chosen essential oils. Choose from the following:

FOR DRY OR DAMAGED HAIR: 2 drops carrot seed oil, 1 drop clary sage, 4 drops lavender, and 2 drops geranium.

FOR FINE HAIR: 4 drops lavender essential oil, 2 drops rose, and 2 drops marigold mint (*Tagetes lucida foeniculum*).

FOR OILY HAIR: 3 drops lemongrass, 3 drops rosemary, and 3 drops peppermint.

FOR DARK HAIR THAT IS GRAYING: 6 drops sage, 2 drops rosemary, and 2 drops bergamot.

FOR LIGHT HAIR THAT IS GRAYING: 3 drops lemongrass, 1 drop thyme, and 1 drop carrot seed oil.

FOR GROWING HAIR: 6 drops rosemary and 2 drops sandalwood.

Castille Shampoo Blend Variation

Make an herbal oil with gotu kola leaves to increase hair growth.

- 1 tablespoon olive oil
- 2 teaspoons fresh or dried gotu kola leaves

Heat oil. Add gotu kola leaves. Simmer at low heat 5 minutes. Strain. Add to ½ cup castille shampoo.

Mild Shampoo Blend

For those who would like to make a gentle shampoo, here's one that encourages healthy hair and new growth. Mild shampoo causes less breakage and damage to hair.

- 2 cups water
- 4 tablespoons soapwort stems
- 4 tablespoons rosemary

In a small sauce pan, heat water to a boil. Add soapwort stems and rosemary. Simmer 15 minutes. Remove from heat. Steep 30 minutes. Strain and bottle in a clean glass jar. Add essential oils as desired. Suggestions: 6 drops of rosemary, 3 drops lemon, and 1 drop thyme or tea tree oil.

VARIATION: Substitute 4 tablespoons lavender leaves or flowers for rosemary. Add the following essential oils: 6 drops lavender, 4 drops rose or sage, and 1 drop sandalwood.

Natural Conditioner

A therapeutic conditioner can be made in your kitchen.

- ⅓ cup jojoba oil
- ⅓ cup aloe gel
- 1 egg yolk, beaten

Blend ingredients together. Add an essential oil blend matching your hair condition or color, or create a new one. Apply to towel-dried hair. Leave on 5 minutes or longer before rinsing thoroughly. Refrigerate leftover conditioner up to 5 days.

Hair Rinses

Herbal Vinegar Hair Rinse for Normal Hair

4   tablespoons rosemary, or an herb of your choice
1   cup vinegar, heated
1   cup distilled water

Steep rosemary in vinegar for 30 minutes, covered. Strain and add water. Use as a rinse after an herbal shampoo.

Chamomile Rinse for Dull Hair

Another therapeutic rinse to brighten lifeless hair can be brewed with fresh or dried chamomlie flowers.

2   cups distilled water
4   tablespoons chamomile flowers

Heat water to boil. Remove from heat. Add chamomile flowers. Steep 30 minutes. Strain and comb through clean hair. Leave in.

Hair Rinse to Prevent Hair Loss

Use this infusion daily and watch your hair grow.

2   cups water
2   tablespoons each southernwood, (*Artemesia abrotanum*), rosemary, and gotu kola leaves
2   teaspoons sea salt

Heat water to a boil. Remove from heat. Add southernwood, rosemary, and gotu kola leaves. Cover and steep for 20 minutes. Strain. Add sea salt and shake well before rinsing your hair. Leave in.

Herbal Sleep Pillow

Prepare this aromatic pillow and sleep with the angels.

1   linen or muslin pillow case lining (found at fabric stores)

    Lemon verbena leaves, scented geranium leaves, lavender leaves and buds, sweet woodruff leaves, sweet annie (Artemesia annua) leaves and buds, lemon thyme leaves, rosemary leaves, fennel leaves, and chamomile leaves

1   tablespoon hops

Leave one side of the pillow case lining open. Fill the case loosely with any combination of the above sweet smelling, dried herbs. Add hops to ensure sound sleep. Sew the open end closed. Cover with a pretty pillow case. Sprinkle with a favorite essential oil.

A Note About Essential Oils

(Editor's note: Essential oils are concentrated essences of herbs, and are much stronger than the herb leaves, flowers, or stems. Never ingest essential oils or put undiluted essential oils on bare skin. Consult a holistic health practitioner before using any type of essential oil if you are pregnant, epileptic, or have a heart condition. If you have any reason to feel concerned about using a particular essential oil, consider substituting the herb plant itself where possible. If you are pregnant or have sensitive skin, consider substitutions for the following oils. Basil, eucalyptus, and bergamot oils are toxic. Rosemary, peppermint, marjoram, sage, oregano, clary sage, and fennel oils should not be used by pregnant women. Epileptics should avoid rosemary, fennel, and sage, and people with high blood pressure should avoid thyme. Lemon balm, lemon verbena, lemongrass, sage, cinnamon bark, peppermint, thyme, basil, oregano, and ginger oils may be skin-irritating. When making beauty recipes using essential oils, try rubbing a small amount of the finished product on your inner arm and wait for several hours to determine if you are sensitive to the oils before trying the product elsewhere.)

Bee Really Beautiful

~ By Leeda Alleyn Pacotti ~

Anyone doubting the love of Earth for her children, anyone blind to the majestic forces in nature, anyone deaf to the eternal communion of creation on this planet, should seek and experience the tantalizing gifts from bees. Without bees we would never smell the heady perfumes of wildflower fields or showy roses; we would never savor the quenching sweetness of pulpy, ripe fruits; we would never watch the bountiful growth of verdant gardens or tasty, delectable vegetables. Spring would be silent—no longer that joyous release from winter's ache.

We are fortunate in this world although we often fail to see it. We prefer to be terrified by stories of killer bees, a raging planet, and a malignant universe. But, every warm day of 60 degrees or more, from March through November, nature's dutiful, toiling

bees search for nectar. Flying from source to source, siphoning sweet liquids, and reducing the watery sugars, they make an unripe honey. Cleansing themselves at the hive entries, they drop pollen from their bodies and deposit the new honey to feed future broods and secure the hive against winter's famine. Through enzymatic processes with nurse bees, honey becomes an extraordinary life-extending substance, reserved exclusively for nature's prized monarch, the queen.

What we humans take for granted is the cornucopia of sweet edibles, disease protection, and longevity nourishment that comes from bees. For the bees not only produce abundantly for themselves, but plenty for us, too.

Gifts From the Monarchy

Many books and articles recount testimonials of aged populations, with the more sagacious among them reaching 130 to 160 years of age. Invariably, these people live in less modern areas, away from routine and mechanized stresses, without conveniences, fast foods, and freezer fare. They feast on what they cultivate or tend, working with the sun and limiting their table times. In every instance of long-lived villages and secreted valleys or meadows, these people keep bees, utilizing and selling every edible component from the hive, and leaving plenty for the bees and themselves.

Through the foresight and wise virtue of beekeepers, who oversee nature's six-legged pollinators, any of us can enjoy and benefit from bee products.

Bee pollen is collected for human consumption in a pollen trap, which gently strips pollen pellets from bees' legs as they enter the hive. The pollen drops through a screen into a clean receptacle for daily gathering.

This highly concentrated, antibacterial, antiallergenic food substance has a base composition of 20 percent proteins and amino acids because bees select high-quality pollens that are rich in nitrogenous matter, with the remainder composed of fatty acids and carbohydrates from natural sugars. It contains Vitamins B-1, B-2, B-3 (as niacinamide), B-5 (pantothenic acid), B-6, and B-12 (folic acid), and Vitamins A, C, and E. Glucosides naturally occur in bee pollen, acting as transport for the proteins and vitamins into the bloodstream. The special nutrients in bee pollen feed the endocrine glands, which promote a strong sense of wellbeing and enhance work and socializing.

During times of stress, the body rapidly uses up B vitamins, which cannot be retained beyond twenty-four hours. Vitamin B-2 helps to correct splitting nails and reverse aging symptoms, especially the disappearing upper lip. The content of Vitamin B-5 is the greatest of all the nutrients in bee pollen. This antistress vitamin prevents consequences of premature aging, changing hair that is gray due to stress back to its natural color.

Interestingly, bee pollen has a beneficial effect on anyone who needs to normalize weight. An underweight person should take a teaspoon of bee pollen after each meal to assist food absorption in the intestines. An overweight person needs to take a teaspoon of bee pollen before each meal to curb the appetite and supply highly digestible nutrients. One teaspoon of bee pollen is only fifteen calories, the equivalent of one teaspoon of refined sugar.

Bee Propolis

Bee propolis is sometimes referred to as "bee glue." Instead of collecting pollen, bees gather the sticky resin from poplar trees and conifers to mix with wayward pollen and their wax secretions and enzymes. The resulting mixture is antibacterial, antibiotic, antifungal, antiseptic, and antiviral. It is the primary protectant for the hive, which is, after all, a brood nursery. Bees use propolis to line the interior of the hive and the queen's brood cells, sealing cracks and holes. Throughout the gathering season, bee propolis barriers at the entryways to the hive disinfect each incoming bee. During the winter, this resin-wax is accumulated at hive entrances to reduce their size, inhibiting wintry winds from lowering the hive's internal temperature.

Bee propolis contains caffeic acid and galangin and is a source of nonallergenic bioflavonoids. German studies show caffeic acid compounds are effective against certain viruses, including the human herpes virus strain. Galangin, a flavonoid, strengthens the thymus gland, which influences the entire immune system. Investigative research in Romania shows that bee propolis suppresses the multiplicative rate of abnormal cells and restores activity of normal cells, which suggests that bee propolis may be a deterrent to the growth rate of some cancers.

To take advantage of antibacterial effects, many medicines contain a component of bee propolis. However, bee propolis is perfectly edible. When chewed, it significantly reduces throat inflammation, inhibits drainage from the sinuses and nose, and soothes gum and inner mouth problems. Digestive problems, arising from an abundance of mucus in the stomach or poor dentation, are also inhibited when bee propolis is chewed. Applied as a salve, bee propolis benefits abrasions and bruises. When bacterial infections are present, bee propolis seems to stimulate phagocytosis, which is the process of white blood cells' destruction of bacteria in the body.

Raw Honey

Raw honey, which is rich in pollen, is a natural antiseptic and disinfectant. Raw honey is what the bees are all about, predigesting nectars as food for new bees in the brood. It is a concentrated sweetener, taking on fragrance, color, and taste from different flower sources. The raw honey we use is excess, never used by the brood. Antiseptic, raw honey has been used since the times of the Sumerians, Babylonians, and Egyptians as a skin salve for burns and wounds.

When dieting, replace sugar with raw honey, which soothes the digestive tract and burns more slowly, producing prolonged energy. Honey, added to unheated foods and drinks or taken by the tablespoon, can be a significant relief for allergies. Raw honey can also be substituted in food recipes calling for refined sugar.

Because it is nearly twice as sweet, use an amount of raw honey equal to one-half the amount of refined sugar. However, when raw honey is heated through cooking or baking, expect its enzyme or nutrient content to be neutralized. One tablespoon of raw honey equals sixty calories; one-quarter cup equals 240 calories. Compare this to 360 calories in one-half cup of refined sugar, the amount necessary to replace one-quarter cup raw honey.

Caution: Never give honey to infants under the age of one. Honey is particularly dangerous for infants because it contains spores of bacteria that can cause botulism and will colonize in a baby's digestive tract.

Beeswax

Beeswax is the sealant for hive cells filled with honey. Sometimes, raw honey may be sold with a piece of honeycomb containing beeswax and unextracted honey.

Although beeswax has no nutritional value, the lingering honey taste makes it a pleasant replacement for chewing gum, helping to exercise the gums and lightly cleanse teeth. For over 200 years, beeswax has been the sole choice of thoracic surgeons to rejoin ribs split for chest surgery. Beeswax slowly disintegrates in the body, permitting ribs to knit without a need for a torso cast. In many lotions, creams, and mascara, beeswax is added as a stiffening agent.

Royal Jelly

Royal jelly is a creation of nurse bees, which combine honey and pollen into a milky, acidic, protein-rich food. Royal jelly, as it is secreted and fed directly to the queen by these nursing worker bees, is the queen's sole diet. As the only reproductive female, the queen lives between six to seven years, or about fifty-five times longer than the forty-day life span of worker bees (drones, which are males, live for one season, dying shortly after copulation with the queen). This remarkable longevity and exclusive diet have earned royal jelly the reputation as an anti-aging food.

Royal jelly is predominately Vitamin B-5 or pantothenic acid, with a concentration of Vitamin B-6, and all the other B-complex vitamins. It is a natural source of acetylcholine, an important neurotransmitter that stimulates the adrenal glands to produce hormones. Pantothenic acid also activates these glands to produce hormones, which maintain the body's vigor; a noticeable effect is its ability to recolor hair grayed by stress. In the composition of royal jelly, gamma globulin strengthens the immune system to fight bacterial and viral infections. Normally, royal jelly is taken orally, but can also be applied to the skin, neutralizing alkaline reactions.

Detecting Allergies

Start using any bee product in a small amount, about one-half teaspoon, after a meal. If you detect no allergic symptoms, like discomforts, rash, sneezing, or wheezing, take another one-half teaspoon after your next meal. The next day, try one-half teaspoon before breakfast. No allergic reactions mean you can safely dosage with these products, following package directions. If you have any questions, talk with your health-care provider.

Beauty and the Bee

As you can see, bee products contain many elements to enhance the body and fight infection. Their use in medicines and salves makes them ideal for natural cosmetic remedies. Try the following "recipes" for beauty and adapt them for your use.

Facial Mixtures

Lip Balm

Mix a half cup almond oil, a half cup canola oil, and a quarter cup cocoa butter. Melt and stir the mixture over low heat. Add one tablespoon honey and two ounces of beeswax, and your preferred food flavoring, if desired. After all are well mixed, test for a firm consistency, adding more beeswax for stiffening.

Facial Mask for Normal to Dry Skin

Mix equal parts of cornstarch, raw honey, and milk (or equal parts of raw honey and egg whites, well mixed, or equal parts of raw honey and mashed bananas). After cleansing your face, apply the mask, avoiding the area around your eyes. Elevate your feet and lie back without a pillow for about a half hour. Rinse off the mask and continue your facial cleansing routine.

Acne Mask

Blend one teaspoon clay powder and one teaspoon raw honey. Gently apply the mixture to your face, avoiding the area around your eyes. After fifteen minutes, rinse well with lukewarm water.

Pore Treatment

Mix two tablespoons egg whites, one tablespoon milk powder, and a half teaspoon raw honey, gently beating to blend. Apply the mixture to your face, avoiding the eye area, and let dry. Rinse with clear, warm water and pat your face dry.

Hair Conditioner

Gradually mix a half cup of mayonnaise with two tablespoons olive or canola oil and two tablespoons raw honey, gently warming the mixture in the top of a double boiler. Apply the warm mixture to your scalp and work it throughout your hair. Cover your hair with a plastic wrap or bag. Wrap a towel around the plastic cover to keep in warmth. Leave the mixture on for a half hour to two hours. Afterward, you may need to use a gentle shampoo two or three times to remove sticky residue.

Hands

Nail Restorer

Mix equal parts of honey, avocado oil, and egg yolk, adding a pinch of salt. Apply the mixture to nails, yellowed or brittle from polishes or chemicals, and leave on for about a half hour. Rinse off with clear, warm water. Repeat until you see results.

Cuticle Softener

Mix two tablespoons olive oil with one tablespoon raw honey. Massage the mixture into your cuticles and nails.

Skin

Bedsores or Itch Salve

Mix equal parts of goldenseal root powder or extract and Vitamin E oil, adding enough raw honey to make a paste. Apply the salve as frequently as necessary for relief and healing. Additionally, for bedsores, alternate the salve with royal jelly or aloe vera gel.

Fungal Ointment

Alternate applications of raw honey and crushed garlic to the affected skin area.

Nature's Bandage

For simple wounds and small cuts, dab on raw honey, which dries to form a natural bandage.

Simple Ointment

Apply royal jelly gently on your skin's surface to restore a slightly acidic condition, to soothe or heal dermatitis, eczema, impetigo, and other dermal disorders.

Skin Lotion

Cover one cup rose petals with olive or canola oil, and place in a glass pan over low heat. Cover and steep for four to six hours. Strain out the petals, and add one ounce of melted beeswax, stirring until creamy. Test for consistency, adding a small amount of oil if the lotion is too stiff.

Waxing Into Good Health

All of the "recipes" above directly affect the skin, which is regenerated every twenty-seven days. What you have eaten or experienced in the preceding month, you are seeing in your skin now. Your skin lets you know whether you are caring for yourself internally, responding to positive changes in diet and lifestyle more readily than any other organ.

Hair is also a good indicator. Problems with dull, dry hair or mousy color come from inadequate diet and counterproductive daily habits. Without making a few necessary and positive changes, you could spend your way into a cycle of conditioners and treatments that have no lasting effect.

The best remedy for poor skin, hair, and nails is a nourishing diet of whole and natural foods, from which your body can derive the proper vitamins, minerals, proteins, and essential fats. While on the road to a healthier body, you can supplement your diet with bee foods, reducing the effects of stress from physical changes and life's unexpected moments.

The Economical Buzz

When purchasing bee products, try to obtain them raw from a local keeper who lives no further than ten miles from your home. Finding a beekeeper is not a hard task. Look under "apiarists," "bees," or "beekeepers" in the yellow pages. If you find nothing, call your USDA County Extension Service, and ask about beekeepers who sell products in your area. The products will have minute doses of local pollen, to which you will become gradually desensitized.

Fresh bee pollen should not cling or form clumps. Be sure it is sold in a tightly sealed container. Raw honey has not been treated, processed, or heated, which will destroy the fragile vitamins and other nutrients. Royal jelly spoils very easily and must be combined with raw honey to preserve potency. Be sure it is tightly sealed when purchased and keep it refrigerated.

When purchasing bee products from a keeper, consider the advantages. Capsuled bee pollen may have been gathered in another part of the country; processed bee propolis has reduced antibacterial power; and processed honey has limited or no antiseptic properties.

You'll receive bargain rates from beekeepers compared to the costs of grocery prices and lost benefits. Expect prices to vary by locality and season, or when bee populations have been significantly reduced by disease or parasites. Bee pollen costs about ten dollars per pound; raw honey, purchased in quantities when you bring your own container, is about fifty cents per pound. You can request beeswax, but expect to find only small quantities. Beeswax is normally sold to medical supply manufacturers and candle makers. Both bee propolis and royal jelly are now popular in health articles and diets. Commercial prices for these products go from premium to exorbitant. While bee propolis is more abundant, royal jelly enjoys a very limited production. Expect to pay a beekeeper about one-half to three-fourths the commercial price.

When purchasing raw honey, it is not true that aged honey is superior to freshly extracted honey, especially when both have been properly bottled and stored. The preference for aged honey is a European taste, where honey is routinely aged at least one year prior to putting it up for sale. Aging in no way deteriorates the properties of raw honey unless it has been improperly stored and allowed to become filthy or infected. Inspect raw honey carefully, and plan on buying it in gallon quantities (one gallon equals sixteen cups or about twelve pounds).

Although you may balk at the idea of using honey in cosmetics and salves, think about how much you spend for a sixteen-ounce bottle of rejuvenating skin lotion or a four-ounce jar of wrinkle cream, chemically preserved and powerfully scented to mask the lack of freshness. Two ounces of raw honey, when you buy in a large quantity, will cost about seven cents.

From nutrition to food to medicine to cosmetics, bees have enriched our lives with their bountiful products. As these blessings pass your lips, give silent thanks to Earth's magnificent servants.

Herb
Crafts

An Herbal Wedding

≫ By Roslyn Reid ≪

*Y*ou say you're getting married? Or perhaps handfasted? You want a nice traditional ceremony, but you just checked out the prices for flowers and found yourself lying on the floor?

Join the stunned crowd. On this special occasion, money is usually the last thing you're thinking about—until the real world comes crashing in. But all is not lost—by using herbs, you can follow the ancient traditions on your big day without busting the bank.

Before we begin—sexist alert! Although the association between herbs and weddings is a very old and long one, this article is written from a woman's perspective because I am one. If you are a man, you can adapt the ideas given here for the bridal bouquet into a garland for your suit (or whatever attire you wish to wear—even a necklace for the skyclad wedding!). For

gay couples, please feel free to substitute whatever terminology you wish for the use of "bride" and "groom" in this article.

An Old Tradition

Even though the use of herbs with or without flowers in wedding decorations has been traditional for centuries, research is necessary to determine which herbs are appropriate. For instance, in ancient times certain herbs were strewn about the feasting hall to keep the insects down. Fortunately, we have the board of health to do that nowadays. Nevertheless, this probably isn't the kind of message you want to send to your wedding guests!

Garlic (sometimes known as "the stinking rose") was used in old times to ward off evil spirits, but these days you could really knock 'em dead by carrying a garlic bouquet down the aisle in June! So as you can see, when following ancient traditions, it is necessary to choose your herbs judiciously.

This is not the only caveat, either. There are many different sources offering folklore on the meaning of each herb, and their interpretations can differ widely. Although lavender is typically mentioned as part of wedding celebrations, one herbal I checked out gave its meaning as "distrust!" Be sure to make a note of your sources, if only for your own use in keeping the symbolism straight. See "Resources" at the end of this article for sources.

The Ancient Language of Herbs

Now that you have become aware of these precautions, here is some information on the associations of herbs to get you started on your choices. Some herbs associated with the planet Venus are feverfew, mint, mugwort, myrtle, pennyroyal, plaintain, thyme, and verbena (European vervain). Herbs associated with love in general are lavender, mistletoe, myrrh, periwinkle, and valerian.

Aphrodesiacs

Coriander, ginseng, and yohimbe are aphrodesiacs. Some of these are obvious choices, such as mistletoe, which we kiss under;

An Herbal Wedding

ginseng, a well-known stamina enhancer; and yohimbe, an African herb with the same reputation as ginseng. But the inclusion of some of the others are less clear. Pennyroyal, for instance, was designated by Pliny as a flea chaser, although well-known herbalist Mrs. Grieve informs us that it is "...an old-fashioned remedy for...menstrual derangements." Culpepper says it is good for swoons, which sounds like something useful to have around at a wedding. The following lore is from British naturopath John Lust, whose *Herb Book* is a good source of information in choosing herbs to use at your wedding.

Basil

Basil is reputed to stimulate sensuality, and is associated with Erzulie, the Haitian goddess of love. Lust also asserts that in rural New Mexico, a wife is told to dust basil powder over her husband's heart and other parts of his upper body to cure a wandering eye—he will then become a loving and faithful spouse. However, if you're starting out like this on your wedding day, perhaps it's a good idea to reconsider!

Dandelion

An old poem reads, "To carry your thoughts to your sweetheart, blow the feathered seeds off the puffball of a dandelion." This is a romantic thought, but not a good idea if any of your guests have allergies.

Elder

This tree is the abode of Freya, Norse goddess of love. A few sprigs in your boquet or in the centerpiece might be appropriate.

European Vervain

Vervain supposedly originated from the tears of Isis while she wept for her slain husband. Charming.

Maidenhair Fern

In Roman mythology, this fern was said to represent the hair of Venus when she emerged from the sea. This was because when the fern is dipped into water and then pulled out it appears not to have gotten wet at all.

Marjoram

According to Greek legend, Aphrodite first cultivated the marjoram. Therefore, to honor and invoke her presence, the ancient Greeks wore wreaths of it as wedding flowers.

Myrtle

New England Witch Elizabeth Pepper relates a charming story about myrtle: "In a tenth-century romance, Ogier the Dane was the knight chosen by the enchantress Morgan le Fay to dwell with her on Avalon. To erase the memory of his past life, she placed on his head a garland woven of myrtle and laurel—the crown of forgetfulness. The herb has kept the lovers' theme of forsaking all others for centuries."

Plantain

According to yet another romantic myth, plaintain originated from a maiden who spent so much time by the side of the road watching for the return of her absent lover that she eventually turned into this common roadside plant.

Rosemary

This herb has been associated with remembrance since the days when the ancient Greek students would wear it to help them remember the answers to heir exams. It has a long association with love and weddings, and has been used in wedding bouquets from the time of Charlemagne. Even today it is still popular with brides in Europe. This is another instance where interpretation can vary considerably. Rosemary is also a funeral flower, and some say it causes domestic dissention.

Some Ideas for Using Herbs

Now that you know what herbs you want, what do you do with them? Well, fortunately you don't have to be Martha Stewart to think up ideas for using herbs at your wedding—although it might help to consult one of her books to save wear and tear on the brain at this stressful time!

Herbs can be used in several different ways: in food, drinks, and decorations, for a start. In ancient Persia, a tray of multicolored herbs called *atel-o-batel* was often present at weddings. The tray consisted of seven elements, some of them herbs, which were thought to ward off evil spirits—including gunpowder.

Decorations

The most obvious use of herbs is in the bouquets of the bridal party. The use of the bridal bouquet stems from ancient times when it was believed that strong-smelling flowers and herbs would keep the evil spirits away. The Romans extended the wearing of flowers to the men in the party. Brides' bouquets often contained dill, which was thought to promote lust; but for obvious reasons, you might not want to promote such symbolism uniformly in every bridesmaid's bouquet.

Fortunately, all the bouquets in the wedding party do not have to match, so it should be easy enough to choose appropriate herbs for each member. You might want to keep it simple by choosing just one herb. Consider ivy, which stands for fidelity and is easy enough to find. A sprig of jasmine, the symbol of femininity, would add color. Decide on a theme for each bouquet. You can have fun choosing herbs you think are suitable to each bridesmaid, or hand them a copy of a good herbal and let them choose their own! There are other decorations to consider besides bouquets—for instance, garlands for the men. Here again, rosemary would be appropriate for the groom, and perhaps a bit of ginseng (whose name comes from the Chinese words for "likeness of man"). If you are using headpieces and necklaces, consider weaving a few herbs into braided lengths of ivy, the symbol of fidelity; or just using ivy alone. Centerpieces are another opportunity to use your imagination. Because centerpieces do not have to be carried, larger herbs can be used here. If the tables are sizeable enough, this is a chance to go completely wild by using herbs with size and presence, or herbs that would not survive the tossing of the bouquet, such as mushrooms. Decide on an overall theme for centerpieces. Branches of birch and ash, both reputedly used for Witches' broomsticks, can be fashioned into interesting frames from which to hang smaller herbs. Wire some peat or a chunk of stiff green florist's foam into a pot (dampen the foam first for better handling), stick a few of these branches into the peat or foam along with some ferns, and you have the start of a marvelous centerpiece.

Sometimes a garland is used for the wedding table or various other parts of the room, such as a bannister. If so, the garland should be in keeping with the theme of the centerpieces. For smaller tables without enough room for a spectacular centerpiece, Bertha Reppert suggests placing wine glasses or candlesticks with floral foam in them to hold various herbs.

Miscellaneous

Herbs can even be burned as incense. Try using verbena and other herbs sacred to Venus during handfasting ceremonies. Another idea is to toss a few dried lavender blossoms into each wedding invitation, or perhaps rub the place cards with lavender flowers.

Speaking of scents, another good use of fragrant herbs is for potpourri, a practice dating from ancient Egypt. Here is another tradition that survived due to practical use. In ancient days, bathing was not always in fashion, refrigeration was unknown, and it's likely that households just reeked. Potpourri served to make things more bearable. Fragrant herbs may be placed around the hall in small jars or saucers—even seashells—or tied in small mesh bags. For an outdoor wedding, you can choose a fragrant part of a garden. One old custom was to sprinkle or strew potpourri on the floor so the fragrance would be released when people stepped on it. As I mentioned previously, this was more likely done to keep the critters at bay than out of any romantic notion—although you don't have to tell that to the guests!

Potpourri can be fresh or dried, but if you make it ahead of time, keep it in an airtight container until you're ready to use it.

Everyone knows the tradition of throwing rice, which has now largely been replaced by birdseed. But why not throw herb seeds instead? Clover was associated with the sacred sun wheel of the ancient Celts, and clover seeds are easy to obtain at garden centers. Dried lavender flowers can be a charming substitution for rice or birdseed. Celery seed, which can be found at the supermarket, might be an interesting choice for this task. Celery was used as a calmative, but it also supposedly induces menses.

Favors

Favors are sometimes put out on the tables for wedding guests to take home as keepsakes. A charming favor would be a small pot of herbs for every guest. A local nursery can supply many of these quite cheaply, or you can transplant cuttings from neighbors' gardens or your own into pots found at garage sales. One warning here, though: do not use parsley! Although it is quite popular with gardeners and easy to grow, transplanting this herb is associated with domestic disaster. Choose a more appropriate (and useful) herb such as thyme or mint.

At many weddings, the favors consist of a bag of almonds. The tradition behind this comes from the following Greek fable as told by Servius. Deserted on her wedding day by her lover Demophon, a young maiden named Phyllis died of grief. To reward her constancy and compensate for her misery, the gods changed her into an almond tree. Later, when Demophon eventually returned and the leafless, flowerless, and forlorn tree was pointed out to him as the memorial of Phyllis, he embraced it in his arms, which caused it to burst into bloom. Ever after, the almond has become an emblem of true love inextinguishable by death. OK, so the woman had to die first—but who could resist such a romantic tale?

Sprigs of rosemary can be tucked into folded napkins at each table. The only limit to the possibilities of decorating with herbs is your imagination. The arrangements don't have to look professionally perfect. In fact, many people like the homemade look better because of the personal effort involved.

Food and Drink

Dill, the herb of lust, can selectively be put into the food. The dill from the bridal bouquet was traditionally eaten after the wedding ceremony for the purpose of arousing the couple's passion for each other. Here again, use the herb judiciously—if you're into polyamory, spread it around; but if not, you might want to use restraint lest trouble start among the guests!

Z. Budapest has some unusual culinary suggestions, such as grinding up coriander and adding it to the couple's wine glasses to increase their desire for each other. This might make a nice little ceremony during the initial toast to the bride and groom.

Anise is an herb that was thought to ward off the evil eye. At the end of a meal, the ancient Romans brought out a cake called *mustacae*, spiced with anise to promote digestion (thereby chasing the evil spirits out of one's digestive tract). Eventually this cake became a tradition at the end of their wedding ceremonies. If you don't like spiced cake, an after-dinner anisette will do the same trick.

Another good idea for an after-dinner drink is sambuca, made from elderberries—the tree of Freya, Norse goddess of love. Sometimes a coffee bean is floated in the sambuca. If you choose to follow this tradition, be aware of an interesting fact about coffee—in ancient Turkey, a husband whose wife who did not keep him supplied with enough coffee could divorce her. (Guess we could say that he had the grounds.)

Speaking of stress—don't forget the chamomile tea as a soother for yourself!

Sources of Herbs

Finally, you must locate the herbs you wish to use. Fortunately, herbs are so easy to grow that most of us know a few folks who can supply them. If you don't, there are several sources of fresh herbs available. During the growing season, one of the most economical sources is pick-your-own farms. There should be a list of these available from your local county extension agent, located in the blue pages of your phone book. If you go this route, and wish to use fresh herbs, be sure to enlist plenty of friends—the herbs must be picked as close to use as possible.

Some of these herbs can be found in the wild. Plantain and dandelion can be found in your own back yard. If you have no back yard, try someone else's—they will be glad to let you pick all you want of these herbs commonly regarded as weeds! If you choose to pick fresh herbs and dry them, allow at least ten days for drying, or longer if the weather is cold or wet. I find they dry very well hanging in a closed car parked in the sun! As I mentioned before, don't forget the supermarket. There are plenty of herbs to be found there! Ethnic markets are an especially good source of herbs because they usually offer a wide selection not found in ordinary supermarkets. You can easily find fresh or dried herbs.

Dried herbs are an alternative for those fresh herbs that you just can't find or when there is no time to pick them just before use. If you can't find what you want at the supermarket or gourmet shop, try a mail order herbal dealer or an occult store. Just make sure any mail order dealer you choose knows you have a deadline for obtaining them.

Finally, if you have the time (thyme?), use your herbal lore source notes to print out a listing of all the herbs used in the wedding, along with their meanings according to your sources. This is a keepsake your guests will use for many years to come, and may even find helpful when it comes time to plan their own weddings! Best of luck, and may your rosemary grow tall.

Books

Indispensable to any event in which herbs are to play a central part is a book called *Herbs for Weddings and Other Celebrations* (see bibliography, below). This book is a wealth of ideas on the many ways to use herbs in your wedding.

Websites

The Queensland Herb Society's website offers some interpretations of herbal lore at http://www.powerup.com.au/~sage/The%20HerbalWedding.html.

A site called "Celebrating with Herbs" can be found at http://www.wholeherb.com/HAC/HTM. The Medieval and Renaissance Wedding Information Page, a fascinating and comprehensive collection of lore, is at http://paul.spu.edu/~kst/bib/bib.html.

Bibliography

Budapest, Zsuzanna. *Holy Book of Women's Mysteries*, Volume 1. Oakland, CA: Z. Budapest, c. 1986.

Campanelli, Dan, and Pauline Campanelli. *Circles, Groves, and Sanctuaries*. St. Paul, MN: Llewellyn Publications, 1992.

Cooper, J.C. *Illustrated Encyclopedia of Traditional Symbols*. London: Thames and Hudson, 1978.

Cunningham, Scott, and David Harrington. *Spell Crafts*. St. Paul, MN: Llewellyn Publications, 1993.

Grieve, M. *Modern Herbal*. New York: Hafner Press, 1974.

Jacob, Dorothy. *Witch's Guide to Gardening*. New York: Taplinger Publications, 1965.

Lust, John. *The Herb Book*. New York, Bantam Books, 1974.

Reppert, Bertha. *Herbs for Weddings and Other Celebrations*. Pownal, VT: Storey Books, 1993.

Starhawk. *The Spiral Dance*. San Francisco: Harper and Row, 1989.

Potpourri

⤞ By Caroline Moss ⤝

*T*here can't be many people
who have not come across
brightly-colored potpourri,
now found in every gift shop and supermarket in shiny bags. The scent of
some of these mixes can be overpowering in the extreme, and certainly not
recommended for anyone with a sensitive nose. Most of these very commercial offerings are a long way from the
original idea, which developed in Europe over the past several hundred
years. Of course, fragrant perfumes and
oils have been used for many thousands
of years as well as in the early civiliza-
tions of China, India, Greece, Egypt,
and the Americas, but potpourri, in a
form we would recognize, is a largely
post-sixteenth-century creation.

Potpourri literally translated from
the French means "rotten pot," and
evolved for two main reasons. One
was, obviously, to scent the home. At a

time when bathing and clothes washing, even among the aristocracy, was not what it is now, flowers and herbs played a major role as air fresheners. Leaves and small branches of herbs were laid on the floor to release their scent when walked upon. These "strewing herbs" had the added benefit of repelling insect pests and keeping the dust down. When out and about, European aristocrats would carry tussie-mussies, which are small posies of scented flowers and herbs. These could be sniffed regularly when the street smells became too much. They were also thought to give some protection against disease and are still carried today on ceremonial occasions by English High Court judges.

The early potpourris were made by layering fragrant flower petals, often simply roses, in a lidded crock with salt. The petals broke down and a dark, heavily scented paste was formed, which would last many, many years. On entering a room the lid could be removed, and it would be replaced on leaving, thus extending the life of the mixture. Today, we are more familiar with the dry potpourri. This form needs four main elements to be successful: color, texture, fixative, and fragrance. Of course, some ingredients will fulfill more than one requirement. For example, rose petals will give both scent and color, whereas dried orange slices will simply provide color and texture.

Creating a Long-Lasting Scent

Although many petals and leaves have a lovely fragrance when dried, if kept out in a bowl of potpourri for long they will gradually lose their aroma. In order to both maintain the scent for a far longer period and also to create new scents and blends, we want to use both oils and fixatives. Many books will tell you that you must always use only essential oils. These are the pure, unadulterated oils extracted from plants. They vary in price depending on the rarity of the plant and the ease of extraction, from a reasonable price for lavender to a price past the Moon and rising for rose. I would say that if you come across a synthetic oil that you like, then go ahead and use it. Do check the scent first, though—

essential oil of rose will be wonderful, synthetic oil may or may not be. Synthetic oils do allow you have fun at a reasonable price. I once found a little brown bottle of something labelled "Christmas Carol" in a market stall for $1.50 that was quite lovely. A selection of holiday fragrances for me to create my own Christmas mix, say frankincense, myrrh, bayberry, and cinnamon, would have cost around forty times that! If you do start to build a little collection of oils just remember to use and enjoy them. Although very precious, they do not last forever, so don't leave them in a cupboard for years awaiting the "perfect" use.

Having acquired some scented oil, the most effective way to be ensure adequate distribution throughout the mix and a long-lasting fragrance is to mix the oil with your fixative material (see below). After the oil has been dropped onto the chosen vehicle, such as orris root powder or fir cones, this should be sealed in a plastic bag or airtight glass jar for at least two days, and up to a couple of weeks. This allows the true marriage of oil and fixative and for the fragrance to mature.

Mixing the Potpourri

This is the really fun bit. All the ingredients will be assembled and combined. You may be following a precise recipe, or you may be simply using what you have available. In either case, once everything is in a large bowl, one with plenty of room for tossing and turning, you need to mix it thoroughly with a large metal spoon (wood absorbs the oils). Then store the potpourri in a airtight container to mature until needed.

You may well find at this stage that you want to adjust either the looks or the fragrance of your mixture. If things look too dull, simply add more color, like some deep red petals. If the texture looks too "bitty," try to incorporate some larger pieces for a bolder texture, like cones, dried fruit slices, and large cinnamon sticks. All you need to remember is that you just cannot go wrong. Whatever so-called mistake you make can be adjusted. I have included a few recipes at the end for those who want a starting point. However, why not just look at the following lists of color, texture, fixatives, and fragrances, pick something from each group, and get going? The only small piece of advice is to start simple. You can always add things, but a mix of too many fragrances or ingredients is difficult to get right.

Color and Texture

Petals for color and texture can include rose, lavender, marigold, tiger lily, tulip, or salvia. If collected from the garden, they need to be picked at their peak and dried quickly. Many make the mistake of collecting falling petals that do not have the quality required. To make any quantity of potpourri it is often preferable to buy petals in bulk from a specialist supplier. Most will sell in small (say one- or two-cup) quantities. Drying herbs at home needs a small book's worth of advice in itself, and I would direct you to the library for further information.

Flower heads and buds for texture can include rose, carnation, globe amaranth, bergamot, everlasting flowers, bachelor's button, statice, aster, or chamomile. Even if you are purchasing most of your materials from a dried flower specialist, this is a good opportunity to incorporate just a few flower heads from a special bouquet or garden visit. How about a gift of potpourri to a new bride containing some of the buds from her wedding posy?

Leaves are most useful both in terms of scent and bulk. Those of particular note include scented geranium, bay, lemon balm, mint, rosemary, artemisias, lamb's ear, lemon verbena, tansy, woodruff, pine, spruce or balsam needles, and alecost/costmary. At Christmas, I like to line a large, flattish wooden bowl with cypress sprigs and lay my seasonal potpourri on top. This gives bulk, color, and a lovely winter scent.

Seeds, seed heads, and pods come into their own for texture. Look out for rose hips, juniper, star anise, allspice, nigella, honesty, pussy willow, chile peppers, poppy, tonka bean (tonquin), cloves, and vanilla pod. Use the final three items in this list with caution as they are extremely highly scented.

Wood and bark give wonderful natural textures and pieces can be brought back from any country walk (although be sure just to collect small pieces or those already dead—stripping a living tree of its bark will kill it). Other barks also give warm scents associated with a masculine, winter mixture. These include cinnamon and sandalwood.

Cones are the highly decorative seed pods of a number of tree species and come in a wide variety of sizes and colors. Some retain a fresh, forest fragrance, while others can be used simply for their aesthetic properties. Those to look out for include pine, larch, and the tiny bunches of alder cones.

Citrus can form the basis of a lovely fresh potpourri and, indeed, the essential oil is to be found in the list of fragrances below. These versatile fruits can also provide color and texture very cheaply. The peel can be dried easily, either just left to air dry or placed on top of a radiator. As you have eaten the fruit this costs nothing, and you can just pick out the best looking pieces. Slices of dried citrus fruit are now widely available to buy, and they look very effective in potpourri. You can dry slices at home either in a very low oven or on a heater. However, they are not always successful unless you have a home dehydrator. In addition to orange you can use other citrus fruits such as lemon or lime, although they do not have such an attractive color. Grapefruit tends to have too thick a skin to work well.

Depending on what sort of mix you have, you may well be able to incorporate grated scented soaps and candles, incense ash, and even old pot pourri that has lost its fragrance but still has useful bulk and color. You will find that many commercial potpourris nowadays use dyed wood shavings. These are very cheap and take color and fragrance easily, but will immediately reduce the mixture to a coarse and vulgar concoction and I personally would not include them. I also do not find the need to dye any of my mixtures. Work with what nature provides and you will find the variety more than sufficient.

Fixatives

As mentioned above, fixatives enhance the longevity of potpourri and some add their own aroma. If not following a tested recipe, start with one fixative, which is quite sufficient for the purpose. Although I would normally suggest sticking to natural materials, I mention the synthestic fixative now available as some are allergic to orris root, which is one of the most popular and traditional of mediums. With any of the powder fixatives, such as orris root, or violet powder, the watch word is moderation. A teaspoonful will be more than adequate for a mixing bowl full of potpourri. Too much results in a white powdery look to the finished product.

Options available include frankincense or myrrh (granules), oak moss, orris root, patchouli, sandalwood chips, synthetic fixative (from specialist herb suppliers), vetiver root, or violet powder (an old mix including starch, orris, bergamot, and clove, but no violets). Your choice will depend on what is available and also whether you want it purely as a fixative, in which case use orris root or to add scent in its own right, like sandalwood.

Essential Oils

We have looked at the benefits of essentail oils over synthetic above. Simply look at what is available, what you can afford, and what it smells like. Just be aware that some oils smell rather odd in the bottle and the final result can only really be ascertained when just a few drops are combined with other materials. Remember that if you want your oils to be used for aromatherapy purposes as well, then only essential oils will do.

Popular scents for potpourri include: bayberry, bergamot, bay, cinnamon, citrus (lemon, orange, or lime), clove, jasmine, lavender, lemon verbena, musk, neroli, patchouli, peppermint, pine, rose, rose geranium, sandalwood, vanilla, violet, wintergreen, and ylang-ylang.

As well as being combined with a fixative when making a new batch of potpourri, oils can also be added to an ageing mixture to rejuvenate the scent. The oil can simply be sprinkled over the top, which is best if using a synthetic oil. Alternatively, an oil-fixative mixture can be made up and mixed in to the existing potpourri after the fixative has matured for a week or two.

Uses

Having made a lovely batch of potpourri, it is fun to find a few uses for it other than simply putting it in a bowl. Here are some suggestions:

- Cover polystyrene balls, wreaths, or hearts with glue and coat with a fairly fine potpourri.

- Fill clear glass baubles.

- Stitch or stick three sides of a card, fill with potpourri, and seal the final edge.

- Sandwich between material and lace and catch material in an embroidery hoop.

- Put a spoonful into old lace hanky and tie with ribbon. This is nice as a tag to a birthday gift or, with name tag attached, as a place setting and party favor

- Put a spoonful in a square of net, gather with ribbon, and attach to dried flower wreaths and arrangements.

- Make up sachets to put into drawers or to hang on clothes hangers.

Recipes

English Country Garden Potpourri

2	ounces lavender
5	ounces red rose petals
½	teaspoon orris root powder (fixative)
15	drops rose oil

Pine Tree Christmas Potpourri

Handful of 2-inch pinecones

Large mixing bowl full of evergreen sprigs

2 ounces cinnamon sticks

½ ounce whole cloves

1 ounce star anise

15 orange slices, dried

4 ounces dark red rose buds

2 ounces bay leaves, dried and painted gold

2 ounces frankincense granules (fixative)

25 drops cinnamon oil

5 drops pine oil

Moonlight Serenade Potpourri

2 ounces white larkspur

1 ounce white globe amaranth

4 ounces lamb's ears

4 ounces white rose buds

1 ounce bay leaves

1 ounce eucalyptus leaves

8–10 freeze-dried gardenia heads

1 teaspoon orris root powder (fixative)

1 teaspoon gardenia fragrance oil

Herbal Dyeing

ᔍ By K.D. Spitzer ᔍ

just recently I read a comment that the herbal world can get along just fine without humans, but that we cannot get along without herbs. This could not be more true. Not only do herbs nourish and heal us and lend the ephemeral beauty of their blossoms and form, but they also bring a more permanent brightness of color into our lives. This has far-reaching implications for those of us who live in northern climates.

A large portion of our world is pretty much black and white for what seems like endless months of the year. Color is a gift that lifts our spirits and brings joy into our hearts. It is an integral part of every culture. In the West, brides wear white, mourners wear black, kings wear purple, and red roses definitely declare a passionate love. Since ancient times, our ancestors have known how to extract the color

pigments from plants and other life forms and attach them to textiles and cosmetics. Thus we are able to extend the sunny days of summer into the long bleak darkness of winter, carrying a lightness of spirit from the very being of the living plant.

Fortunes have been won and lost over the centuries, empires have been built or destroyed, and wars have been fought by the ambitious, the greedy, opportunists, and mercenaries over the dye trade and all its raw materials. If it's true that you can track the history of global exploration and empire by the history of the spice trade and its ruthless, ambitious adventurers, then you must add the history of the dye trade to that mix. It's not just the insatiable demand by the public for flavor and food preservation, but also the almost urgent need for color and ornament that has fueled the endless drive in search of plants.

It's not just plants (and men) that have given up their lives for color. We have lost an entire species of sea snail (*Murex*) to the egos of the rich and powerful of the ancient world. The tiny dye sacs of thousands of these snails combined to yield the color tyrian purple. It was a labor-intensive process that only produced a small amount of dye and drove the entire species into extinction.

With the law of supply and demand actively working even in the ancient world, only a very exclusive few could afford to trim their clothing with cloth dyed purple, and thus contributed the saying "born to the purple," which has lasted to modern times. The search for purple continued, intensely at times, less so at others. In some parts of the world lichens offered a heathered purple, but it was difficult to extract reliably, and once again there was not much of it.

In the 1960s there was a rumor that traveled across the U.S.A. among textile artisans that the common dandelion, under certain conditions, would yield purple. There was even a published recipe in the 1970s, and lots of dandelions were sacrificed fruitlessly upon the altar of this need for an accessible purple.

It seems that almost simultaneously in the New World and the Old it was discovered that a scale insect could produce clear reds in relatively prodigious amounts. If you can produce a clear red and a clear blue, then you can also produce purple. In the Mediterranean, kermes (*Kermes spp.*) was successfully cultivated on oak trees and a flourishing trade developed with the Low Countries, which were the center of not only the dye trade, but also tapestry ateliers. Wools dyed with kermes are still vividly red in surviving tapestries from the fourteenth century.

In the New World, in South America, cochineal (*Dactylopius coccus*), another scale insect, was discovered thriving on prickly pear cactus. This was such an important red dye stuff that it is said that Montezuma himself received some of his tax tributes in cochineal.

The red coats of the British army were dyed with madder (*Rubia tinctorium*), also called "turkey red." Wealthy British adventurers tried to establish cochineal as a thriving trade in Australia in order to take over the supply of red dyes for the British army. They lost their shirts and colonial plantations in this venture. Cochineal, however, retained its importance as a dye stuff and is, today, along with annatto (*Bixa orellana*), often used to color beverages and other foods red or orange. It does grow in the deep South, especially Florida, and, of course, the prickly pear-laden American southwest.

Almost all plants yield some pigment, but some plants are most important to the commercial dye trade: red madder, which has been mentioned, but also the two blues, woad (*Isatis tinctoria*) and indigo (*Indigofera suffruticosa*). After his conquest of Britannia, Julius Caesar mentions how the native Britains painted their bodies blue to frighten their enemies. At that time there was already a thriving woad trade, and a very smelly business it was. Between the fermenting leaves and the stale urine used to draw the pigment, the dyers' guild was relegated downwind of urban centers.

Although indigo is a very ancient dye, especially in India, it was many centuries until it found a place on the palettes of northern European dyers. The woad lobby kept even the most ruthless indigo entrepreneurs out of England until the 1700s. It was much in demand, as less indigo yielded more and clearer blues than woad.

It took a woman, Eliza Pinckney, to establish indigo as a cash crop in North America—South Carolina to be exact. By 1747, she had such an established crop that she was able to ship the harvest to England. This continued until the American Revolution, when the land was needed for food crops. After the war, India had moved into the world market with a cheaper product, and cotton moved in as King in the American south.

Clear yellows are the last component of primary dye colors and weld (*Reseda luteola*) ruled supreme in England. Weld and woad together produced Saxon green, or Robin Hood green, or British racing green, even forest green—that particular green that we associate with England in its "merrie ole" days. Clear yellows would not be complete without the mention of two other important contributions. Quercitron, or black oak (*Quercus velutina*), was exported to Europe from the eastern U.S. right up through the early 1900s. Its inner bark and bark were ground finely and used by the colonists as a yellow dye. It is colorfast and a tough match for its chief competitor, turmeric (*Curcuma spp.*) which, while a cheap substitute, fades easily.

Turmeric is often used for top dyeing. This is a process that takes dyed cloth or fibers and dyes them again to obtain a third color. Something blue, top dyed with turmeric, would probably result in a green hue. Top dyeing is a pretty common process in the cloth trade. Quite often several disparate colors will be top-dyed and blended together into a cohesive whole that now works well in a woven or knitted fabric.

Mordant

Another term that is used by dyers is mordant. To mordant a fiber is to process it so that color pigments will adhere to that fiber, and different fibers mordanted with different metals will produce a variety of colors in one dye pot of plant pigments.

The amount of the mordant is an important measurement as it can cause fibers to break down.

Alum

Alum (potassium aluminum sulfate) is often combined (but not necessarily) with cream of tartar (potassium acid tartrate) to mordant wools and silks. Cotton and other vegetable fibers do not absorb metallic salts readily and thus need tannic acids, which can be obtained from oak leaves or staghorn sumac. You can dump this under the hydrangeas or broad-leafed evergreens when you're finished. It's a soil acidifier.

Tin

Tin, or stannous chloride, brightens colors, but can also cause the fibers to become brittle. It is often added to alum-mordant-ed wool or silk just before it is drawn from the dye bath. Dispose of this appropriately.

Iron

Iron is said to sadden colors. That is, it grays them. Ferrous sulfate or copperas can be added to the wool, but not too much as it will also make the fibers brittle. Better yet, extract the pigments from the plants in an iron kettle or throw in a handful of iron nails. I recommend cleaning it well when you are finished. Alexis de Tocqueville, a French statesman touring the newly independent United States, wrote in his memoirs that when he was traveling through New Jersey, had by chance a wonderful stew served to him for his lunch. It was remarkable, as he wrote acerbically in his journal, because the cook had used the iron cauldron for an indigo dye bath the day before and all the vegetables were blue!

Copper

Copper (copper sulfate or blue vitriol) can lend a green tint and is less harsh than other metals. Try throwing a copper scrubbie into the dye pot to achieve a darker green. Organic farmers use copper as a fungicide. It's also used to eat tree roots in sewers.

Chrome

Chrome, or potassium dichromate, is a neon orange. Mostly used for wools only, it really brightens colors. It has even been used, supposedly, as a dietary supplement. Do not dispose of chrome at home.

Care should be taken in the use of all mordants. Don't lean over the pot to inhale or let the steam near your eyes. Treat chrome and tin as you would any other hazardous waste.

Harvesting Plants

Care should also be taken in harvesting plants. Never use any poisonous plants or plants that have a reputation for causing allergies. Never harvest plants on the endangered list when wildcrafting. Also, never take the largest or the smallest plants of a particular species, and take only thirty percent of the plants in that locale. Harvesting just the useful parts, leaves or flowering tops, of the plant can also make the plant bushier and prolong its life in the garden.

How to Begin Dyeing

If you've ever dyed Easter eggs with onion skins, then you have been introduced to the merest possibilities of plant dyeing. If it engendered a thirst for more information, then you are well on your way to being hooked on a most fulfilling hobby. If you only produce a color card, you will have the satisfaction that comes from exploring the most basic properties of herbs.

On the other hand you may launch a project like a friend has just completed for her authentically restored 1700s colonial home: crewel embroidered curtains. The linen curtains were purchased, but the crewel yarn was hand spun and hand dyed with plants from her garden. It took a while because she has a full-time job and teenagers (another full-time job), but now she has something that she can point to with pride and satisfaction. The curtains are permanent proof of her labors while so much else in her life is temporary.

If you're going to experiment with herbal dyeing, then you will probably want to start with 100 percent white or natural wool. Certainly think about cotton, silk, linen, or even basket-making materials. You'll need to wash the material, and of course it should be wet when it goes into the mordant or dye pot. You can make small skeins to experiment with. Figure on no more than four ounces in each pot with these recipes.

Mordant Recipe

4   quarts water
1   tablespoon alum
1   teaspoon cream of tartar or ½ teaspoon tin, copper, iron, or chrome

Combine water, alum, and cream of tartar. Bring the mordant to a simmer and keep it there for about 15 minutes. Stir with a paint stirrer that you can discard when your project is done. Add the wool and let it simmer for 1 hour. Take it off the heat and let cool to lukewarm. Rinse well, and at this point you can store it in the fridge or dry it until ready to use. You can also put it in the dye bath if it is ready.

Dye Bath

Chop plant materials so they release their pigments easily. Simmer about an hour. Use about one pound of the plant to one pound of wool; probably a half pound of plants will easily dye four ounce skeins. When it's cool, strain the dye bath before adding the wool. Toss in the wool and bring to a simmer; stirring occasionally. Keep it simmering. Let it cool down, and rinse the wool well. The big thing to remember here is that wool will felt if it is subjected to abrupt temperature changes. The dye bath probably still has plenty of pigment in it and you can continue to start new batches until it or you is exhausted.

Record Keeping

Always keep records of where you gathered your plants and when. You also need to keep careful notes of what you did. Plants, especially indigo and woad, have more pigment when they are in bloom, although it is the leaves you are harvesting. Other plants keep their color in the blossoms or in the roots. Raw wool needs to have the lanolin washed out before it will take mordant or dye.

Home dyeing with plants almost became a lost art. The arrival of modern synthetic dyes was greeted with great joy because they were more reliable, easily transported, had a good shelf life, and in many instances were colorfast. The old ways are being kept by people excited by the beauty and surprise of the plant world, who are energized by working in the woods and fields and garden, and who have a commitment to sustaining old traditions. They revel in the challenge of research and rediscovery and enjoy the deep satisfactions that come from the open-ended communication with plants and their devas.

A Dyer's Herb Garden

COMMON NAME	LATIN NAME	PART USED
Calendula	*Calendula officinalis*	Flowers
Coreopsis	*Calliopsis tinctoria*	Flowers, whole plant
Cosmos	*Cosmos sulphureus*	Flowers
Dandelion	*Taraxacum officialis*	All parts
Dyer's broom	*Genista tinctoria*	All parts but roots
Dyer's knotweed	*Polygonum tinctuoria*	Leaves, roots
Dyer's chamomile	*Anthemis tinctoria*	Flowers
Dyer's woodruff	*Asperula tinctoria*	All parts
Elderberry	*Sambucus canadensis*	Berries, leaves
Fustic (old)	*Chloraphora tinctoria* *Morus tinctoria*	Bark, chips

Common Name	Latin Name	Part Used
Goldenrod	*Solidago spp.*	Flowers, leaves, stems
Henna	*Lawsonia inermis*	Leaves
Indigo	*Indigofera tinctoria*	leaves
Lily of the valley	*Convallaria majalis*	leaves
Madder	*Rubra tinctorum*	dried and ground roots
Milkweed	*Asclepius spp.*	flowers, stems, leaves
Onions	*Allium cepa*	dried skins
Osage orange	*Maclura pomifera*	bark, leaves
Pokeweed	*Phytolacca americana*	berries
Safflower	*Carthamus tinctoria*	flowers
St. John's wort	*Hypericum perforatum*	leaves, stems, flowers
Soapwort	*Saponaria officinalis*	leaves in mid July for gentle suds
Sumac, staghorn	*Rhus glabra*	leaves for mordant, berries for dye
Tansy	*Tanacetum vulgare*	flowers, leaves, tops
Weld	*Reseda luteola*	leaves, seed
Woad	*Isatis tinctoria*	leaves

Suppliers for Dye Herbs

SUNNYBROOK FARMS NURSERY
P.O. Box #6, 9448 Mayfield Road
Chesterland, OH 44026
216-729-7232

DABNEY HERBS
Box 22061
Louisville, KY 40252
502-893-5198

HERBFARM
32894 Issaquah-Fall City Road
Fall City, WA 98024

Suppliers for Mordants and Natural Dye Stuffs

THE MANNINGS
P.O. Box # 687
East Berlin, Pa 17316

RUMPELSTILTSKIN
1021 R Street
Sacramento, CA 95814

EARTH GUILD
33 Haywood Street
Asheville, NC 28801
800-327-8448

Bibliography

Androsko, Rita. *Natural Dyes and Home Dyeing.* New York: Dover Publications, 1971.

Bliss, Anne. *North American Dye Plants.* New York: Interweave Press, Inc., 1993.

Buchanan, Rita. *A Dyer's Garden.* New York: Interweave Press, Inc., 1995.

Herbal Soap-Making

✺ By K.D. Spitzer ✺

Of course the origins of soap-making are lost in the mists of time, not to mention the myths of time. My favorite legend puts the discovery of soap and its cleansing qualities in Rome, at Mount Sapo. There was a beautiful temple there, dedicated to the Goddess Sapo and situated high on a hill over the River Tiber. Animal sacrifices were made there to obtain the attention and blessings of the Goddess. Naturally, proper etiquette demanded that animals be offered to the Goddess cooked. Today we refer to this kind of sacrifice as "burnt offerings," but truth be told, it was actually dinner for the temple handmaidens, and whatever was left was distributed to the poor.

The animals were ritually slaughtered and then roasted over wood fires. On rainy days, the ashes and rendered fats that had dripped into the

fires would wash down from the temple to the river below. Roman women who washed their laundry on the banks of the river very quickly noticed that when the river had sudsy lumps floating in it, their clothing got a lot whiter very quickly.

The combination of wood ashes, fats, and rain water mixed together on the trip down the side of Mount Sapo thus magically creating a new substance, and clean clothes surely were a blessing from the Goddess. If you doubt this, when next you do laundry, agitating clothes and Tide™ together in your electricity-powered washer, remember the lifetime when you dunked your laundry in river water and beat it on a rock.

The alchemical process of mixing lye (which is sodium hydroxide that has been leached from hard wood ashes with rainwater) and fats into a cake of soap is called—what a surprise— saponfication. Because of our colonial history, we think of fats as tallow, which was rendered from animal fats, usually beef or pork. Actually, ancient records show that olive oil and other vegetable oils were routinely used as the fats in soapmaking.

Clay tablets from Sumer dated about 2500 B.C. reveal a recipe using lye, water, and cassia oil (obtained from the barks of a genus of trees and shrubs indigenous to warm climates, and one of which is cinnamon) to make a soap for washing wool. (If the lanolin is not removed from the wool, it will resist taking a dye, and you need soap to remove lanolin, not to mention all the other stuff that sheep pick up in their perambulations.)

The Phoenicians were trading soap by at least 500 years B.C., and by the first century A.D. Galen, who was a Greek physician, was recommending bathing as a means of promoting good health. When Pompeii was excavated, a complete soapmaking factory was discovered, along with bars of soap ready for sale. Pompeii was lost intact in 79 A.D. As you have seen, the legend that the Spanish developed Castile soap, named for one of their capital cities, with olive oil as its principal constituent, is largely erroneous. On the other hand, they did notice a good thing when they saw it and then capitalized on it, if you'll notice the pun.

In the Middle Ages, it appears that people who could afford it purchased luxury cakes for bathing from the guilds. Laundry soap was made at home, and was a very smelly affair. The soap was rather soupy and probably dark in color. Even today you can't rely on consistent results in soapmaking, although with care, you can produce a fine product. You know that making soap at home has become rather trendy when you find molds, pigments, and other ingredients at your local Walmart.

Milling Soap

Many recipes produce enough soap in one recipe to supply your entire town for years. You may want to either halve the recipe or plan on milling it in small batches to experiment with various herbal additives. Milling, or French milling, is a refinement in soapmaking. The "mother" batch is grated and melted with water, herbs, spices, scents, exfoliators, and color pigments and poured into molds. Milling also produces a harder, longer-lasting soap.

Milling is often the most effective means of retaining the special qualities of fresh herbs in soap, because they are added just before the soap sets. Grind them finely as this means that, however attractive, the herbs will really be in the soap, but then also in the sink. This is also true of melt-and-pour glycerin soaps. Milled soaps can be colored and then scented with essential oils, and fresh herbs like lavender flowers added for sunburned skin.

Infusing Oils

If you plan ahead, you can infuse oil with fresh herbs using your favorite method. These oils can be used in your soap. Use about six ounces of fresh herb to two cups of olive oil. Either heat the oil in the sun for a couple weeks and the light of the Moon for one night, or bring to 100°F, turn off heat, and let steep. Do this every day for two weeks. The method will depend somewhat on the best way to extract the particular constituents of each herb. Strain the oil before adding to soap.

Calendula will produce a bar that is soothing for skin with minor scratches or abrasions. Infuse oil with comfrey and wintergreen leaves and use the penetrating oil to produce a soap with pain-relieving qualities for muscle aches, joint tiredness, and arthritis. Succulent plants like jewelweed can actually be put in a juicer, and the resulting liquid used to replace water in a skin-soothing soap if you've gotten into a poison ivy patch.

Other Additions

Whipping air into your soap with your handmixer will cause it to float. Use oatmeal, cornmeal, or poppyseeds as exfoliators. If you live near the seashore, gather kelp and bladderwrack to add to your soaps. Study the qualities of oils from almond to wheat germ to determine the best emollients for your particular needs in skin care. Experiment with herbal dyes: take a look at alkanet, annatto, paprika, and turmeric. The first two can be infused in oil to release their color and added to the end of the milling process. The last two, along with ground cinnamon, cloves, and other dark spices, will give good color as well as healing properties to bars in their powdered form.

Milk soaps are very popular right now with the designer soap set. A quarter cup of instant powdered milk added to a milled soap recipe, along with a quarter cup of honey (cut back on the water), will produce a silky complexion bar. Some health food stores sell powdered goats' milk, and most grocery stores sell a powdered buttermilk. You need to add one tablespoon of powdered benzoin as a preservative and scent fixative. Milk soaps need scenting; use a good essential oil. Of course, you can substitute fresh milk for the water in milling. Don't forget the benzoin. By the way, any soaps using fresh fruits and vegetables need benzoin.

Some Further Advice

- Definitely buy a scale for measuring lye, fat, and water.
- Plastic needlepoint canvas makes a great drying screen.

- Rubbermaid makes a great container with a snap-top lid that's perfect for the first few days of curing.

- Try to find a thermometer that measures below 100 degrees.

- Use a small plastic pitcher for mixing the lye, and don't use it or your wooden spoons for anything else.

- Wearing plastic goggles is a sensible addition to your wardrobe when mixing lye. Always wear rubber gloves, even when grating soap for hand milling.

- I hate to say it, but Walmart does carry most of what you need for a small amount of money.

Lye

Use only Red Devil™ lye, which you should be able to find in your local grocery store. When you weigh the lye, place a container on the scale and adjust to zero. This sets the scale so that you only end up weighing the lye. You can use this same procedure to weigh the oils. Give mixing the lye your full and careful attention as it is a dangerous substance. Always pour the lye into the water (not the other way around) and don't stick your face over it while mixing.

Rendering Animal Fat

Planning ahead is definitely important in soapmaking. If you choose to use tallow as one of your ingredients because it produces a mild but hard soap, you'll need to render it from a high-quality suet; near the kidneys produces the best. Any animal fats will do, but beef and pork are the best. Chicken fat softens the soap. Cut it up, mince in the food processor, or push it through the meat grinder. Cover it with water and cook in the crock pot, bake in a covered roaster in the oven at 200°F, or nuke it in the microwave. (*Editor's note:* Be careful if you put this in the microwave; fats catch fire easily.)

This is a smelly process. Open the windows. When all the fat has been rendered, pour it through several layers of cheesecloth. Refrigerate. When the tallow has hardened, pour off the water and scrape, rinse, and discard any meat scraps or gelatin from the pure tallow. Store in the fridge or freezer. Eight pounds of suet will yield about two-and-a-half pounds of tallow.

Making Soap

Here's the basic procedure. Choose a day when the Moon is in a fixed sign. Dissolve lye in water. Melt fats over low heat. Bring both mixtures to the same temperature, between 95 and 100 °F. They MUST be at the same temperature. To get these two to match up, you may need to put their containers into ice water or hot water to raise or lower their temperature to match the other. The lye will be very hot and will need to be cooled to 100°F. You'll need to carefully raise the temperature of the melting fats and oils to just reach 100 degrees. Then add the lye slowly to the fats. The success of your project depends upon this step, so take your time to get it right.

Once the lye and fats are combined, stir like crazy until the soap begins to thicken and trace. (*Editor's note:* You will probably have to stir for at least fifteen minutes; don't skimp on this part.) Lift the spoon, and if the drips leave a trail in the soap, or if a line drawn in the soap stays (in other words, it doesn't smooth out immediately), that's tracing.

Then it's time to pour the batch into the primary mold. If you've stirred for an hour and you don't think it has traced, dump it into the primary mold anyway. You can always remelt and stir again another day! (*Editor's note:* you might want to line the primary mold with wax paper so that the hardened soap is easier to remove.)

Cover the container and wrap in it blankets—no kidding! The soap needs to cool slowly and be kept out of drafts. You need to check it every day, and it may be several days before you can remove the blankets and lid. When it is solid enough, you can turn it out on the plastic canvas and let it dry until it is as solid as cheddar or Swiss cheese. At this point either cut into bars or grate for handmilling. Use rubber gloves when handling the soap (*Editor's note:* This is because until the soap has fully cured the lye is still caustic.) Allow the soap to cure (dry) for four to six weeks.

Great White Soap

This soap traces and sets very quickly and is just fine as a hand-cut bar or grated for milling. It also takes shape very well in a mold with fine details.

16	ounces blended oils or olive oil
38	ounces tallow
1½	ounces cocoa butter
7	ounces lye
20	ounces water

Sensitive Skin Soap

This is a versatile soap. It's a great moisturizer, mills easily, and is a good base to build on. Use comfrey-infused olive oil with vitamin E and scent with flowers for a good shaving soap for yourself, or with sandalwood or bay rum for your menfolks.

12	ounces coconut oil
6	ounces palm oil
10	ounces almond oil
8	ounces olive oil
4	ounces wheat germ oil, cold-pressed
14	ounces water
	Scant 6 ounces lye

Milled Soaps

Place grated basic soap in a pot and add water. Let it melt over low heat without stirring. When it is soft and lump-free, and at the last moment, add additional ingredients from the recipes below and pour into secondary molds. It's a good idea to have one large secondary mold ready in case the soap sets up before you have a chance to divide it into smaller containers.

Gardener's Grit Milled Soap

This is not only a great cleanser, but antifungal, antimicrobial, and analgesic; perfect after a day in the herb garden.

- 12 ounces grated great white soap
- 9 ounces water (before weighing the water, put ¼ cup lemon juice in the container and add enough water to make 9 ounces).
- 1 ounce corn meal
- ¼ ounce patchouli essential oil
- ¼ ounce lemongrass essential oil

Milled Baby Soap

You'll need to make your herbal infusion in late June. Cure soap for a full six weeks.

- 12 ounces grated soap for sensitive skin
- 9 ounces water
- 2 ounces infused oil (Infuse 2 cups of olive oil with 2 ounces each of fresh plantain, chickweed, and elder flowers; strain)

Goat's Milk Milled Soap

Tres chic and oh so soft!

- 12 ounces grated white soap
- 9 ounces goats' milk or buttermilk
- 2 teaspoons powdered benzoin

  Several drops peppermint or lavender essential oil

Rosemary-Lavender Milled Soap

You'll need to infuse 2 cups olive oil with 3 ounces each fresh rosemary leaves and lavender blossoms before making this soap.

12	ounces grated white soap
9	ounces water
2	ounces infused oil
	Several drops rosemary essential oil
	Several drops lavender essential oil

Bay Rum Milled Soap

Here's a little something for the menfolk.

12	ounces grated soap for sensitive skin
7	ounces water
2	ounces bay rum
2	ounces dark rum
1	heaping tablespoon ground allspice
1	heaping tablespoon ground cinnamon
2	ground bay leaves
1	ounce bay essential oil
1	ounce sweet orange essential oil

Mix ingredients together and cover tightly. Let stand for 48 hours to a week to let the scents marry. Don't skimp on the time.

Ritual Cleansing Milled Bath Bar

12	ounces grated soap for sensitive skin
9	ounces water
2	ounces infused ritual oil (see directions)
	Several drops lavender and rosemary
	Pinch of valerian

Use this for bathing before any magical ritual. Start at the New Moon in Taurus or Scorpio. To make the infused ritual oil, finely grind 2 tablespoons each lavender and rosemary, 1½ tablespoons each thyme and basil, 1 tablespoon each fennel and hyssop, and 1½ teaspoons each mint and vervain, and a pinch of valerian. Place dried herbs in 2 cups olive oil and heat to 100°F. Turn off heat and let cool; repeat every day for two weeks. Present it to the Goddess at the Full Moon in Scorpio or Taurus and dedicate it for ritual use. Strain the oil before adding to the soap. Double the amounts for fresh herbs.

(Editor's note: Pregnant women should avoid using peppermint, rosemary, and bay essential oils.)

Soap-Making Supplies

POURETTE
1418 Northwest 53rd Street
Seattle, WA 98107
800-888-9425
Molds, oils, and glycerin.

CREATION HERBAL PRODUCTS
P.O. Box 344
10492 U.S. Highway #421
Deep Gap, NC 28618
704-262-0006
Herbs, oils, and glycerin.

LAVENDER LANE
7337 #1 Roseville Road
Sacramento, CA 95842
916-334-4400
Oils, fragrances, and jars.

Herb
History,
Myth, and
Magic

Herb Lore

ᵅ By Verna Gates ᵅ

When the natural world was more magical than it is in our scientific day, the plants themselves led exciting lives and reflected the spirits of the gods. These plants held the power to cure or curse, to nourish or season, to protect or attract. Most of these herbs are in popular use today, even if we no longer remember why.

Parsley

When you place that spring of parsley on your plate, you are repeating an old Roman custom. They believed that parsley sanitized food simply with its presence. No matter how little you care to eat that parsley, you should never give it away, for giving away parsley gives away your luck. The finely-cut parsley leaves originate with angry fairies. There once was an old woman who grew tulips for fairy beds. They

especially preferred these swinging beds as cradles for fairy babies. When the old lady died, her son took over and decided to make a profit. He tore down the tulips and planted parsley. The angry fairies stomped the leaves in protest and parsley still bears the scars, but legends persist that babies come from parsley beds.

Chicory

The wonderful bitter herb that seasons Cajun coffee in New Orleans is not a native American plant. In fact, Thomas Jefferson was almost tried for treason for importing chicory seeds during the War of 1812. He knew the value of this bright blue flower for seasoning and medicine. All bitter herbs are cleansers. The plant is also a good luck charm and is especially potent on exploring trips. Many of the early settlers, particularly the prospectors, carried a root of the plant in their pocket for luck. It still possesses the power to open locks and remove obstacles.

Evening Primrose

Called the "little keys to heaven" in German, this plant is featured in an old Bavarian tale of sin and non-redemption. Once there were three sinners—good sinners—so good they had never been caught. Their brand of sin was stealing, and as thieves they had retired rich men. One day they heard that the king had built an impenetrable castle. They couldn't resist. The three thieves found their way in and found the king's treasure, but couldn't get out. They were sent to their deaths. However, these unrepentant sinners figured that God's house was pretty much like the king's—there had to be a back door ajar, a window cracked, or a servant to be bribed. So they went gaily to their deaths and actually were making their way into the back door to heaven. Saint Peter found out and got so upset that he dropped the keys to the pearly gates to earth. They turned into the evening primrose, which, due to its heavenly origins, opens any lock. The evening primrose is also the only known source outside of human breast milk for a certain hormone, making it an excellent herb for women.

Saint John's Wort

This plant isn't really a plant, it is a day disguise for fairy horses. If you step on it during the day, it will come by your bed and force you on a wild ride through the countryside. Wherever it stops when the sun comes up, it will sink back into the ground. You will be left for a long walk home to breakfast.

This plant was once considered a powerful medicinal. It was believed that all you had to do was pin it to your clothes to keep diseases away. Besides, if it is worn in your clothes, the devil cannot approach within the space of nine paces. If you gather it on a Friday and wear it around your neck, it will cure melancholy. Actually, it is a cure for depression, as studies in Europe are showing. It is prescribed three to one over Prozac in Germany. *Wort* is an old Anglo Saxon word for medicinal plant.

Rue

Sorrow and repentance were the emblems of this plant. When someone committed a sin against you, it was customary in Britain to throw a handful of rue at them. Accompanying the toss is this curse, "May you rue this day as long as you live." However, it can be useful in preventing malevolence. If maids eat it when tempted, they can avoid the seductions of their lovers. As a medicinal, it is supposed to make eyes keener and wits sharper, and just a sniff of it keeps the plague away.

Rosemary

This plant was blessed on Christmas when Mary laid out the freshly washed swaddling clothes to dry on it. The fragrant aroma is supposed to come from the sweet scent of the Christ child. Rosemary was supposed to be an herb that improved the memory. In Hamlet, Ophelia carries it before her death, saying "rosemary is for remembrance." As it is a funeral flower, Shakespeare warns his audience of her fate. A sprig of rosemary worn in the buttonhole will guarantee success in all tasks. Supposedly, the plant will only grow where a woman is head of the household, in name or will. Also, if a pinch of it is dropped into a barrel of beer, no one will get drunk.

Sage

If a girl goes out into the garden on All Saints' Eve and picks nine sage leaves on the stroke of midnight, one at every stroke, she will see the face of her future husband. If you would like to live a long life with your husband, the advice says to eat sage in May. However, you should never let sage bloom, for it brings bad luck to the family. It does serve as an omen of health—when someone leaves on a long journey, hang a spring of sage and watch it. As long as it stays healthy, the absent person is well and happy. Sage is the symbol of wisdom and will strengthen the memory.

Basil

The only correct way to sow basil seeds is to scream at them. There is an old French expression that translates literally as "sowing the basil" that idiomatically means "raving like a lunatic." Thus properly sowed, your basil plants should bring you the joy of well-seasoned foods. In India, where the plant is native, it is a holy herb, dedicated to the god Vishnu. His wife, Lakshmi, lives disguised in the plant, so beware of picking a sprig of it as it causes Vishnu pain. He will not hear your prayers if you harm it. You can pick the seeds and make a prayer rosary. Individual leaves are also allowable for picking. All devout Hindus go to their final resting place with a basil leaf ready to show at the gate of heaven.

Marjoram

Called "happy-minded" by the Germans and "joy-of-the-mountain" elsewhere in Europe, marjoram is a creation of the goddess Venus herself. This savory spice cradles the sweet scent from the touch of her fingers. It was also given to antiseptic value and sweetened the chambers of the sick. Not only will it ward off disease, but can also be used as a charm against the devil and his minions, as no one who has sold himself to Satan can abide the plant.

Valerian

Valerian root tea is often used to bring sweet slumber to tired heads. Centuries ago, the Magdalene soothed Christ by pouring valerian on his feet. This perfume has long been burned on the altars of the Roman church, whisking upward the prayers of the believers.

Dandelion

When you see Flemish paintings of the crucifixion, look below to see a dandelion painted at the foot of Christ. Supposedly, this plant gets its bitter taste because it absorbed the bitterness of Christ's suffering on the cross. It is also considered one of the original seven bitter herbs of the Passover. Just a few decades ago, this was the one of the most important plants in America. The natives and pioneers both used it as a food. It is one of the most nutritious foods you can eat. You can eat every part of it and even make coffee, tea, and wine with it. Two colors of dye can be made from the plant. It is also a serious medicinal, with gentle cleansing action on the kidneys and liver. If you ever see anything on a French menu called *piss-en-lit*, it's dandelion, and the French for "wet the bed."

Soapwort

A priest arrived back in England after a trip to France and announced that God had told him they should all bathe. He had discovered the soapy suds you get from rubbing the soapwort leaves. At the time, the plant, because of its pleasant scent, was sarcastically called the "pride of London" because of its unpleasant smell of the city's open sewers. This plant is sometimes called "bouncing bet" because its cluster of flowers resembles someone bent over a washtub.

Yarrow

When Achilles was born, his mother, a Titan, wanted to ensure his immortality, since his father was a human. She dipped the child in the river running through Hades, but had to grasp the child by the ankle, giving rise to the Achilles heel. When the Greeks battled Troy, Achilles, with his virtual invulnerability, served as a warrior and a medic. He treated many of the soldiers with yarrow, a plant with proven antiseptic and blood-clotting properties. It is often called soldier's wort or wound wort. Achilles was killed by an arrow to his ankle by the cowardly Paris, but his legend lives on in the *achillea millefolium*, the Latin name for the yarrow. The yarrow is also sometimes called "old man's pepper," as in "to pep up," the Viagra of herbs.

Mandrake

This herb is the most controversial plant that has ever been grown on this earth. Marijuana and opium poppies have nothing on the mandrake. As late as 1630, three women in Germany were burned at the stake just for having the plant in their yard. The maligned herb has a root shaped like a person, with arms, legs, a torso, and some say they've seen them with noses, ears, and full beards. It grew from the Medusa head when Perseus buried it in the temple. In Iceland, they believe it only grows from the throat of a rascal who was hanged for stealing a penny from a poor widow on high holy days, in church, between the reading of the gospel and the epistle. This plant was associated with the devil and evil spells. One recipe for flying involves mixing together bat's blood, viper tongues, mandrake root, and the fat of dead children.

Many rituals evolved regarding the storage of the mandrake root, including keeping a noose around its neck and keeping it in a tiny velvet coffin. One of the reason for this herb's many legends is its power as a medicinal. It is currently being tested as an anti-cancer drug and is showing some promise.

Communicating with Plants

⇜ By Penny Kelly ⇝

*I*magine having children and never speaking to them, or going to work every day and not talking to your coworkers. You probably wouldn't dream of ignoring anyone so rudely. It would seem unnatural and awkward simply because, in both cases, you have a relationship to maintain and communication is natural between those involved in relationships.

For this same reason, we are, by virtue of our existence here on planet Earth, in a relationship with plants. From corn to cantaloupe, our relationship with plants forms the foundation of security that brings us food, clothing, shelter, medicines, and the hundreds of useful daily items that make our lives more pleasant. So how is it that most of us do not communicate with plants?

The most common excuse is that plants do not talk. Infants, dogs, and grizzly bears do not talk either, but each gets its message across using various sounds and behaviors. One way or another, we end up getting the idea and responding correctly. Although plants make sounds, these sounds cannot be heard without the assistance of a computerized voice box. Hooking up a few sensors to a plant and attaching these to an amplifier and speakers reveals that plants make an amazing array of sounds.

The next most common reason for not talking to plants is that we do not think of them as intelligent beings. Intelligence is the ability to learn from experience, or the ability to respond successfully to changing situations. Since a plant continually assesses its environment and adapts itself and its output, it is clear that plants are capable of perception. If a plant can perceive and respond to its environment—and you are part of that plant's environment—it will perceive and respond to you. All that is needed is for you to communicate that you are open and receptive.

I have been talking with my plants for about seven or eight years now. It started innocently one day when trimming my grapevines. I was just moving along from plant to plant, muttering things half under my breath like, "Stand up here!" "I want you to grow this way." and "What do you need?" I didn't stop to listen for an answer because I didn't think plants could communicate, but the following year when I went for a walk among the vines in the early spring, they invited me back with great excitement and passion. For once I forgot to be doubtful, and spontaneously entered into a brief conversation with them in which I promised to come back and trim them, and they promised to grow perfectly for me. Later, when the conversation had long been over and I was examining it from a logical arm's length away, I simply could not conjure up enough doubt to discount the experience. The whole thing had been too real.

Since then, talking to the other living things around me has become as natural as talking to my children; an intimate, two-way affair. One of the more dramatic exchanges was with my aloe plant. I bought a small aloe plant that grew beautifully. When it was too big for the pot it had always been in, I decided to transplant it. Having never transplanted a cactus-type plant before, and having heard that they were finicky and difficult, I wasn't sure it would survive. Nevertheless, I bought a large, round, pink-and- white glazed pot to put it in, and one warm summer day I made the switch, also christening her with the name Chloe.

At first she looked fine in her new home. Then she began to look dull. I watered, worried, and watched. The thick green leaves began to look slack, then they turned brown. For a week or so, each time I walked by the plant I was painfully aware that she did not look good. About to abandon hope, one day on my way out the door, I stopped, touched the once-beautiful plant and said, "What do you need? I want you to live and be healthy again." Then I hurried off. A few days later she was turning green again and began to grow.

Eventually she filled the entire pot, and two years later it was obvious the new pot was now too small. This time I realized I would have to separate her into at least half-a-dozen other pots. I bought the pots, brought them home, got out the potting soil, and went to get Chloe. Unfortunately, she wouldn't come out of the pink and white pot. I pulled gently, then more forcefully, breaking one of her thick arms. Then I turned her and the pot upside down, shook everything, at first a little, then a lot. Nothing came out except dirt. Setting the pot back down and eyeing its shape, I realized it would have been better if the sides had flared out like a normal flower pot. Instead they curved in, firmly holding Chloe inside. If I wanted to get her out, I would have to break the pot or pull her out forcibly, risking severe damage to her roots and leaves. Not sure I was ready to hurt her, I ended up postponing the transplant and said to her, "Look, I need to get you out of this pot without breaking the pot or hurting you. So I would like to give you some time to get yourself ready. I'll check back with you in a few days, okay?"

The few days came and went, then a week went by, then two. One day I was walking through the entryway and heard a distinct voice say, "I'm ready!"

I looked around, realized it was Chloe, and stopped just long enough to say, "Not today, Chloe! I'm scheduled from now until seven tonight. I'll get back to you, though."

About two more weeks went by and still I put off the transplant. She called out to me again that she was ready but I was still too busy to stop running long enough. Another couple of weeks went by and one day we had a serious ice storm. The electricity went out and we had no heat, water, lights, or modern conveniences. I had been asked to be part of a video that was to be taped at the farm, and we still had no electricity the morning of the scheduled taping. When the power suddenly came back on two hours before the taping was supposed to begin, I ended up running around like a madwoman, filling the dishwasher, flushing toilets thankfully, and vacuuming wildly. When I went into the entryway to vacuum, I heard Chloe say once more, "I'm ready!"

"Oh no! Not today, Chloe. I've got company coming and definitely don't have time," I said as I sailed past her with the vacuum. But when the entryway was finished and I turned around to leave, there was Chloe standing on her head on the floor outside the pot, roots in the air, and dirt scattered everywhere over the carpet I had just vacuumed. I stared, disbelieving.

Finally, I caved. "Well, okaaaay, I guess it's going to be today, isn't it?" I said with a sigh of resignation, and by the time the video crew arrived, Chloe had been neatly divided into eight pots instead of the original six I'd planned for.

Other communication with other plants has been just as interesting and productive. While buying young fruit trees at the local Quality Farm and Fleet, I picked up a pear tree and then put it back when I saw a large diseased area on the main trunk. Immediately the little tree spoke up saying, "Please, please take me with you. I'll heal. I promise you. Please!" With misgivings I decided to buy it in spite of the disease. To my surprise it did heal, with absolutely no sprays or medications on my part.

A young peach tree that I had planted in what I thought was the wrong place insisted that she was in exactly the right spot, and has done beautifully in spite of my concerns. A flower garden that I insisted was in the right spot, even though the trees, the weeds, and the soil itself kept suggesting I find a different place, has refused to thrive.

While these may be some good solid, economic reasons for communicating with plants, other reasons are even more important. The most obvious has to do with healing. Every human being has a unique energy system. Every plant is unique as well. If you shy away from modern chemical medicines and depend mainly on herbs, it is well worth it to take the time to personally get to know the plants and herbs in your local area. This is valuable because one herb may have an affinity for your particular energy system, activating several healing mechanisms in your body, even though folklore and reference books indicate other plants as traditionally more important for your condition.

Plants in any given area are quite aware of the people who live among them. They are aware not only of your physical, mental, emotional, and spiritual condition, they are also quite sensitive to the kinds of external conditions you and they are subject to. This includes conditions such as local animals, birds, insects, wind, sun, rain, cold, soil types, and the millions of bacteria and fungi that share life in your area. Like humans, each plant has a purpose, a reason for being, and a gift to give. Like us, each member of the plant family hopes to be of service by offering a unique kind of help to those around it. Some offer food, some make good medicine, some provide wood for houses or tools, some renew soil, some are multitalented and offer several of these services for you as well as the local animals, birds, and insects.

Although it was customary in many older cultures to talk to plants in order to find out what that plant's personality was like, what gift it offered, and whether or not it was willing to be of service in a specific healing situation, very few of us take the time today to nurture a relationships with plants. It isn't difficult to talk to plants and hear their responses. It just isn't done very much any more.

If you would like to reestablish relationships with plants, whether out of curiosity, a love of old tradition, or a serious interest in healing, there are several ways to proceed and each works well. One way to start is to choose a plant that you are interested in, or that seems to be growing everywhere in your yard or locality. Try to choose a plant whose medicinal properties are not well known so you do not end up telling yourself, "Well, that's what I thought it would say anyway." For instance, do not choose echinacea or ginseng because these are too well-known.

Once you have picked out your plant, go outside and sit down near it. Quiet yourself as much as possible, then touch the plant and say a mental "Hello." Then introduce yourself by stating your full name, preferably using the format "I am (your name)." Tell the plant you would like to get to know plants better and to establish working relationships with them. Ask the plant if it would be willing to communicate with you, then pause. Sometimes you will hear in your mind's ear a clear "yes" or "no," and other times you may simply get a feeling of being welcome. At other times there will be no sense of an answer, but you'll feel compelled to go on with your communication. Surprisingly, the answer is seldom "no," but when it is, it is quite clear and uncomplicated. Usually this is because the plant is already aware that you have a special affinity for another plant in the area, and is anticipating your need by withdrawing so that you will reach out to the plant that is best suited to you.

You normally do not have to wait a long time for an answer from a plant. Usually it is responding almost as soon as you introduce yourself. When you feel you have opened communication with the plant, offer it a small gift. The customary gift is tobacco, which is considered to have a good balance of both male and female energies. If you do not have anything handy, at the very least offer it a hair from your head, which is full of your own personal energy, is symbolic of your thoughts, and shows your good will. Then ask the plant as clearly and simply as possible, "What kind of healing would you offer me?"

Following this, sit very still and quiet, listening in your head for the delicate communications that will be sent telepathically. Also notice any pictures that come to you and pay special attention to how your body feels. Everything you experience immediately after asking the plant about its healing abilities is neither accidental nor imaginary.

If you are too nervous or skeptical, you may not be able to relax enough to get the information you have asked for. In this case, you need to practice relaxing. If you get words, pictures, or feelings that are clear but don't make sense, then you need help interpreting what you have been given. Talking to someone who is skilled with either herbal medicine or intuitive information may help.

The things that I have found to be most potent in setting up relationships with plants are a notebook, and a sense that this will be a lifetime relationship, not just a quick thrill. When I want to get to know a plant, I take my notebook and a pen and go to sit by the plant. After a moment I say "Hello" and offer a small gift. Then I begin sketching the plant, noting the date so I know how the plant looks in that season. When I am done sketching, I tell the plant my name and state that I am interested in having a relationship with it. I ask if I may have permission to take several leaves with me for awhile, carrying them in my pocket, setting them on my dresser, or putting them next to me while I eat or sleep so the plant can get to know how I live. I promise to return the leaves and to honor the plant's presence at all times. If permission is given, I take the leaves, sometimes keeping them with me for months before I return them to the plant.

On my return, I either enhance my original sketch or make a new one if the plant looks very different because it is a new season. Then I ask the plant if it is still interested in having a relationship with me. If the answer is yes, I ask the plant what kinds of healing it offers me personally. Next, I inquire as to what kinds of healing it might offer to others besides myself. Finally, I ask what I can do for the plant. Usually the plant is quite happy with recognition or the relationship itself, but sometimes it will ask for something like water or food in the form of compost or another material. After finding out when the plant would most like to have the water or food, I try to provide it in a timely way.

After that the relationship is established and needs only to be respected and nurtured like any relationship. This is especially rewarding when you are working with vegetables, herbs, or fruits in your garden. If you have a vegetable garden, take the time when planting your seeds to make contact with the intelligence of each plant. This intelligence is sometimes referred to as a "deva," and she is responsible for the growth of the plant, its health, and potency. Taking a moment to send a message to the Carrot Deva, the Lavender Deva, or the Raspberry Deva and asking them to help your carrots develop into healthy food that will nourish you at all levels—physical, mental, emotional, and spiritual—will often result in vegetables that are superbly healthy, herbs that are extraordinarily potent, and fruits that are sweet.

Finally, be aware that taking time to establish connections with the intelligent energy that fills each plant has at least one or two more perks. You will often find that at least one of the plants from the group that you have made efforts to communicate with becomes more than a good friend, it becomes almost a blood brother with you, bringing you information, teaching you about other plants and sometimes where to find them. Quite often, if you don't have the kind of plant handy that you need for a specific kind of healing, you can ask your blood brother plant for help and discover that miracles can take place as it alters its own energy to perform the requested healing.

Communicating with plants is something that you can easily learn, and for anyone interested in growing things, or in healing, it would seem to be one of those skills that is not only useful, but enlightening in its own right. For the deeper you travel into nature, the more you find yourself.

The Plant Familiar

≈ By Raven Grimassi ≈

Many people are accustomed to the concept of the Witches' familiar spirit. Most people think of this in terms of an animal or spirit companion. In this article I will present an older form of the familiar, that which dwells as the spirit within a plant. Since ancient times, the belief in a "mana" or "numen" spirit has been widespread. It is this indwelling consciousness that gives a plant its occult powers and properties.

The purpose of the following technique is to raise or grow a plant as a "familiar spirit" or a magical plant for spellworking. In ancient times, a circle of small stones was set around the chosen plant to "bind" the numen spirit there. Then a hole was dug toward the roots (being careful not to damage them) and a chosen power stone was set in place to "charge" the plant with the intent of one's magic.

Over the passing of the centuries the method has evolved somewhat. Today it is a bit different, but equally as effective. You can begin with a seed or young sprout/plant. Prepare the soil for planting in a secluded area, one that is appropriate for the needs of the plant. Take the stone or crystal that you have selected to fit your purposes, and place it three inches deep in the soil.

Fill in the soil over the crystal and plant the seed (or plant) as is appropriate. Lay a circle of eight marking stones around the plant site. At each of the four quarters (of the stone circle) place a crystal or stone of the same type you buried in the soil. The other four stones may be of the same type, or may be assorted. If you have selected stones or crystals possessing occult powers make sure that they are harmonious in nature to one another. The spacing of the stones is determined by the physical needs of the plant, so allow for the growth of the plant.

Method One

If you planted a seed, wait seven days after the sprout appears to proceed with the following. If you used a young plant, wait seven days after planting. Remove the stones between the quarter stones and plant a seed at each point. Next bury the quarter stones where they lay, at least an inch deep. The seeds may be of the same type as the plant within the circle, or an assortment of plants.

Each day, for seven days, place both palms on the ground within the circle, forming a triangle with your fingertips (index fingers and thumbs touching). The stem of the plant, or the buried seed, will be in the open center of the triangle. Using you imagination and visualization, sense your power flowing out through your arms and into the soil. The "source" of the power can begin from one (or more) of your personal power centers, or you may employ personal techniques for drawing/raising power.

It is important to talk to the plant and send it visual images. Communicate your needs and desires to the plant through mental pictures. This is the foundation stage, and it is vital that you "inform" the indwelling spirit with the intent of your magical charge. This will align the entity and create a rapport between you and the plant. It is in this stage that both you and the plant become familiar to one another.

As the plant grows, you must take good care of it. This is essential to the relationship you are forming. Learn as much as possible about the needs of the plant. Water and fertilize it as is suited to its natural environment. Check it daily for insects and protect it from damage of any kind. For a deeply intimate connection with the plant's spirit you can create a strong bond by adding three drops of your blood to a quart of water, using this water for your plant during its routine care.

On a magical level, what you have accomplished through these techniques is as follows. First you've amplified the power level of the spirit numen or mana through placement of the stones or crystals. Secondly, you have extended its power and influence to the other plants around it. This is because the seeds within the ring became alive under the emanating influence of the center crystal/stone and the plant. They were bathed in the cross-quarter current of energy, controlled from the center entities, through the quarter crystals you placed.

Whenever you need to use the leaves, flowers, or roots of the plant for spells or potions, use only the circle plants (never the center plant). The center plant is the familiar. The other plants are simply extensions of its power. This is the principle of contagion magic. Whatever is in close proximity with another thing, or mixed with something else, takes on some of the neighboring power. This is also one of the reasons for employing stones or crystals in creating a plant familiar.

The final step in creating this plant familiar is to establish your link and strengthen your rapport. To do this you must sit comfortably in front of the plant at the north quarter facing south. In the Old Religion, north is the place of divine power and the south is the realm of the astral forces. Sitting in this position makes you the bridge between these worlds, from which you can direct the flow of energy.

Stare comfortably at the plant and then allow your vision to slightly blur. In this state observe the general shape of the plant. Do not force or rush the process. Try to leave your mind blank and receptive. Eventually the plant will transmit an image to you mentally as you gaze at it. You will receive this "formed thought" as a physical distortion of the plant. Its shape will shift and transform so that it begins to resemble something else. It may appear as an animal, insect, or some other creature.

Whatever shape is revealed to you will be the familiar spirit, the magical bond between you and the consciousness of the plant. The familiar will give you extra power in any magical work whenever you summon it. House plants can become protective entities for your home through this technique. Plants given as gifts can be very useful for magical purposes as well. You can harvest the leaves and flowers of the circle plants and make magical sachets for friends and loved ones.

To summon your familiar, simply imagine your plant in its setting and visualize it becoming the transmitted image of the spirit familiar originally revealed to you. Mentally draw it to you and allow it to merge within your thoughts. Do this by picturing it moving to you in the way the creature would animate itself in nature. Choose a "word of calling" or a "beckoning gesture" to accompany the summoning visualization. Then mentally receive the creature into your body and spirit through your forehead. Experience the entity form, imagining that you are that creature. See yourself as the entity form, be the form, and act like the form. This is how it becomes a familiar spirit. Once you can perform this successfully, then you truly possess a familiar spirit.

Method Two

On the night of the New Moon, place a seed or a plant over a buried crystal or personal power stone. Each day, after sunset, focus your power through your hands as you did in method one. Your source of power must be evoked and focused before you begin. To do this, perform the following: Sit comfortably in front of the plant, at the west quarter facing east. Close your eyes and visualize the Full Moon above you. Using imagery, mentally draw the Moon down until it sits just above your head. Next, visualize its light glowing brightly. Then mentally move the Moon down to your stomach area, seeing it glide softly downward through your body. Once the Moon is resting just below the navel, visualize it expanding outward until it encloses you totally in a sphere of light. The image would be similar to sitting inside a glowing white balloon.

At this point, begin to pour the light out through your hands into the soil, as though your arms are hoses. You may drain the light out completely if you wish, or simply a portion of it, releasing the rest back into the air. In any case you must rid your body of the gathered power. Then begin to send your visual communications to the plant, establishing what is desired of the familiar spirit. This method works extremely well for the formation of magical plants in general.

Create an "image play" for the plant, mentally transmitting images of how you will use the plant familiar. This is very much like daydreaming, so feel free to indulge yourself. Picture the successful outcome of the spell, potion, or work of magic, and transmit this to the plant. Include the summoning of the familiar, and picture the intended work of the familiar in your visual communication. As in method one, you must take good care of the plant. Add other plants to the stone circle for this method also.

On the night before the Moon is Full, perform the following: Set out an open jar beneath the Moon, containing the water you are using for the plant. If possible, use a green glass jar or a green filter over the jar. Leave this out for the night and be sure to remove it before sunrise. On the night of the Full Moon, pour this water out over the plant. Then take some white flour and sprinkle it in a waxing crescent shape on the soil. The plant will occupy the inner center of the crescent. The stones of the circle surround the crescent image. If you desire, you can set a crystal at each tip of the crescent to enhance the power focused on the plant. This technique will make the chemical properties of the plant more potent, increasing its magical potential as well. Being attuned to lunar energy in this way allows the plant to work well within the astral and subconscious spheres of influence.

Working With the Plant Familiar

In method one you were shown the technique for summoning the familiar. Now we will look at some techniques for using the familiar in the Witches' craft.

Incense

For powdered or herbal bulk incense, summon the familiar and send it to rest on the material. Mentally see it move across the surface, occasionally digging down into the material and then reappearing through the surface. Visualize the material beginning to glow with the symbolic color of the desired magical effect (see chart below) until it seems fully charged. Then recall the familiar and return it to the plant. Color correspondences for incenses are:

BLUE: peace, contemplation, and spirituality.

RED: passion, motivation, lust, vigor, and vitality.

GREEN: growth, healing, balance, abundance, and love.

YELLOW: mental activity, excitement, and stimulation.

PINK: friendship, relationships, and forgiveness.

PURPLE: magical energy, unseen forces, and decisiveness.

BLACK: absorbing, compelling, binding, and disintegrating.

BROWN: grounding and solidifying.

GRAY: neutralizing, discerning, and disenchanting.

SILVER: enchanting, enhancing, blending, and changing.

GOLD: success, victory, enrichment, and purifying.

Potions

Set the potion before you and summon the spirit familiar. After you have successfully linked, mentally project the familiar out into the potion. See it enter the potion, swimming and diving within the liquid. As it performs these acts, see the liquid begin to glow with a color that corresponds to the desired magical effect. Through such visualizations you help the familiar impart its magical energy to material objects.

Amulets and Talismans

Summon the familiar and project it onto the amulet or talisman. Visualize it grasping the edges and see it glowing with the symbolic color of the desired effect. Mentally picture the familiar being absorbed into the object, and then have it reform, still grasping the item. Carry the amulet or talisman with the familiar attached to it. However, be sure to return the familiar to the plant within two days. The spirit needs to revitalize itself within the living plant. A spirit needs a physical form in order to remain within the material world.

Mental Influence

Familiars can be used to influence the thoughts and emotions of other people. Through your familiar you can lend someone else some creativity, inspiration, motivation, or whatever. Normally, this is most effective when the person is asleep or under the influence of a drug, as in the case of major surgery. Even when the person is fully conscious this method can still be effective.

Summon your familiar and project it into the mind of the person desired. See it "perched" upon the crown of the head, then mentally see it enter through the forehead, the "third eye" power center. Leave it within the person's mind while they sleep (or for several hours if the person is conscious) and then recall it, returning it to the plant. As always, you must instruct the familiar mentally (or verbally) as to what it is to accomplish, and you must direct it through imagery during the work.

Healing

Summon the plant familiar and project it into the body of the person concerned. Visualize it being the same size as the patient and see it merge with his or her physical body. Mentally see the patient glowing with the symbolic color of the desired effect. If a specific area of the body is concerned, then focus the familiar there and mentally reduce its size so that it is compatible with the area requiring healing. See it move in and out, removing and discarding the illness. This can be visualized as bits of dark material or whatever may seem appropriate. Intensify the magical color in this area for the healing. Finally, recall the familiar and return it to the plant.

Plant and Herbal Correspondences

BINDING: holly, ivy, mullein, shepherd's purse, and solomon's seal.

BLESSING: acacia, hyssop, orris, pennyroyal, and rosemary.

MAGICAL DEFENSE: basil, clove, dragon's blood reed, fennel, garlic, nettle, peppers, rue, thistle, vetivert, and wormwood.

PURIFICATION: angelica, bay, centaury, eyebright, lovage, mint, myrrh, pennyroyal, rue, sage, St. John's wort, and vervain.

RELATIONSHIPS: columbine, cowslip, daisy, dittany of crete, feverfew, lady's mantle, periwinkle, primrose, thyme, vervain, and yarrow.

PSYCHIC NATURE: camomile, cinquefoil, heliotrope, jasmine, and rosemary.

DIVINATION: camphor, goldenrod, ivy, mugwort, orris, and wormwood.

PERSONAL POWER: carnation, dittany of crete, gentian, ginger, pennyroyal, and solomon's seal.

HEALING: cinnamon, gardenia, garlic, goldenseal, and vervain.

Smudge 101

≈ By Bernyce Barlow ≈

S mudging is an age-old tradition using the smoke of herbs to purify the aura of the body or a space. It is believed by some cultures that evil spirits are chased away by the smoke of specific herbs. Other cultures feel smoke from sacred herbs is a sign to spirit that prayers are being spoken.

Smudging can be done several different ways. A smudge stick is often used, as are abalone shells filled with burning herbs. I have seen coffee cans with holes punched into the bottom and a makeshift wire handle. These are filled with smoking cedar or dried angelica (which pops and sparkles)—a poor man's smudge burner! On a larger scale, I have seen ceremonial fire tenders smudge entire groups of people using large amounts of herbs for the occasion.

Smudge smoke is usually distributed by fanning. Feathers, fans, or

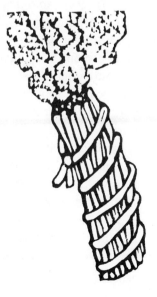

appropriate leaves can all be used to wave the smoke in the direction you want it to go. There is no wrong way to smudge unless it is unsafe.

To make a smudge stick, choose an herb that is known for its purifying or medicinal properties, like sage, mugwort, sweetgrass, or lavender. In the early morning, harvest the tops of the plants just before they flower or go to seed. If you are selecting a loose smudge ingredient such as cedar or juniper, morning is again the best time to harvest. An ideal smudge stick is about two to three inches in diameter and approximately eight inches long, so make your cuttings an inch or two longer if possible, just in case your smudge stick needs grooming. When you have enough herbs, align the tops and bottoms and shape them into a loose bundle that looks like a fat cigar. Secure the bundle by winding a piece of yarn or wet willow bark around it like a candy cane stripe, and set it aside for a few days to dry. If you wrap the bundle too tightly the center will not dry, possibly causing mold. If the yarn is too loose after the bundle dries, rewrap it. Thank the plant for its sacrifice and Spirit for the plant's creation.

After your smudge stick has dried, it is ready to burn. Light one end and hold the other like a sparkler. You may have to blow on it to get it smoking. Once the smudge stick has caught fire and is producing smoke (not flames), bathe your body in the smoke just as you were taking a shower. Wave the smoke over all parts of your body, including the bottoms of your feet. Breathe the smoke lightly and take small amounts into your lungs. You do not have to inhale the smudge through any other way than natural breathing. Cleanse each chakra, then consider yourself purified! When you are done with your smudge stick extinguish it by blotting it out on an appropriate surface, or leave it in an abalone shell or some other fireproof container to burn out on its own. You can trim the burnt end of the smudge stick if you wish to tidy it up after use.

Loose smudge is often placed in abalone shells or containers like the above-mentioned coffee can. There are also fancy incense and smudge burners that you can buy at stores. Often these are made of brass and have a handle or chain that comes in handy during the smudge process. Sometimes treated charcoal rounds are put at the bottom of the container holding the loose smudge to keep it burning as fresh herbs are added. Dried needle boughs and leaf clusters from cedar, pine, juniper, sage, sagebrush, spruce, and angelica work well as loose smudge, as does lavender and certain blends of resins like pinion pine, dragon's blood, or amber. By the way, angelica pops and cedar can irritate the lungs and skin, so go easy on these two herbs, especially if you are smudging an enclosed area like a sweat lodge or small room.

Some folks want to get creative and use all kinds of plants for smudging, such as eucalyptus, lemongrass, or bay laurel leaves. Like cedar, these plants can be irritating to mucus membranes when profusely burned, so before you get too creative check out the properties of the plants you are using in your smudge. If you are smudging with cedar inside a damp sweat lodge, make sure to rinse off between rounds as the cedar smoke/oil can cause an itchy rash to break out when exposed to sunlight.

Personally, I burn sweetgrass, mugwort, lavender, amber, or sage for smudging. Traditionally in North America, sage, sagebrush, and mugwort have been used in smudge for centuries. Medically speaking, these plants have either an antiseptic or antihistamine constituent in them. Some have both. In the Southwest, ranchers sometimes give their livestock sage tea to dry up mothers in milk. The histamine property of sage is not the only medicine that the plant possesses. It is also an antiseptic. No wonder sage smoke is thought of as a cleansing essence! Sage smoke is not harsh. Its aroma is like a sweet wood spice, almost addicting at times. It's a heady, endearing scent that settles heavy on the senses.

A good smudging can leave you feeling as if an invisible field of protection has been placed around you. Some folks feel ceremonially purified after an herbal smudging, and for good reason. Herbal smoke has been a part of all our tribal cultures.

The smoke helps us to connect on a spiritual level that which we are seeking within ourselves. Smudging also has physical benefits that compliment a smoky spiritual cleansing. It appears just on their own, the histamine and antiseptic properties of various sage plants are worth lighting up over, ceremony or no ceremony.

So, next time you are feeling like you need a good smudging, go ahead, light up, and start fanning. You might find the smoke bath an unique way to cleanse any unwanted energy from your body as well as a very earthy aromatherapy treatment. While you are at it, say a prayer or a positive afirmation or two because it is taught smudge smoke is a signal that prayers are being said, and indeed, Spirit will come where there is sacred smoke. Author's note: When smudging animals take special care not to drop ashes or burning bits of stem on their fur. Do not smudge birds or fish.

Mitakuye Oyas'in, all my relations.

Bold, Beautiful Borage

By Elizabeth Barrette

History

The cultivation of this useful and attractive plant dates back hundreds of years. Its names hint at its properties: Pliny, a famous Roman scholar, called it *euphrosinum;* the Welsh *llanwenlys* translates to "herb of gladness," and another Celtic name, *borrach,* means "courage." Both Roman and Celtic warriors relied on borage for assistance in battle. Later on, women floated borage flowers in the cup traditionally given to a crusader upon departure. This herb also appears in many medieval manuscripts. Look for it in old herbals, if you collect such things.

Habits

Borage stands erect on thick, hollow stems and grows two to three feet high. Prickly hairs cover both the stems and its large, wrinkled leaves. These leaves, oval in shape, form a basal rosette and

then alternate on the stalks. Another common name for borage, beeflower, hints at this plant's powerful attraction to bees. Honeybees in particular love the sky-blue, star-shaped blossoms, which appear around Midsummer. Each flower bud opens to reveal five-pointed petals, and they appear in droopy clusters at the end of the stems. These blooms mature to produce large, brownish-black seeds with three sides. The seeds can remain viable for as long as eight years; for best results, collect them carefully and store in a cool, dry place. (Moisture and heat cause seeds to mold or sprout prematurely and die.) The native habitat spans Europe, Asia Minor, and Africa. Due to its popularity, people raise borage widely in North America as well. In the wild, borage grows in wastelands and ravaged places. You can often find it alongside country roads or in abandoned lots.

Cultivation

Borage grows best when sown directly from seed instead of transplanting. It likes bright sunshine and open air, with soil around pH 6.6. In companion planting, this amiable herb combines well with almost anything, but strawberries and borage are mutually beneficial. It also blends perfectly with roses. Although technically an annual because it dies back every winter, borage reseeds itself so vigorously that its role in the landscape more closely resembles that of a perennial.

To grow borage as a container plant, give it a large pot of medium depth and broad mouth; make sure this container provides adequate drainage. Blend a potting mix of sand, vermiculite, and manure compost to give this herb the rich but light soil it prefers. Press the seeds gently into the soil after danger of frost has passed. Keep moist. Thin the seedlings to stand about two feet apart. Borage tends to ramble if not trimmed, so give it room to sprawl. You can take the pot indoors during the winter, too; stagger plantings for year-round flowers. Another trick: use pots of borage to bring the bees to other flowering plants in your garden or orchard.

Medicinal Properties

Herbalists today rely on borage for a wide range of purposes. Externally, a poultice of the leaves can soothe bruises and inflammation; their emollient properties also make the leaves popular in face packs to treat dry skin. The dark, lozenge-like seeds yield an oil useful against such complaints as irritable bowel syndrome and menstrual complaints. Some herbalists recommend it for eczema, arthritis, and even hangovers as well.

Magical Applications

Borage has an ancient reputation for bolstering courage, lifting spirits, and enhancing psychic abilities. Modern science suggests that the first of these may come from the plant's high potassium content, since potassium can stimulate the adrenal gland. Historically, people invoked this power by drinking wine flavored with borage, but you can get similar results by simply wearing or carrying the flowers. According to folklore, women would sneak borage into the beverage of a potential husband, in hopes of giving him the courage to propose marriage! The euphoric effects prove harder to explain, but some herbalists still recommend borage to fight depression. For this you may wear the flowers; it is certainly worth exploring as a magical application. Because of the affinity bees have toward borage flowers, I also find it useful for communicating with them and other beneficial insects.

Courage Charm

Walking around with a dried flower or leaf loose in your pocket can get a bit messy, so consider this alternative. I often make herbal charms by enclosing a bit of the plant in decorated embroidery cloth.

- 2   pieces of Aida cloth, 1 blue and 1 green
- 1   piece of tissue
- 2   skeins of embroidery floss, one blue and one green

Silver blending filament

9   dried borage flowers

Pinch of dried borage leaves.

I find Aida cloth ideal for encasing charms because its regular weave makes it easy to get the cutting and stitching even; plus, it is 100 percent cotton and comes in all colors. The tissue serves as a lining and keeps the herb from sifting out through the holes; for this purpose you could also use a bit of unbleached coffee filter or a teabag. The colors blue and green echo the powers of borage. Light blue offers clarity of mind, calm, and healing; fresh green increases ambition and helps you meet challenges, yet also supports the healing theme of blue while adding a grounding note of its own. The silver blending filament brings light to the embroidered symbols, enhancing their power. While you collect your supplies, repeat this verse to yourself:

Blue-starred borage, your embrace
Grants me courage, joy, and grace.

First gather all your supplies together. Cut out two 1½-inch by 2-inch rectangles of Aida cloth, one each of blue and green. Next, cut two pieces of embroidery floss, one blue and one green, of a comfortable sewing length. Split each piece in half (embroidery floss has six strands) and combine one blue half with one green half, so that you have three strands of each blended together into one piece. Thread your embroidery needle with the blue-and-green floss. Now put the rectangles of Aida cloth together and match up the edges; sew up the two long sides and one short side to make a little pouch, leaving abouta quarter inch of the side seams undone at the top so you can fold the top edges in later. For this I use a cross-stitch, which makes a very strong seam. After you finish these seams, turn the pouch right-side-out. Use the eraser end of a pencil to push the corners all the way square.

To decorate your pouch, thread your needle with three strands of green floss and one strand of silver blending thread. Use this to embroider a symbol of clarity (such as the ogham

Nion for ash, or the rune Ansuz) on the blue side of the pouch. Then rethread your needle with three strands of blue floss and one of silver. Use this to embroider a symbol of confidence (such as the ogham Ailm for silver fir, or the rune Sowelo) on the green side of the pouch. Set the pouch aside for a minute.

Now spread out the tissue and place your borage in the center. Take a little while to meditate on your purpose. Focus your mind on thoughts of courage, happiness, and clear vision. Imagine yourself taking bold action, with a smile on your face. Then carefully fold up all the edges to wrap the herb securely: start by folding the top edge toward you, then turn the tissue a quarter to the right and fold the new top toward you, repeating the process until you have a neat packet. Slip this inside the pouch.

At this point, you have several options. If you want to carry your pouch, you can proceed directly to closing the top. If you want to hang it, you will need to make a short braid; and if you want to wear it, you will need to make a long braid. For a hanging loop, cut two six-inch pieces of embroidery floss, one blue and one green; for a wearing loop, cut two thirty-six-inch pieces. Separate each piece into three sets of two strands; then combine pairs of blue with pairs of green so that you have three pieces of blue-and-green floss, each with four strands. Knot these at one end and braid them, then knot the other end.

To close the top, thread your needle with three blue and three green strands—for this I usually use leftovers from an earlier step. (If you need to cut more floss, you only need a little.) If you have a braid, place the knots inside the mouth of the pouch about a quarter inch down the left and right side seams. Fold the rest of the braid outside of the pouch where it won't get in your way. Now fold the top edges down inside the pouch and press the mouth closed, making sure to trap the knots inside if you have a braid. Hold the pouch closed and sew across the top. I use a simple whip-stitch which is just a spiral: in one side, out the other, over the top, and back in on the first side. Afterwards, use your fingers to plump the pouch into a nice even shape.

Your finished charm will measure about one and a quarter inch by one and three quarters inch, which is just the right size to hide in the palm of your hand or tuck in your pocket. Wear or carry it to job interviews, dates, tests, important meetings—anywhere you need a boost of confidence and clarity. Alternatively, hang the charm in your bedroom or keep it on your altar.

Altogether, its many virtues make borage a wonderful plant to have around, and it deserves a place in any herb garden. Working with it can teach you some exciting things. To learn more about borage, look it up in a good guide to plants, or ask a qualified herbalist. With this herb on your side, you can accomplish almost anything you set your mind to do!

References

Bremness, Leslie. *The Complete Book of Herbs*. New York: Penguin Books, 1988.

Bremness, Leslie. *Herbs: The Visual Guide to More Than 700 Herb Species from Around the World*. New York: DK Publishing, Inc. 1994.

Cunningham, Scott. *Cunningham's Encyclopedia of Magical Herbs*. St. Paul, MN: Llewellyn Publications, 1991.

Kowalchik, Claire and William Hylton, editors. *Rodale's Illustrated Encyclopedia of Herbs*. Emmaus, PA: Rodale Press, 1987.

Nicholas Culpeper, Renegade Herbalist

⪼ By Susan Wittig Albert, Ph.D. ⪻

O f all the herbalists of the last five hundred years, Nicholas Culpeper is still probably the most infamous. Reviled in his lifetime by the powerful Royal College of Physicians for daring to translate their learned *Pharmacopoea* from Latin into English, and villified after his death for his "superstitious" blend of astrology and herbalism, his name is almost synonymous today with the idea of folk superstition and quasi-magical beliefs in astrological botany.

Yet we owe a very great debt to this renegade herbalist who made—for his own time and for all time—an extraordinarily valuable and courageous contribution to the history and lore of herbs and astrological herbalism, a fascinating tradition of orally transmitted superstitions and folk uses of plant medicines that dates back through the Middle Ages and into the time of

classical antiquity. Much of this oral lore belonged to "Witches," the wise ones of the villages who understood the ancient healing uses of plants and passed on these teachings to others, whom they trained to recognize and use local plants. From the beginnings of organized medicine in Europe and Great Britain, these healers (most of them women) were actively persecuted by physicians, surgeons, and the Church, who accused them of witchcraft if they used their healing knowledge to treat others and made strenuous efforts to eradicate the traditional knowledge of plant medicines. This wasn't difficult to do, of course—when the witches were eradicated, their knowledge was lost with them, for most could neither read nor write and thus could leave no record of the plants they used. Nicholas Culpeper was born and died at a time when it was dangerous to possess and share the knowledge of green medicine and beliefs in astrological herbalism that were held by the village wise women.[1] It is to him, however, that we owe much of our understanding of the details of these traditional practices, particularly those that relied on the astrological relationships of herbs. If it had not been for his systematic documentation and preservation of this knowledge, the information would almost certainly have been lost, and that would have been a very great loss indeed.

Nicholas Culpeper was born in 1616, in Surrey, England. The Culpepers were an aristocratic family whose history went back to the time of King John and who owned a great deal of property in the south of England. Nicholas' father, a clergyman, died thirteen days before his son's birth. Nicholas' mother took the boy to live near her family, where he was much influenced by his grandfather, also a clergyman, who taught him Greek and Latin. Nicholas, whose family intended him for the Church, was sent off to Cambridge, where he distinguished himself in classics and was recognized as a brilliant scholar with a great deal of promise. He was something of a young man about town, however, and within the year he had squandered his father's legacy and fallen passionately in love with a rich young woman. The pair planned to meet at Lewes for a clandestine marriage, but on the way to the wedding, her coach was struck by lightning and she was killed.

This tragedy was a life-changing event for the nineteen-year-old Culpeper, who seems to have been an impulsive man, driven by his passions and his need for personal independence. He abruptly left Cambridge, abandoned all plans of entering the Church, and gave up the inheritance his grandfather would have left to him if he had behaved himself. Instead, he devoted his life to providing medicines and medical advice to the poor of London, apprenticing himself to a Bishopgate apothecary and beginning a serious study of herbal medicines and of astrology. In 1640, he married a fifteen-year-old girl named Alice Field and used her small fortune to set up his own apothecary practice in Red Lion Street, Spitalfields, in London's East End.[2] There, he ministered to the poor, treating them with herbal medications and continuing to collect and record as much as he could about the uses of medicinal plants that were native to England. He undoubtedly got a great deal of this information from the "herb women" who gathered local herbs and sold them to the London apothecaries, who in turn used the plants to fill the prescriptions set down by physicians in the *London Pharmacopoeia*, the "secret handbook" of medical recipes. During the English Civil War (in the early 1640s), he sided with Cromwell and the Puritans against the forces of the Crown—yet another renegade act for this aristocrat-turned-apothecary. During this time, too, he was accused of witchcraft. While details are sparse, we can surmise that this occurred at least in part because of his great fascination for the lore and traditions of local herbs and because of his traffic in herbs with the village wise women.

Culpeper had apparently always had difficulty in holding his tongue, and in 1649 his plainspokenness got him into even deeper trouble. In this year, the unorthodox pharmicist enraged the entire London medical establishment by translating the Latin *London Pharmacopoeia* into English and publishing it as *The*

London Dispensatory. His motives: to expose the secret practices of the exclusive guild of physicians and to make herbal medicines available to people who were unable to pay the exorbitant physicians' fees. Undaunted by the physicians' ire, he went on to publish the first English textbook on midwifery and childcare, *The English Midwife* (1651), which emphasized nutrition and cleanliness and offered a variety of herbal remedies for common problems of pregnancy and childbirth. Also in that year, he published a diagnostic manual entitled *Judgement of Disease*, and in 1652, brought out his famous herbal, *The English Physician*, an easy-to-use manual designed to teach ordinary people how to find and use commonly-available herbal medicines. Nicholas Culpeper died in 1654 (apparently of tuberculosis), at the age of 38, but his wife Alice, whom he had tutored in the art of herbal medicine, continued to publish his books. *The English Physician* became enduringly popular. It was the first medical text printed in North America and has appeared in over a hundred editions in the 350 years since its publication.

When we glance through *Culpeper's Dispensatory* (which is contained in the facsimile of the 1814 edition[3]) it isn't difficult to see why the College of Physicians was so enraged by his open publication of their tightly held secrets. More than that, though, they were afraid of him, with very good reason. Nicholas Culpeper was smart, outspoken, and self-assured, ready to take on the medical establishment and to point out that the emperor had no clothes. He was vehement in his rejection of the expensive imported exotic plants that the College preferred, pointing out that there were plenty of herbs free for the picking in field and heath that would do just as well. But he went even further, listing, in plain English, the "pharmaceuticals" that the surgeons required apothecaries to stock in their shops. These included such unhelpful products as the fat of a beaver, stork, hedgehog, or lion; thirteen kinds of dung, including dog and sheep dung; the brain of a sparrow, the heart of a stag, the horn of a unicorn, the skull of a man killed by a violent death, fox lungs, and the testicles of a horse. It isn't hard to imagine the disgust people must have felt when they read such nonsense.

In his translation, Culpeper also includes the detailed prescriptions and provides an explanation of the ailments they are designed to treat, which the College had intentionally omitted in order to keep apothecaries from making unauthorized use of the medications. Often, instead of an explanation, he provides a sarcastic remark. For example, at the end of one prescription, which includes three pounds of earthworms, two gallons of snails, powdered hart's horn, and powdered ivory (among other ingredients), he adds tersely: "Tis a mess altogether." Commenting on a prescription for "Tincture of Strawberries" that takes twelve days to prepare, he says, "A fine thing for Gentlemen that have nothing else to do with their money." About a recipe for "Syrup of Agnus Castus," he remarks wryly, "A pretty Syrup, and good for little." About "Neopolitan Ointment," he says, "Hundreds are bound to curse such ointments and those that appoint them." In fact, once translated from their mystifying Latin into English, many of the College's prescription medicines seemed very much like Witches' brews!

But it was Culpeper who was said to be a Witch. The accusation must have easy to make, given his first-hand knowledge of plants that were used by the rural folk of England and his great interest in astrology, especially in medical astrology. Astrology is an ancient belief system, of course, going back to the dawn of civilization, and the fundamental precept of medical-botanical astrology—that certain parts of the body are ruled by certain planets, which correspondingly rule the plants that provide relief for diseases of these body parts—had long been accepted as a basis for medical practice. By Culpeper's day, the ideas of astrology were being replaced by the new science of astronomy, and the "old medicine" was being reinterpreted through a more scientific understanding of physical anatomy, the circulation of blood, and the nature of infectious disease. Culpeper's astrological explanations of the various uses of plants made him an easy target for his bitter enemies among the College of Physicians, who attempted to make him appear dangerous on the one hand (accusing him of witchcraft) and ludicrous on the other (calling him a superstitious fool, a "frowsy-headed coxcomb," an ignorant quack). As time went on, the astrological material that underpins his presentation of the healing herbs made Culpeper seem out-of-date and old-fashioned, and he was more and more often considered an herbal charlatan whose work smacked of witchcraft. Eleanour Sinclair Rohde, who studied old herbals, calls his *English Physician* an "absurd book," and describes Culpeper as "an old rogue standing at the street comer," haranguing the crowd about herbs and astrology.[4] Others deride his use of herbal astrology as "ridiculous old wives' tales" and "arrant and outlandish nonsense."

But it is exactly Culpeper's extensive documentation of these "outlandish" astrological beliefs that makes his work so fascinating to us today. To his valuable reports of the various folk uses of native plants, many of them previously unreported, Culpeper added what he had teamed from his studies of medical astrology (the relationship between the planets and the human body), combined with astrological botany (the relationship between the planets and plants). There was nothing new in this combination, of course—the idea that all created life was governed by the stars was a long-held philosophy. What is new in Culpeper's work, though, and what sets him apart from other herbalists, is his application of these principles to plant medicines widely available in the England of his day and his insistence on writing for common people who would put his instructions to immediate and practical use.

Culpeper's ideas about medical and herbal astrology are fairly clearly defined and in line with the beliefs of earlier physicians who shared this philosophy—Hippocrates, Galen, and Paracelsus, among many others. It had long been held that the human body exhibits four humors, each related to one of the four elements: choleric (fire), phlegmatic (water), sanguine (air), and melancholic (earth). In medical astrology, these humors and elements are ruled by planets, as are all body parts, all physiological processes, all diseases, and all medicinal plants. In most works of medical astrology, plants governed by an opposing planet or planets were recommended to treat the diseased part. Culpeper was convinced, however, that the use of "opposites" was only one way to treat a disease. Some ailments, he said, should be treated by "sympathy"—that is, by selecting medicinal plants ruled by the same planet that governed the diseased part. In his discussion of the herb dodder (which is ruled by Saturn) he writes:

> Sympathy and Antipathy, are the two Hinges upon which the whol Moddel of Physick sums, and that Physitian which minds them not is like a Door off from the Hooks, more likely to do a man a mischief than to secure him: then all the Diseases Saturn causeth, this [dodder] helps by Sympathy, and strengthens al the parts of the Body he rules, such as caused by Sol it helps by Antipathy, what those diseases are see my Judgment of Diseases by Astrology...[5]

This approach gave Culpeper a great deal of flexibility in prescribing herbal medicines and required more "art" on the part of the herbalists who copied his methods. It probably also increased the chances for success because the more plants an herbalist might choose from, the more likely it was that one of them might have some effect. Culpeper made it easy for others to follow him in the practice of medical-botanical astrology by publishing two definitive handbooks. In *Judgment of Disease* (1651), he specified which planet or planets governed different parts of the body and different diseases. In his *English Physician* (1652), he catalogued all the English herbs known to him, specified their planetary associations, and described their uses in treating various diseases. Using these companion volumes, it would have been a relatively easy matter for any reader to determine which planet was "responsible" for the disease, and then to choose the applicable herbal remedies—remedies that would have been readily available in the gardens, fields, and forests of England, rather than imported from some faraway place and compounded with a variety of unsavory ingredients by apothecaries who knew next to nothing about what they were doing.

In *The English Physician*, each herb is annotated with a physical description, an indication of where the plant grows and when it is in season, and an extended comment on its various uses (its "virtues"). By telling his readers where the plant may be found (wall rue, for example, "grows at Dartford, and the bridge at Ashford in Kent, at Beaconsfield in Buckinghamshire..."), Culpeper made it easy for them to locate and harvest it, as well as prepare it for use. In his introduction, Culpeper gives a full example of his method, using the herb blessed thistle:

> The Herb is Carduns Benedictus, or blessed Thistle or holy Thistle...It is an Herb of Mars, and under the Sign Aries; now in handling this Herb, I shall give you a rational Pattern of all the rest, and if you please to view them throughout the Book, you shall to your content find it true.
>
> It helps Swimming and giddiness of the Head, or the Disease called Vertigo, because Aries is the House of Mars.
>
> It is an excellent Remedy against the yellow Jaundice, and other infirmities of the Gall, because Mars governs Choller.
>
> It strengthens the attractive faculty in man, and clarifies the Blood, because the one is ruled by Mars.
>
> The continual drinking the Decoction of it helps red Faces, Tetters, and Ringworms because Mars causeth them.
>
> It helps Plague sore, Boils and Itch, the Biting of mad Dogs and venemous Beasts, all which infirmities are under Mars. Thus you see what it cloth by Sympathy...

He goes on to list several applications "by antypathy." In opposition to Venus, it cures the French pox; to Saturn, it cures deafness and melancholy. Once the astrological rulerships and relationships are learned (and Culpeper's audience would certainly have been familiar with them), the logic behind the applications of various herbs is not difficult to understand. In fact, it often seems that what Culpeper is really searching for in his work is the *why* of herbal medicine: "If you please to make use of these Rules," he says in his introduction, "you may be able to give a Reason of your Judgment to him that asketh you." The astrological model is certainly mnemonic, if nothing else, and must have made it easier to remember which herbs were associated with which parts of the body. Sometimes, too, I suspect that Culpeper is writing with his tongue firmly in his cheek, making fun of the astrological connections even as he uses them:

> Wormwood is an herb of Mars . . . I prove it thus: What delights in martial places, is a martial herb; Wormwood delights in martial places (for about forges and iron works you may gather a cart-load of it), ergo, it is a martial herb.

A reader who takes this kind of exaggerated logic seriously (and there are many remarks of this kind in *The English Physician*) might indeed think that Culpeper was a fool or a quack. Personally, I think he was neither. I think, rather, that he was a maverick with a renegade wit and a sharp tongue, who often wrote the way he talked, with an intemperate sense of humor and a strongly ironic twist.

When we look at Nicholas Culpeper in the context of his own time and political situation, it is easy to see the scope of his valuable contribution to our knowledge of the history of medicinal plants Culpeper understood, far better than any other medical man of his day, that it is important for people to know how their bodies function, what readily available herbal remedies they might apply to various physical ailments, and how to obtain or make and use these simple remedies for themselves. His use of medical astrology was very much in keeping with the traditional "physick" he practiced and familiar to the audience of ordinary people that he wanted to reach. Without a doubt, his books and treatises give us the best-documented report available to us of the uses of medicinal plants in Great Britain and northern Europe at the beginning of the Age of Enlightenment. For those of us who read him in later centuries, I think we should be very glad that this renegade pharmacist chose to use the astrological model to explain the relationships between the plants and the planets. If he had not, all the fascinating information contained in his work—which tells us the logic behind the application of certain plants to certain physical conditions—would certainly have been lost, swept away by the avalanche of chemical medicines and scientific practices that came into use in the eighteenth century. And that, I believe, would have been a tragedy.

Endnotes

1 In Europe, the Catholic persecution of Witches was fueled by the notorious *Malleus Malleficarum* ("Hammer of Witches"), written in the late 1400s. In England, Protestant persecutions did not get off to a good start until the time of King James I, who wrote a witch-hunting handbook called *Daemonologie* less than twenty years before Culpeper's birth. In America, the frenzy raged throughout the seventeenth century, reaching its peak with the Salem witch trials in 1692, forty years after Culpeper's death.

2 At the time, the apothecaries treated the poor, who could not afford the exorbitant fees charged by members of the College of Physicians. If the apothecary read Latin and could afford to stock the often exotic ingredients recommended by the College, he employed their book of prescriptions; if he could not, he used whatever knowledge he had to make his own medicines from

available plants. Although apothecaries were supposed to be trained in an apprenticeship, there was a great deal of abuse of the system, and many were indeed quacks.

3 Culpeper, Nicholas. *Culpeper's Complete Herbal & English Physician Enlarged.* Glenwood, IL: Meyerbooks, 1990.

4 Rohde, Eleanor Sinclair. *The Old English Herbals*, p. 165. The source for this and other quotations from Culpeper is the original edition of *The English Physitian: Or an Astrologo-physical Discourse of the Vulgar Herbs of This Nation.* London: Peter Cole, 1652. The reader needs to be aware that subsequent editions (from which the currently available "facsimile" editions are copied) contained material added by Alice Field Culpeper and later students of Culpeper's method. It is only by studying the edition that appeared in the author's lifetime that we can see what Culpeper himself wrote and approved. The 1652 edition (keyed by Richard Siderits and colleagues from a copy at the Historical Library, Cushing/Whitney Medical Library, Yale University) is on the Internet at www.med.yale.edu/library/historical/culpeper/culpeper.htm.

Culpeper's Herbs

Here are some of the more familiar of Culpeper's herbs, arranged according to their ruling planets (only five planets, plus the Sun and the Moon, were known at the time) and zodiacal signs. Culpeper's astrological designations are sometimes idiosyncratic. Where he differs from other writers, he usually offers an explanation.

Mars (Aries, Scorpio)

Basil, garlic, hawthorn, hops, mustard, onions, radish, horse radish, rhubarb, thistles, tobacco, and wormwood.

Sun (Leo)

Chamomile, eyebright, St. John's wort, lovage, marigold (calendula), peony, rosemary, rue, and saffron.

Venus (Taurus, Libra)

Ladies' bedstraw, chickweed, cowslips, daisies, elder, goldenrod, ladies' mantle, mint, plantain, sorrel, strawberries, tansy, violet, and yarrow.

Mercury (Gemini, Virgo)

Dill, fern, fennel, horehound, lavender, licorice, maidenhair, sweet marjoram, parsley, and southernwood.

Moon (Cancer)

Cabbage, columbine, watercress, ivy, lettuce, moonwort, poppy, purslain, white roses, and willow.

Jupiter (Sagittarius, Pisces)

Agrimony, bay, bilberry, borage, costmary, dandelion, dock, hyssop, liverwort, red roses, and sage.

Saturn (Capricorn, Aquarius)

Cleavers, comfry, dodder, goutwort, hemlock, hemp, henbane, horsetail, mullein, and nightshade.

The
Quarters
and Signs
of the
Moon and
Moon
Tables

The Quarters and Signs of the Moon

$\mathscr{E}$veryone has seen the Moon wax and wane through a period of approximately twenty-nine and-a-half days. This circuit from New Moon to Full Moon and back again is called the lunation cycle. The cycle is divided into parts, called quarters or phases. There are several methods by which this can be done, and the system used in the *Herbal Almanac* may not correspond to those used in other almanacs.

The Quarters

First Quarter

The first quarter begins at the New Moon, when the Sun and Moon are in the same place, or conjunct. (This means that the Sun and Moon are in the same degree of the same sign.) The Moon is not visible at first, since it rises at the same time as the Sun. The New Moon is the time of new beginnings, beginnings of projects that favor growth, externalization of activities, and the growth of ideas. The first quarter is the time of germination, emergence, beginnings, and outwardly directed activity.

Second Quarter

The second quarter begins halfway between the New Moon and the Full Moon, when the Sun and Moon are at right angles, or a 90 degree square to each other. This half Moon rises around noon and sets around midnight, so it can be seen in the western sky during the first half of the night. The second quarter is the time of growth and articulation of things that already exist.

Third Quarter

The third quarter begins at the Full Moon, when the Sun and Moon are opposite one another and the full light of the Sun can shine on the full sphere of the Moon. The round Moon can be seen rising in the east at sunset, and then rising a little later each evening. The Full Moon stands for illumination, fulfillment, culmination, completion, drawing inward, unrest, emotional expressions, and hasty actions leading to failure. The third quarter is a time of maturity, fruition, and the assumption of the full form of expression.

Fourth Quarter

The fourth quarter begins about halfway between the Full Moon and New Moon, when the Sun and Moon are again at 90 degrees, or square. This decreasing Moon rises at midnight, and can be seen in the east during the last half of the night, reaching the overhead position just about as the Sun rises. The fourth quarter is a time of disintegration, drawing back for reorganization and reflection.

The Signs

Moon in Aries

Moon in Aries is good for starting things, but lacking in staying power. Things occur rapidly, but also quickly pass.

Moon in Taurus

With Moon in Taurus, things begun during this sign last the longest and tend to increase in value. Things begun now become habitual and hard to alter.

Moon in Gemini

Moon in Gemini is an inconsistent position for the Moon, characterized by a lot of talk. Things begun now are easily changed by outside influences.

Moon in Cancer

Moon in Cancer stimulates emotional rapport between people. It pinpoints need, and supports growth and nurturance.

Moon in Leo

Moon in Leo accents showmanship, being seen, drama, recreation, and happy pursuits. It may be concerned with praise and subject to flattery.

Moon in Virgo

Moon in Virgo favors accomplishment of details and commands from higher up while discouraging independent thinking.

Moon in Libra

Moon in Libra increases self-awareness. It favors self-examination and interaction with others, but discourages spontaneous initiative.

Moon in Scorpio

Moon in Scorpio increases awareness of psychic power. It precipitates psychic crises and ends connections thoroughly.

Moon in Sagittarius

Moon in Sagittarius encourages expansionary flights of imagination and confidence in the flow of life.

Moon in Capricorn

Moon in Capricorn increases awareness of the need for structure, discipline, and organization. Institutional activities are favored.

Moon in Aquarius

Moon in Aquarius favors activities that are unique and individualistic, concern for humanitarian needs, society as a whole, and improvements that can be made.

Moon in Pisces

During Moon in Pisces, energy withdraws from the surface of life, hibernates within, secretly reorganizing and realigning.

January Moon Table

Date	Sign	Element	Nature	Phase
1 Sat.	Scorpio	Water	Fruitful	4th
2 Sun. 4:32 pm	Sagittarius	Fire	Barren	4th
3 Mon.	Sagittarius	Fire	Barren	4th
4 Tue.	Sagittarius	Fire	Barren	4th
5 Wed. 5:24 am	Capricorn	Earth	Semi-fruit	4th
6 Thu.	Capricorn	Earth	Semi-fruit	New 1:14 pm
7 Fri. 5:53 pm	Aquarius	Air	Barren	1st
8 Sat.	Aquarius	Air	Barren	1st
9 Sun.	Aquarius	Air	Barren	1st
10 Mon. 4:59 am	Pisces	Water	Fruitful	1st
11 Tue.	Pisces	Water	Fruitful	1st
12 Wed. 1:48 pm	Aries	Fire	Barren	1st
13 Thu.	Aries	Fire	Barren	1st
14 Fri. 7:38 pm	Taurus	Earth	Semi-fruit	2nd 8:34 am
15 Sat.	Taurus	Earth	Semi-fruit	2nd
16 Sun. 10:25 pm	Gemini	Air	Barren	2nd
17 Mon.	Gemini	Air	Barren	2nd
18 Tue. 11:01 pm	Cancer	Water	Fruitful	2nd
19 Wed.	Cancer	Water	Fruitful	2nd
20 Thu. 10:58 pm	Leo	Fire	Barren	Full 11:40 pm
21 Fri.	Leo	Fire	Barren	3rd
22 Sat.	Leo	Fire	Barren	3rd
23 Sun. 12:07 am	Virgo	Earth	Barren	3rd
24 Mon.	Virgo	Earth	Barren	3rd
25 Tue. 4:09 am	Libra	Air	Semi-fruit	3rd
26 Wed.	Libra	Air	Semi-fruit	3rd
27 Thu. 12:01 pm	Scorpio	Water	Fruitful	3rd
28 Fri.	Scorpio	Water	Fruitful	4th 2:57 am
29 Sat. 11:17 pm	Sagittarius	Fire	Barren	4th
30 Sun.	Sagittarius	Fire	Barren	4th
31 Mon.	Sagittarius	Fire	Barren	4th

February Moon Table

Date	Sign	Element	Nature	Phase
1 Tue. 12:10 pm	Capricorn	Earth	Semi-fruit	4th
2 Wed.	Capricorn	Earth	Semi-fruit	4th
3 Thu.	Capricorn	Earth	Semi-fruit	4th
4 Fri. 12:31 am	Aquarius	Air	Barren	4th
5 Sat.	Aquarius	Air	Barren	New 8:03 am
6 Sun. 11:02 am	Pisces	Water	Fruitful	1st
7 Mon.	Pisces	Water	Fruitful	1st
8 Tue. 7:17 pm	Aries	Fire	Barren	1st
9 Wed.	Aries	Fire	Barren	1st
10 Thu.	Aries	Fire	Barren	1st
11 Fri. 1:21 am	Taurus	Earth	Semi-fruit	1st
12 Sat.	Taurus	Earth	Semi-fruit	2nd 6:21 pm
13 Sun. 5:23 am	Gemini	Air	Barren	2nd
14 Mon.	Gemini	Air	Barren	2nd
15 Tue. 7:45 am	Cancer	Water	Fruitful	2nd
16 Wed.	Cancer	Water	Fruitful	2nd
17 Thu. 9:11 am	Leo	Fire	Barren	2nd
18 Fri.	Leo	Fire	Barren	2nd
19 Sat. 10:53 am	Virgo	Earth	Barren	Full 11:27 am
20 Sun.	Virgo	Earth	Barren	3rd
21 Mon. 2:21 pm	Libra	Air	Semi-fruit	3rd
22 Tue.	Libra	Air	Semi-fruit	3rd
23 Wed. 8:58 pm	Scorpio	Water	Fruitful	3rd
24 Thu.	Scorpio	Water	Fruitful	3rd
25 Fri.	Scorpio	Water	Fruitful	3rd
26 Sat. 7:10 am	Sagittarius	Fire	Barren	4th 10:53 pm
27 Sun.	Sagittarius	Fire	Barren	4th
28 Mon. 7:45 pm	Capricorn	Earth	Semi-fruit	4th
29 Tue.	Capricorn	Earth	Semi-fruit	4th

March Moon Table

Date	Sign	Element	Nature	Phase
1 Wed.	Capricorn	Earth	Semi-fruit	4th
2 Thu. 8:14 am	Aquarius	Air	Barren	4th
3 Fri.	Aquarius	Air	Barren	4th
4 Sat. 6:30 pm	Pisces	Water	Fruitful	4th
5 Sun.	Pisces	Water	Fruitful	4th
6 Mon.	Pisces	Water	Fruitful	New 12:17 am
7 Tue. 1:54 am	Aries	Fire	Barren	1st
8 Wed.	Aries	Fire	Barren	1st
9 Thu. 7:01 am	Taurus	Earth	Semi-fruit	1st
10 Fri.	Taurus	Earth	Semi-fruit	1st
11 Sat. 10:46 am	Gemini	Air	Barren	1st
12 Sun.	Gemini	Air	Barren	1st
13 Mon. 1:51 pm	Cancer	Water	Fruitful	2nd 1:59 am
14 Tue.	Cancer	Water	Fruitful	2nd
15 Wed. 4:43 pm	Leo	Fire	Barren	2nd
16 Thu.	Leo	Fire	Barren	2nd
17 Fri. 7:48 pm	Virgo	Earth	Barren	2nd
18 Sat.	Virgo	Earth	Barren	2nd
19 Sun. 11:57 pm	Libra	Air	Semi-fruit	Full 11:44 pm
20 Mon.	Libra	Air	Semi-fruit	3rd
21 Tue.	Libra	Air	Semi-fruit	3rd
22 Wed. 6:17 am	Scorpio	Water	Fruitful	3rd
23 Thu.	Scorpio	Water	Fruitful	3rd
24 Fri. 3:43 pm	Sagittarius	Fire	Barren	3rd
25 Sat.	Sagittarius	Fire	Barren	3rd
26 Sun.	Sagittarius	Fire	Barren	3rd
27 Mon. 3:51 am	Capricorn	Earth	Semi-fruit	4th 7:21 pm
28 Tue.	Capricorn	Earth	Semi-fruit	4th
29 Wed. 4:34 pm	Aquarius	Air	Barren	4th
30 Thu.	Aquarius	Air	Barren	4th
31 Fri.	Aquarius	Air	Barren	4th

April Moon Table

Date	Sign	Element	Nature	Phase
1 Sat. 3:12 am	Pisces	Water	Fruitful	4th
2 Sun.	Pisces	Water	Fruitful	4th
3 Mon. 10:22 am	Aries	Fire	Barren	4th
4 Tue.	Aries	Fire	Barren	New 1:12 pm
5 Wed. 2:29 pm	Taurus	Earth	Semi-fruit	1st
6 Thu.	Taurus	Earth	Semi-fruit	1st
7 Fri. 4:58 pm	Gemini	Air	Barren	1st
8 Sat.	Gemini	Air	Barren	1st
9 Sun. 7:16 pm	Cancer	Water	Fruitful	1st
10 Mon.	Cancer	Water	Fruitful	1st
11 Tue. 10:16 pm	Leo	Fire	Barren	2nd 8:30 am
12 Wed.	Leo	Fire	Barren	2nd
13 Thu.	Leo	Fire	Barren	2nd
14 Fri. 2:19 am	Virgo	Earth	Barren	2nd
15 Sat.	Virgo	Earth	Barren	2nd
16 Sun. 7:36 am	Libra	Air	Semi-fruit	2nd
17 Mon.	Libra	Air	Semi-fruit	2nd
18 Tue. 2:35 pm	Scorpio	Water	Fruitful	Full 12:41 pm
19 Wed.	Scorpio	Water	Fruitful	3rd
20 Thu. 11:58 pm	Sagittarius	Fire	Barren	3rd
21 Fri.	Sagittarius	Fire	Barren	3rd
22 Sat.	Sagittarius	Fire	Barren	3rd
23 Sun. 11:47 am	Capricorn	Earth	Semi-fruit	3rd
24 Mon.	Capricorn	Earth	Semi-fruit	3rd
25 Tue.	Capricorn	Earth	Semi-fruit	3rd
26 Wed. 12:42 am	Aquarius	Air	Barren	4th 2:30 pm
27 Thu.	Aquarius	Air	Barren	4th
28 Fri. 12:06 pm	Pisces	Water	Fruitful	4th
29 Sat.	Pisces	Water	Fruitful	4th
30 Sun. 7:54 pm	Aries	Fire	Barren	4th

May Moon Table

Date	Sign	Element	Nature	Phase
1 Mon.	Aries	Fire	Barren	4th
2 Tue. 11:54 pm	Taurus	Earth	Semi-fruit	4th
3 Wed.	Taurus	Earth	Semi-fruit	New 11:12 pm
4 Thu.	Taurus	Earth	Semi-fruit	1st
5 Fri. 1:23 am	Gemini	Air	Barren	1st
6 Sat.	Gemini	Air	Barren	1st
7 Sun. 2:14 am	Cancer	Water	Fruitful	1st
8 Mon.	Cancer	Water	Fruitful	1st
9 Tue. 4:01 am	Leo	Fire	Barren	1st
10 Wed.	Leo	Fire	Barren	2nd 3:00 pm
11 Thu. 7:41 am	Virgo	Earth	Barren	2nd
12 Fri.	Virgo	Earth	Barren	2nd
13 Sat. 1:27 pm	Libra	Air	Semi-fruit	2nd
14 Sun.	Libra	Air	Semi-fruit	2nd
15 Mon. 9:16 pm	Scorpio	Water	Fruitful	2nd
16 Tue.	Scorpio	Water	Fruitful	2nd
17 Wed.	Scorpio	Water	Fruitful	2nd
18 Thu. 7:09 am	Sagittarius	Fire	Barren	Full 2:34 am
19 Fri.	Sagittarius	Fire	Barren	3rd
20 Sat. 7:01 pm	Capricorn	Earth	Semi-fruit	3rd
21 Sun.	Capricorn	Earth	Semi-fruit	3rd
22 Mon.	Capricorn	Earth	Semi-fruit	3rd
23 Tue. 8:00 am	Aquarius	Air	Barren	3rd
24 Wed.	Aquarius	Air	Barren	3rd
25 Thu. 8:07 pm	Pisces	Water	Fruitful	3rd
26 Fri.	Pisces	Water	Fruitful	4th 6:55 am
27 Sat.	Pisces	Water	Fruitful	4th
28 Sun. 5:08 am	Aries	Fire	Barren	4th
29 Mon.	Aries	Fire	Barren	4th
30 Tue. 10:02 am	Taurus	Earth	Semi-fruit	4th
31 Wed.	Taurus	Earth	Semi-fruit	4th

June Moon Table

Date	Sign	Element	Nature	Phase
1 Thu. 11:34 am	Gemini	Air	Barren	4th
2 Fri.	Gemini	Air	Barren	New 7:14 am
3 Sat. 11:30 am	Cancer	Water	Fruitful	1st
4 Sun.	Cancer	Water	Fruitful	1st
5 Mon. 11:45 am	Leo	Fire	Barren	1st
6 Tue.	Leo	Fire	Barren	1st
7 Wed. 1:57 pm	Virgo	Earth	Barren	1st
8 Thu.	Virgo	Earth	Barren	2nd 10:29 pm
9 Fri. 6:58 pm	Libra	Air	Semi-fruit	2nd
10 Sat.	Libra	Air	Semi-fruit	2nd
11 Sun.	Libra	Air	Semi-fruit	2nd
12 Mon. 2:55 am	Scorpio	Water	Fruitful	2nd
13 Tue.	Scorpio	Water	Fruitful	2nd
14 Wed. 1:18 pm	Sagittarius	Fire	Barren	2nd
15 Thu.	Sagittarius	Fire	Barren	2nd
16 Fri.	Sagittarius	Fire	Barren	Full 5:27 pm
17 Sat. 1:26 am	Capricorn	Earth	Semi-fruit	3rd
18 Sun.	Capricorn	Earth	Semi-fruit	3rd
19 Mon. 2:26 pm	Aquarius	Air	Barren	3rd
20 Tue.	Aquarius	Air	Barren	3rd
21 Wed.	Aquarius	Air	Barren	3rd
22 Thu. 2:52 am	Pisces	Water	Fruitful	3rd
23 Fri.	Pisces	Water	Fruitful	3rd
24 Sat. 12:55 pm	Aries	Fire	Barren	4th 8:00 pm
25 Sun.	Aries	Fire	Barren	4th
26 Mon. 7:19 pm	Taurus	Earth	Semi-fruit	4th
27 Tue.	Taurus	Earth	Semi-fruit	4th
28 Wed. 9:59 pm	Gemini	Air	Barren	4th
29 Thu.	Gemini	Air	Barren	4th
30 Fri. 10:09 pm	Cancer	Water	Fruitful	4th

July Moon Table

Date	Sign	Element	Nature	Phase
1 Sat.	Cancer	Water	Fruitful	New 2:20 pm
2 Sun. 9:38 pm	Leo	Fire	Barren	1st
3 Mon.	Leo	Fire	Barren	1st
4 Tue. 10:19 pm	Virgo	Earth	Barren	1st
5 Wed.	Virgo	Earth	Barren	1st
6 Thu.	Virgo	Earth	Barren	1st
7 Fri. 1:47 am	Libra	Air	Semi-fruit	1st
8 Sat.	Libra	Air	Semi-fruit	2nd 7:53 am
9 Sun. 8:48 am	Scorpio	Water	Fruitful	2nd
10 Mon.	Scorpio	Water	Fruitful	2nd
11 Tue. 7:06 pm	Sagittarius	Fire	Barren	2nd
12 Wed.	Sagittarius	Fire	Barren	2nd
13 Thu.	Sagittarius	Fire	Barren	2nd
14 Fri. 7:27 am	Capricorn	Earth	Semi-fruit	2nd
15 Sat.	Capricorn	Earth	Semi-fruit	2nd
16 Sun. 8:27 pm	Aquarius	Air	Barren	Full 8:55 am
17 Mon.	Aquarius	Air	Barren	3rd
18 Tue.	Aquarius	Air	Barren	3rd
19 Wed. 8:44 am	Pisces	Water	Fruitful	3rd
20 Thu.	Pisces	Water	Fruitful	3rd
21 Fri. 7:09 pm	Aries	Fire	Barren	3rd
22 Sat.	Aries	Fire	Barren	3rd
23 Sun.	Aries	Fire	Barren	3rd
24 Mon. 2:44 am	Taurus	Earth	Semi-fruit	4th 6:02 am
25 Tue.	Taurus	Earth	Semi-fruit	4th
26 Wed. 7:01 am	Gemini	Air	Barren	4th
27 Thu.	Gemini	Air	Barren	4th
28 Fri. 8:30 am	Cancer	Water	Fruitful	4th
29 Sat.	Cancer	Water	Fruitful	4th
30 Sun. 8:23 am	Leo	Fire	Barren	New 9:25 pm
31 Mon.	Leo	Fire	Barren	1st

August Moon Table

Date	Sign	Element	Nature	Phase
1 Tue. 8:27 am	Virgo	Earth	Barren	1st
2 Wed.	Virgo	Earth	Barren	1st
3 Thu. 10:31 am	Libra	Air	Semi-fruit	1st
4 Fri.	Libra	Air	Semi-fruit	1st
5 Sat. 4:04 pm	Scorpio	Water	Fruitful	1st
6 Sun.	Scorpio	Water	Fruitful	2nd 8:02 pm
7 Mon.	Scorpio	Water	Fruitful	2nd
8 Tue. 1:30 am	Sagittarius	Fire	Barren	2nd
9 Wed.	Sagittarius	Fire	Barren	2nd
10 Thu. 1:44 pm	Capricorn	Earth	Semi-fruit	2nd
11 Fri.	Capricorn	Earth	Semi-fruit	2nd
12 Sat.	Capricorn	Earth	Semi-fruit	2nd
13 Sun. 2:43 am	Aquarius	Air	Barren	2nd
14 Mon.	Aquarius	Air	Barren	2nd
15 Tue. 2:41 pm	Pisces	Water	Fruitful	Full 12:13 am
16 Wed.	Pisces	Water	Fruitful	3rd
17 Thu.	Pisces	Water	Fruitful	3rd
18 Fri. 12:44 am	Aries	Fire	Barren	3rd
19 Sat.	Aries	Fire	Barren	3rd
20 Sun. 8:31 am	Taurus	Earth	Semi-fruit	3rd
21 Mon.	Taurus	Earth	Semi-fruit	3rd
22 Tue. 1:55 pm	Gemini	Air	Barren	4th 1:51 pm
23 Wed.	Gemini	Air	Barren	4th
24 Thu. 4:59 pm	Cancer	Water	Fruitful	4th
25 Fri.	Cancer	Water	Fruitful	4th
26 Sat. 6:17 pm	Leo	Fire	Barren	4th
27 Sun.	Leo	Fire	Barren	4th
28 Mon. 6:55 pm	Virgo	Earth	Barren	4th
29 Tue.	Virgo	Earth	Barren	New 5:19 am
30 Wed. 8:33 pm	Libra	Air	Semi-fruit	1st
31 Thu.	Libra	Air	Semi-fruit	1st

September Moon Table

Date	Sign	Element	Nature	Phase
1 Fri.	Libra	Air	Semi-fruit	1st
2 Sat. 12:55 am	Scorpio	Water	Fruitful	1st
3 Sun.	Scorpio	Water	Fruitful	1st
4 Mon. 9:08 am	Sagittarius	Fire	Barren	1st
5 Tue.	Sagittarius	Fire	Barren	2nd 11:27 am
6 Wed. 8:47 pm	Capricorn	Earth	Semi-fruit	2nd
7 Thu.	Capricorn	Earth	Semi-fruit	2nd
8 Fri.	Capricorn	Earth	Semi-fruit	2nd
9 Sat. 9:44 am	Aquarius	Air	Barren	2nd
10 Sun.	Aquarius	Air	Barren	2nd
11 Mon. 9:34 pm	Pisces	Water	Fruitful	2nd
12 Tue.	Pisces	Water	Fruitful	2nd
13 Wed.	Pisces	Water	Fruitful	Full 2:37 pm
14 Thu. 7:00 am	Aries	Fire	Barren	3rd
15 Fri.	Aries	Fire	Barren	3rd
16 Sat. 2:05 pm	Taurus	Earth	Semi-fruit	3rd
17 Sun.	Taurus	Earth	Semi-fruit	3rd
18 Mon. 7:22 pm	Gemini	Air	Barren	3rd
19 Tue.	Gemini	Air	Barren	3rd
20 Wed. 11:16 pm	Cancer	Water	Fruitful	4th 8:28 pm
21 Thu.	Cancer	Water	Fruitful	4th
22 Fri.	Cancer	Water	Fruitful	4th
23 Sat. 2:00 am	Leo	Fire	Barren	4th
24 Sun.	Leo	Fire	Barren	4th
25 Mon. 4:02 am	Virgo	Earth	Barren	4th
26 Tue.	Virgo	Earth	Barren	4th
27 Wed. 6:22 am	Libra	Air	Semi-fruit	New 2:53 pm
28 Thu.	Libra	Air	Semi-fruit	1st
29 Fri. 10:30 am	Scorpio	Water	Fruitful	1st
30 Sat.	Scorpio	Water	Fruitful	1st

October Moon Table

Date	Sign	Element	Nature	Phase
1 Sun. 5:50 pm	Sagittarius	Fire	Barren	1st
2 Mon.	Sagittarius	Fire	Barren	1st
3 Tue.	Sagittarius	Fire	Barren	1st
4 Wed. 4:42 am	Capricorn	Earth	Semi-fruit	1st
5 Thu.	Capricorn	Earth	Semi-fruit	2nd 5:59 am
6 Fri. 5:33 pm	Aquarius	Air	Barren	2nd
7 Sat.	Aquarius	Air	Barren	2nd
8 Sun.	Aquarius	Air	Barren	2nd
9 Mon. 5:36 am	Pisces	Water	Fruitful	2nd
10 Tue.	Pisces	Water	Fruitful	2nd
11 Wed. 2:51 pm	Aries	Fire	Barren	2nd
12 Thu.	Aries	Fire	Barren	2nd
13 Fri. 9:06 pm	Taurus	Earth	Semi-fruit	Full 3:53 am
14 Sat.	Taurus	Earth	Semi-fruit	3rd
15 Sun.	Taurus	Earth	Semi-fruit	3rd
16 Mon. 1:19 am	Gemini	Air	Barren	3rd
17 Tue.	Gemini	Air	Barren	3rd
18 Wed. 4:37 am	Cancer	Water	Fruitful	3rd
19 Thu.	Cancer	Water	Fruitful	3rd
20 Fri. 7:42 am	Leo	Fire	Barren	4th 2:59 am
21 Sat.	Leo	Fire	Barren	4th
22 Sun. 10:52 am	Virgo	Earth	Barren	4th
23 Mon.	Virgo	Earth	Barren	4th
24 Tue. 2:30 pm	Libra	Air	Semi-fruit	4th
25 Wed.	Libra	Air	Semi-fruit	4th
26 Thu. 7:23 pm	Scorpio	Water	Fruitful	4th
27 Fri.	Scorpio	Water	Fruitful	New 2:58 am
28 Sat.	Scorpio	Water	Fruitful	1st
29 Sun. 2:40 am	Sagittarius	Fire	Barren	1st
30 Mon.	Sagittarius	Fire	Barren	1st
31 Tue. 1:01 pm	Capricorn	Earth	Semi-fruit	1st

November Moon Table

Date	Sign	Element	Nature	Phase
1 Wed.	Capricorn	Earth	Semi-fruit	1st
2 Thu.	Capricorn	Earth	Semi-fruit	1st
3 Fri. 1:41 am	Aquarius	Air	Barren	1st
4 Sat.	Aquarius	Air	Barren	2nd 2:27 am
5 Sun. 2:13 pm	Pisces	Water	Fruitful	2nd
6 Mon.	Pisces	Water	Fruitful	2nd
7 Tue.	Pisces	Water	Fruitful	2nd
8 Wed. 12:02 am	Aries	Fire	Barren	2nd
9 Thu.	Aries	Fire	Barren	2nd
10 Fri. 6:12 am	Taurus	Earth	Semi-fruit	2nd
11 Sat.	Taurus	Earth	Semi-fruit	Full 4:15 pm
12 Sun. 9:27 am	Gemini	Air	Barren	3rd
13 Mon.	Gemini	Air	Barren	3rd
14 Tue. 11:21 am	Cancer	Water	Fruitful	3rd
15 Wed.	Cancer	Water	Fruitful	3rd
16 Thu. 1:19 pm	Leo	Fire	Barren	3rd
17 Fri.	Leo	Fire	Barren	3rd
18 Sat. 4:15 pm	Virgo	Earth	Barren	4th 10:24 am
19 Sun.	Virgo	Earth	Barren	4th
20 Mon. 8:35 pm	Libra	Air	Semi-fruit	4th
21 Tue.	Libra	Air	Semi-fruit	4th
22 Wed.	Libra	Air	Semi-fruit	4th
23 Thu. 2:33 am	Scorpio	Water	Fruitful	4th
24 Fri.	Scorpio	Water	Fruitful	4th
25 Sat. 10:33 am	Sagittarius	Fire	Barren	New 6:11 pm
26 Sun.	Sagittarius	Fire	Barren	1st
27 Mon. 8:57 pm	Capricorn	Earth	Semi-fruit	1st
28 Tue.	Capricorn	Earth	Semi-fruit	1st
29 Wed.	Capricorn	Earth	Semi-fruit	1st
30 Thu. 9:26 am	Aquarius	Air	Barren	1st

December Moon Table

Date	Sign	Element	Nature	Phase
1 Fri.	Aquarius	Air	Barren	1st
2 Sat. 10:23 pm	Pisces	Water	Fruitful	1st
3 Sun.	Pisces	Water	Fruitful	2nd 10:55 pm
4 Mon.	Pisces	Water	Fruitful	2nd
5 Tue. 9:17 am	Aries	Fire	Barren	2nd
6 Wed.	Aries	Fire	Barren	2nd
7 Thu. 4:26 pm	Taurus	Earth	Semi-fruit	2nd
8 Fri.	Taurus	Earth	Semi-fruit	2nd
9 Sat. 7:50 pm	Gemini	Air	Barren	2nd
10 Sun.	Gemini	Air	Barren	2nd
11 Mon. 8:48 pm	Cancer	Water	Fruitful	Full 4:03 am
12 Tue.	Cancer	Water	Fruitful	3rd
13 Wed. 9:09 pm	Leo	Fire	Barren	3rd
14 Thu.	Leo	Fire	Barren	3rd
15 Fri. 10:30 pm	Virgo	Earth	Barren	3rd
16 Sat.	Virgo	Earth	Barren	3rd
17 Sun.	Virgo	Earth	Barren	4th 7:41 pm
18 Mon. 2:01 am	Libra	Air	Semi-fruit	4th
19 Tue.	Libra	Air	Semi-fruit	4th
20 Wed. 8:12 am	Scorpio	Water	Fruitful	4th
21 Thu.	Scorpio	Water	Fruitful	4th
22 Fri. 4:57 pm	Sagittarius	Fire	Barren	4th
23 Sat.	Sagittarius	Fire	Barren	4th
24 Sun.	Sagittarius	Fire	Barren	4th
25 Mon. 3:54 am	Capricorn	Earth	Semi-fruit	New 12:22 pm
26 Tue.	Capricorn	Earth	Semi-fruit	1st
27 Wed. 4:25 pm	Aquarius	Air	Barren	1st
28 Thu.	Aquarius	Air	Barren	1st
29 Fri.	Aquarius	Air	Barren	1st
30 Sat. 5:27 am	Pisces	Water	Fruitful	1st
31 Sun.	Pisces	Water	Fruitful	1st

About the Authors

SUSAN WITTIG ALBERT, PH.D. is the author of eight China Bayles herbal mysteries, the most recent of which is *Lavender Lament.* Under the pseudonym of Robin Paige, she and her husband Bill Albert also coauthor a series of Victorian mysteries. Look for number six in the series, *Death at Whitechapel.* Susan and Bill live in the Texas hill country. You can find them on the Web at www.mysterypartners.com.

BERNYCE BARLOW is the author of *Sacred Sites of the West,* from Llewellyn. She researches and leads seminars on sacred sites of the ten western states. Bernyce is currently working on a CD of music for the sacred sites. She is also an elder of the Boot-to-the-Head tradition of spiritual enlightenment.

ELIZABETH BARRETTE is a regular contributor to *SageWoman, PanGaia, Circle Network News, PagaNet News,* and *Moonbeams Journal.* Much of her involvement with the wider Pagan community takes place online, where she has helped build networking resources such as the Pagan Leaders mailing list and the Pagan/NeoPagan sections of the NWS Theology Website. Visit her Website at http://www.worthlink. net/~ysabet/index.html.

DEBORAH DUCHON is an anthropologist and ethnobotanist at Georgia State University in Atlanta. She often writes about plant-related issues.

MARGUERITE ELSBETH (Raven Hawk) is a professional diviner and a student of Native American and European folk healing. She is coauthor of *The Grail Castle: Male Myths and Mysteries in the Celtic Tradition* and *The Silver Wheel: Women's Myths and Mysteries* *in the Celtic Tradition* with Kenneth Johnson, and author of *Crystal Medicine: Working with Crystals, Gems and Minerals.* Marguerite is a hereditary Sicilian Strega.

VERNA GATES teaches folklore classes at the University of Alabama at Birmingham and has been featured on *NBC Nightside* as a folklorist. She was a writer for CNN and has been a freelance writer for fifteen years.

JUDY GRIFFIN, PH.D. is an international lecturer, counselor, and author. She has researched indigenous cultures for twenty years and is an authority on medicinal herbs, aromatherapy, natural skincare, flower essences, and organic gardening. Judy has created over 200 chemical-free flower essences and essential oils for North American and European markets. She has written *Mother Nature's Herbal,* a 400-page herbal recently featured on PBS. Judy is presently leading an aromatherapy study at the Baylor Medical Healing Environment Center with bone marrow and stem cell transplant patients. She privately consults as a nutritionist and herbalist.

RAVEN GRIMASSI is a hereditary Italian Witch practicing a family tradition of Stregheria. He is also an Initiate of Pictish-Gaelic Wicca, Gardnerian Wicca, and Brittic Witchcraft. Raven is the author of *Ways of the Strega; The Wiccan Mysteries;* and *Wiccan Magick.*

JOAN HINKLEY has studied herbs for twenty-nine years and homeopathy for ten years, as well as other modalities of the healing arts. She has been in practice for ten years and may be reached at 719-530-0985. As she states, her clientele's cases range from "cough to cancer." Joan is also a teacher and a writer.

ELLEN EVERT HOPMAN is a master herbalist and lay homeopath who holds an M.Ed. in mental health counseling and is a professional member of the American Herbalist's Guild. She is the author of *Tree Medicine, Tree Magic* from Phoenix Publishers; *A Druid's Herbal for the Sacred Earth Year* and *People of the Earth: The New Pagans Speak Out* from Inner Traditions/

Destiny Books; and of the videos *Gifts from the Healing Earth Volume 1* and *Pagans*, both from EFP Services. She has also released three audio tapes from Creative Seminars, including: *The Druid Path: Herbs and Festivals; Celtic Gods and Goddesses;* and *The Herbal and Magical Powers of Trees.*

LIZ JOHNSON provided supplementary herbal proofreading for this almanac. Liz is co-owner of Firewind Herbal Products. Firewind makes high quality incense, candles, soap, jewelry, and other products for Wiccans and magical people. To request a free catalog call 612/543-9065 or find them on the Internet at www.firewindhp.com.

PENNY KELLY has earned a degree in naturopathic medicine and is working toward a Ph.D. in nutition. She is the author of the book *The Elves of Lily Hill Farm.*

GRETCHEN LAWLOR combines over twenty-five years experience as an astrologer with over ten years experience as a naturopath into her astromedical consultations and teachings. She can be reached for consultations at P.O. Box 753, Langley, WA 98260.

HARRY MACCORMACK is an adjunct assistant professor of theater arts, and owner/operator of Sunbow Farm, an organic farm in the Pacific Northwest.

CAROLINE MOSS runs workshops and gives talks on herb growing, cookery, crafts, history, and folklore and designs herb gardens on commission.

LEEDA ALLEYN PACOTTI embarked on metaphysical self-studies in astrology and numerology at age fourteen. Her career encompassed anti-trust law, international treaties, the humanitites, and governmental management in legislation and budget. She now plies a gentle practice as a naturopathic physician, master herbalist, and certified nutritional counselor.

ROSLYN REID is a Druid and a member of the Moonshadow Institute. She is a regular contributor of art and articles to Llewellyn, as well as to Pagan oriented publications such as *SageWoman* and *Dalriada*, a Scottish magazine of Celtic spirituality.

She has also published pieces in consumer magazines like *Tightwad Living* and *Thrifty Times*, and was a contributor to Susun Weed's book, *Breast Cancer? Breast Health!*

K.D. SPITZER has loved herbs all her life. In the years before they became readily available, she wildcrafted plants from woods and abandoned cellar holes and relied on her French mother-in-law to send seeds from Europe. She is master weaver, and one corner of her herb garden is devoted to dye herbs. She teaches and gardens in New Hampshire, where she also reads the tarot.

CARLY WALL, C.A. is the author of *Naturally Healing Herbs, Setting the Mood With Aromatherapy*, and *The Little Giant Encyclopedia of Olde-Thyme Home Remedies* from Sterling Publications. She is a member of NAHA (National Association for Holistic Aromatherapy) and holds a certificate in aromatherapy.

SUSUN WEED is a Green Witch and a Wise Woman known worldwide as an extraordinary teacher with a joyous spirit, a powerful presence, and an encyclopedic knowledge of herbs and health. She is the founder of the Wise Woman Center, editor-in-chief of Ash Tree Publishing, and initiated high priestess of Dianic Wicca. She is the author of *Wise Woman Herbal for the Child Bearing Year, Healing Wise: Menopausal Years the Wise Woman Way*, and *Breast Cancer? Breast Health! The Wise Woman Way*. For information on correspondence courses, apprenticeships, and workshops, write to P.O. Box 64, Woodstock, NY 12498.

Directory
of
Products
and
Services

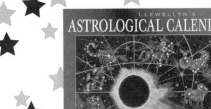

10 Healthy Reasons To Feel Better Fast...

from only $2 each! For new customers only!

#1 Ginkgo Biloba
▶ Helps mental sharpness
▶ Helps boost vitality
30 mg. 60 Caps
Reg. ~~$9.95~~ **Sale!** $3

#2 Saw Palmetto
500 mg. 100 Caps
▶ Promotes prostate health
▶ Helps curb nighttime bathroom visits
Reg. ~~$14.95~~ **Sale!** $3

#3 Bilberry
▶ Soothes eye stress
▶ Enhances night vision
60 mg. 60 Tabs
Reg. ~~$14.95~~ **Sale!** $3

#4 St. John s Wort
260 mg. 60 Tabs
▶ Helps you feel good mentally
▶ Can brighten your day
Reg. ~~$9.95~~ **Sale!** $2

#5 Ginger Root
550 mg. 100 Caps
▶ Nutritionally supports joints
▶ Helps cardiovascular system
Reg. ~~$10.95~~ **Sale!** $3

#6 Red Wine Extract
30 mg. 60 Caps
▶ Contains antioxidants to protect cells
▶ Helps maintain healthful bloodflow
Reg. ~~$17.50~~ **Sale!** $4

#7 Cider Vinegar Plus
300 mg. 100 Tabs
▶ Supports weight loss plans
▶ Helps maintain healthy cholesterol levels
Reg. ~~$9.95~~ **Sale!** $3

#8 Korean Ginseng
▶ Helps physical stamina
▶ Promotes peak energy levels
100 mg. 100 Caps
Reg. ~~$10.95~~ **Sale!** $3

#9 Valerian
▶ Calms you down
▶ Relaxes muscles
500 mg. 90 Caps
Reg. ~~$9.95~~ **Sale!** $2

#10 Butcher's Broom
470 mg. 100 Caps
▶ Promotes healthy veins and circulation
▶ Can help reduce inflammation
Reg. ~~$12.95~~ **Sale!** $3

Yours FREE With Any Order
Collagen & Elastin Skin Cream
▶ Helps restore skin tone and elasticity!
▶ Helps diminish bagging under eyes, crows feet and laugh lines for younger looking skin.
Reg. ~~$3.95~~ Yours FREE! *"It's Marvelous!"*

What Does Your Future Hold?

Feb. 14, 2001

Sept. 8, 2001

July 17, 2002

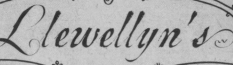

Llewellyn's

HERBAL
ALMANAC

FOR THE YEAR
2000

- Herb Magic & Lore
- Growing & Gathering
- Health & Beauty Herbs
- Herbs for Cooking & Crafts